How the Left and
Right Think

How the Left and Right Think

The Roots of Division in American Politics

BILL MEULEMANS

McFarland & Company, Inc., Publishers
Jefferson, North Carolina

ISBN (print) 978-1-4766-7878-8 ∞
ISBN (ebook) 978-1-4766-3691-7

LIBRARY OF CONGRESS AND BRITISH LIBRARY
CATALOGUING DATA ARE AVAILABLE

Front cover image: Democratic Party and Republican Party symbols
© 2019 cowardlion/Shutterstock

Printed in the United States of America

*McFarland & Company, Inc., Publishers
Box 611, Jefferson, North Carolina 28640
www.mcfarlandpub.com*

Acknowledgments

Portions of this book were started several years ago with the research work of a small group of students who have since then gone on to pursue various careers. A long-overdue thank you goes to Brian Delashmutt, Paula and Bob Glider, Virginia Linder, and Dave Penwell. Together, they spent countless hours reading, taking notes and meeting with me as I put together the ideas contained in this book.

I want to thank the participants who gave of their time when we discussed some of the most controversial topics: Dave DiNucci, Nancy Guenther, Carole Hanna, Ed Jindrich, Craig Mikkelsen, Bill Nelson, Brendan O'Scannlain, Steve Schreiner, Dick Spence, John Taggart, and Dirk Williams.

Several colleagues were very helpful in reviewing the proposed book when help was needed most. I am especially indebted to Hilly Alexander, Nancy Guenther, Judy Jindrich, Earl Starks, Janet Nyn, John Taggart, Bud Thompson, and Steve Schreiner for their advice and counsel. I also wish to express my gratitude to Brian Linger who helped me format materials from an earlier book. And finally, I wish to thank Karen Horton, senior editor of Prentice-Hall, Inc., for giving me permission to use the graphics and portions of other written material that appeared in an earlier edition of my book, *Making Political Choices: An Introduction to Politics.*

This book draws on formal and informal interviews with thousands of people in three countries: the United States, Israel, and Northern Ireland. Without exception, they were generous with their time. But of course, people from all walks of life love to talk about their own political beliefs, especially when they are trying to convert others.

Table of Contents

Acknowledgments   v

Preface   1

Introduction   3

1. What's Happening to Us?   7
   - Secret Money   11
   - Undermining the Electorate   15
   - Why It Happened   17
   - Reformers of the Left and Right   18
   - Nowhere Else to Go   19
   - White Supremacists   24
   - Necessary Reforms   27
   - Questions for You   33

2. Left and Right   35
   - Fixing Society   38
   - Criticisms of the Left   41
   - Criticisms of the Right   45
   - Charges and Counter Charges   47
   - Blind Spots   51
   - Illegal Politics   56
   - Questions for You   61

3. Foundations of Politics   63
   - New Words for Old Ideas   68
   - Eternal Questions   69
   - Outside Threats   76
   - A Poor People's Conference   81
   - Questions for You   86

4. Personal Experiences   89

The Function of Ideologies   90
Learning Political Values   93
An Autobiography of a Liberal   98
An Autobiography of a Conservative   104
Advantages and Disadvantages   110
Morality   120
Questions for You   125

5. Expectations and Deprivations   127

Role of the Central Government   128
Constitutionalism   129
Setting the Scenario   130
Consequences   134
Post-World War II (1945 to the Present)   136
Unfinished Business   142
Attacking the System   143
Success and Anger   145
Questions for You   148

6. Left-Wing Values   150

What They Believe   151
In Their Own Words   153
Basic Problems for the Left   160
Saul Alinsky   164
Revolutionaries on the Left   166
Problems for Revolutionary Radicals   167
The Communist Party   169
Questions for You   171

7. Right-Wing Values   173

What They Believe   173
In Their Own Words   176
Basic Problems for the Right   183
Mitt Romney   186
Revolutionaries on the Right   188
Problems for Revolutionary Reactionaries   190
The Ku Klux Klan   192
Questions for You   197

8. Ideas and People Move to the Right   199

Public Reactions   201
Self-Interest   202
Betrayal of Principles   203

Revolution of the Right or Left?   205
The Flip-Flop   207
More or Less Freedom?   212
Negative and Positive Freedom   215
The New Reactionaries   219
The New Radicals   226
Questions for You   231

9. Moderates, Activists, and Extremists   233
    Moderates: Liberals and Conservatives   236
    Moderates: Characteristics in Common   240
    Activists: Radicals and Reactionaries   241
    Activists: Characteristics in Common   246
    Extremists: Revolutionary Radicals &
        Revolutionary Reactionaries   247
    Extremists: Characteristics in Common   252
    Questions for You   255

10. Beyond Ideology   257
    Left and Right   258
    Predictability   259
    Political Manners   262
    Trump versus Anti-Trump   263
    A Recipe for Disaster   265
    The Dark Corners of America   267
    Questions for You   270

Bibliography   273
Index   277

Preface

How the Left and Right Think is a different kind of book. Much of it is written in the first person in a manner one would expect in a magazine. It enables readers to understand political disagreements and conflicts through the eyes of the author who was physically on the scene. The book deals with issues that reveal how important individual emotions and peer groups are in political affairs. There is an intuitive quality in the writing that touches on basic characteristics that are rarely discussed in traditional books. Extensive field observations from three countries make the subject come alive. Examples are cited that illustrate the inherent advantages and disadvantages of both the right and left in practical politics.

One of the most important missions of the book is to define and compare the major clusters of ideological attitudes and associate them with specific groups that are familiar to the reader. The goal is to provide a working definition of the political labels that help readers *understand* why liberals and conservatives have taken positions on specific issues.

I am familiar with the empirical studies that have been done, but I've chosen to write in a non-academic, conversational style that rests on my own field research over a 40-year period in the United States, Northern Ireland and Israel. My greatest insights have come through situations that are difficult to describe and quantify. Experience gained through this kind of research may be more usable for readers in their daily lives than the information that comes from traditional sources. My approach has been to live and work with the rank-and-file members on both sides of a conflict. I have found that empathy and objectivity have given me a unique understanding of contending points of view that would not have been available through any other means.

Early in my career, I invited people from a wide variety of backgrounds into my college classroom to tell their stories about why they became involved in politics. They ranged from insurgents on the left and right to nearly everyone in between. I developed comparative models to understand individual motives that explained why people see the political world so differently. My

1

methodology has been to contact and interview hundreds of persons in diverse settings, and to analyze their patterns of beliefs and behavior.

A major theme of the book is to focus on a series of specific public issues and to provide the reader with the knowledge to discover why people take political stands. Readers will understand why conservatives favor more restrictions on immigration, and why liberals want universal health care. In follow-up chapters, moderates in elected office are compared with activists protesting out on the street, and with extremists in small cell groups plotting a violent revolution. Numerous real-life examples and stories are cited to support the theories that are presented. In one chapter, a simulation places the reader in the role of a state governor who faces the threat of public violence. One thing is certain: individuals who read this book will discover where they are personally on the political spectrum.

When I was a young professor, I had a psychiatrist come into my classroom to speak about political extremism. He began his remarks by saying, "I've practiced psychiatry for 37 years, and I've never noted a characteristic in one of my patients that I haven't already found in myself. *It's just a matter of degree.*" I've never forgotten that comment because I think it may be true in politics as well. When we see folks in politics that we disagree with, maybe we should take note that: "It's just a matter of degree." We may be surprised to learn that down deep we still share most of the same values. Maybe looking at it that way will make it possible for us to understand each other better. That's really what this country needs, isn't it?

Introduction

Donald Trump and American Politics

It was a perfect storm—all the disabling characteristics were in place before Donald Trump walked on the stage. It was like a theatrical tragedy whereby the plot had already been set to divide the country into warring camps. All that was wanting was a brash leader with no discernable ideology to set the destructive play into motion. In reality, the body politic was already diseased and getting worse. Trump could not have produced such a state of chaos in a healthy political system. He did not cause the paralyzing gridlock—he just knew how to rip off the political scabs that had been festering for years.

The first serious problem that preceded Trump was that campaign contributions had contaminated the political process from top to bottom. The Supreme Court had laid open the gates for uncontrolled sums of money pouring into political campaigns that resulted in unspoken cases of *legalized bribery*. The court decision promoted the notion that unlimited contributions were protected as freedom of speech. As expected, those with the most wealth used the political/economic system to get more than their share. The growing gap of income inequality was remindful of the economic conditions that existed just before the Great Depression of the 1930s. The alarm bells were sounding, but few leaders in power were paying any attention.

Second, the Voting Rights Act of 1965 had been gutted by the Supreme Court, making it possible for state governments to enact state voter suppression laws that targeted specific groups of voters. The laws were not neutral; they restricted voting rights for racial minorities, young people and lower income folks. The number of polling places and times for voting were reduced in specific areas making it more difficult for particular people to vote. Some political leaders argued that the laws were meant to uphold the integrity of the vote, but these laws were clearly enacted to *suppress* the vote for a class of people and to change the outcome of elections.

3

And third, irregular legislative district boundaries (local, state, and federal) had been drawn to over-represent a favored political, racial, economic, or cultural group at the expense of other voters. The result was that some citizens were intentionally under-represented at the local, state and federal level. They were disenfranchised *legally* by a system that undermined their right to be equally represented. Again, the law stacked the deck against specific groups of people.

The first chapter of this book examines a situation that caused angry, frustrated voters to be drawn to a candidate that promised to "Make America Great Again." A lot of people were hurting, but neither political party seemed to care. Donald Trump sought out this special group of voters who felt they were on the outside looking in. He caught their attention with a series of dramatic promises that were simplistic but uplifting. His overall message was that the system was broken and he was "the only one who could fix it."

During the 2016 election campaign, both Donald Trump and U.S. Senator Bernie Sanders got their loudest applause when they said "the system was rigged." Voters didn't always know the legalistic specifics, but they sensed that they had lost their voice in the process. Trump gave them a clear and easy path to follow. In 2016, Trump won. Trust in conventional politics lost.

But this book is not about Donald Trump. It's about the anti-democratic practices that made his kind of claims believable. The major thesis of **How the Left and the Right Think** is to explore and understand the relationship between the left and right in a democracy. The hope of this book is that the American people will demand the return to power of honest conservatives and liberals.

Sometimes people do not realize the value of public trust until it's gone. Often a crisis is necessary to jolt public conscience back into action. Perhaps this is the time that we realize that reforms are necessary to start the long road back to a workable democratic system.

Our Political Family

Politics is both feminine and masculine. Liberals are in the female role, reassuring and helping those left behind. Conservatives act more as the male, concerned with maintaining privilege, order and stability within the system. Ideally these competing characteristics should be in balance as the government demonstrates it has a *heart* for the less fortunate, and a *head* to keep the operations at a manageable level. But today our political family has become wildly dysfunctional. The two sides are far apart on nearly every issue. Leaders in both camps see compromise as surrender. Claims and counter claims are often based on downright lies. There is no trust. And to make matters worse, the Russians are flooding social media with divisive lies that cause us to be even less cooperative with each other.

Many of us remember that our parents had competing roles and different ways of responding to us as children. If you came from a two-parent family it might have gone something like this:

Mother was the helper who sympathized with children in trouble. She was the one who sat down to check the child's school homework. If someone fell down and skinned their knee, she would soothe them with the message: "Everything is going to be all right." She had a special way of reaching out to the child who was handicapped. Mother tried to understand why each child got into trouble and was always ready to give the kid a second chance. She was concerned about equity and made sure everyone felt they were equals. From her position as the peace maker, she tried to eliminate discrimination within the family. Everyone felt they could come to her with their problems; she always seemed to have a helping hand in times of emergencies. Her role was that of nurturing, offering aid and comfort, but she sometimes went too far in trying to shield them from the rough edges of life. Some of the kids became so dependent they had trouble making it on their own. Outside the family, she smoothed over squabbles with neighbors, and was known as one who sought cooperation with relatives in other parts of town. Mother had an interest in keeping the entire community healthy; she was very concerned about the quality of the air we breathed, the water we drank, and the food we ate. She cared about each of us, especially when we needed help.

Father was more concerned about keeping order. He was the disciplinarian. If there was a need, he would reprimand the child who misbehaved. He tried to be fair, but sometimes he became headstrong. Everyone knew he was in charge of the purse strings in the family; he always wanted to know how much something would cost. When he scolded the children, there was often a lecture: "Don't let that happen again," or "You've got to do better." He laid down lessons on how to act. Children respected him, but they knew he expected them to mind the rules and be self-sufficient. His ideal child was someone who could get along without any help. In sports he always told the children to stand up for the home team and win the game. Some of the kids felt he gave too much attention to those who did well, and not enough consideration for those who were less competitive. He brought order to the family, but he sometimes went too far and disregarded weaker children when they needed a hand up in life. Father always stood up for the family if there was any disagreement with the neighbors. It was important for him that he never backed down or was seen as a weak person. But he sometimes cut corners on the quality of life in the family. He was always looking for ways to cut expenses on the health and welfare of those who couldn't fend for themselves. He thought it was fine if the children defended themselves with personal weapons. His view was that each of us was pretty much here on our own, and he seldom offered anyone a helping hand because he thought it would make them dependent and weak.

And so it is in politics: liberalism is the voice of compassion, of nurturing those who need help, of making certain that no one is left behind—conservatism is the voice of maintaining standards, of developing individual initiative, of making sure that competition is rewarded. Politics works well when the two are melded together and operating in unison.

Society, in some ways, is like a larger family. It must have access to both competing ideologies that complement each other—the left and the right. Sometimes we need to stay the course with one philosophy, and at other times, there is a need for a sensible change. The political order can get too much from just one side. The whole idea of democracy is based on sensing when to choose a new direction.

But American politics today is a dysfunctional family; it has become tribal and self-destructive. There is not just disagreement—some folks are trying to destroy each other. The parents are yelling at each other, and no one is listening. The mother no longer seems to have a clear message for those in need; the father has become uncaring, brash, and untruthful. The children treat each other as enemies. No one seems to trust anyone else. Some say the family is inching toward a divorce, and no one knows for sure what will happen then. There is no effort to heal or make peaceful change possible. Some ideas are thought to be too far left and others are too far right. A new, very boisterous father-figure has come on the scene. He proposes a set of disjointed proposed solutions that are neither liberal nor conservative. The balance is gone.

This new leader has come to power because many of the children felt isolated and alienated. They felt no one listened to them so they threw their support to a loud father-figure who promised to knock down the established family relationships that had stood for many years. Now the family is in chaos; some of the children are siding with the father because he gives them favored treatment, while others are talking about ways to get rid of the father and put someone else in charge. Nearly everyone agrees that the family itself is in jeopardy—that the growing division will destroy the union that has held them together.

The lesson for the parents is obvious. Supporters of the mother should formulate a clearly worded plan to help those who feel like they are on the outside; it's not enough to just criticize the irresponsible father-figure—it's time to offer a workable choice. Those who support the father should loosen the purse strings to provide for everyone and stop thinking only of their own welfare. The point is made that there won't be a family anymore if it can't govern itself.

Perhaps there has never been a time when it has been more important to examine the principles of the left and right and how each might shape our ability to govern. We all should familiarize ourselves again with the co-equal halves of liberalism and conservativism to see how they fit together. We need both, you know. If we don't speak up, who knows what will happen to the American family? Which side do you favor? Where do you fit in the American family?

1

What's Happening to Us?

I was born and raised in a small middle-class town in the Midwest, and I've spent my life teaching college students how to get involved in politics. Years ago, I was the first to organize both the Young Democrats and Young Republicans on campus. There was a sincere interest among young people to join opposing campus political clubs; politics was seen as a positive avenue that could improve the world. Students were hungry for knowledge of how to get involved. College was a laboratory for learning how to engage in constructive politics.

But what can I teach them now? Can you imagine trying to convince a classroom of 18-year-olds to have faith in their government? What can I point to with pride? What's happened to our country? How could the envy of the world a few years ago turn so quickly into a country in political chaos? We used to think of ourselves as being exceptional in nearly every way. Now look at us. We have lost our way, and many of us have given up on getting back on track.

There was a time, not long ago, when being an American carried with it a sense of unity, of accepting each other as worthwhile citizens, despite disagreements over policies. While there were many things wrong in that era, there was still a sense of civility. Democrats and Republicans debated each other and offered practical solutions. Problems were solved by bringing both sides together. The public believed the government could work. We didn't see the press or each other as being enemies. But those days are no more.

Today the map of the nation is colored as being either red states or blue states. And within that context, certain states are unfriendly or even hostile to people from the other camp. At the local level there is a growing atmosphere of cultural and political polarization, whereby people think in terms of *them* and *us*. Hardcore partisans even wonder out loud that it might be better if certain states were no longer in the Union. There is a sense of extreme partisanship from the White House right down to the street where you live.

We are divided in almost every way. It's never been this way since the Civil War.

Today when we speak of the left and right in politics there is the assumption that the two camps have little or nothing in common. Local conservatives and liberals have become like boisterous athletic supporters, cheering their side and booing the other team—minds are not open to hearing another point of view. Many make up their minds automatically to support their own tribe even when they know down deep that their side is being self-centered and uncooperative.

Today we are in the era of negative arousals—that is to say we are aroused by what we oppose, not by what we favor. Americans are becoming more and more a people who are motivated by the negative emotions of fear and anger. Some of us think only about what we oppose. There was a time when our strength was our diversity, but now there are some who are intentionally dividing us by race, culture, religion, nationality, and ethnic background.

American politics today has become a blood sport. Our two major political parties are pitted against each other on almost every issue, and the public is sick of the whole mess. There has been a steady decline of ordinary people who see themselves as being either Democrats or Republicans, and there has been a sharp increase in the number of registered Independents, especially among young people. Many Americans are turned off by what they see and hear.

While the percentage of people who identify as Republicans and Democrats has gone down, the intensity of partisanship in both parties has gone up. The result is that the base of each party has shrunk, become more single-minded, and more hostile to anyone who disagrees with them. There are still moderates in both political parties, but they are increasingly outnumbered by members who cheer before they think. Is this true of people you know?

The result is that the most intense, ideologically uncompromising factions of both parties have a disproportionately greater impact on our politics. These hard-core political activists are recruiting candidates who have a black and white view of the world. Stalwarts in both parties dominate the nomination process, hoping to choose the most uncompromising candidates. Campaigns in this category are often funded by billionaires with extreme agendas. The airwaves are flooded with negative messages that are dishonest, or at best misleading. This kind of campaigning causes many moderates to be disgusted and stay home on Election Day, thus increasing the power of the strongly partisan voters who are highly motivated.

Candidates on both sides not only have opposing sets of issues—they each have an opposing set of "facts." Lying is not uncommon and it's hard to find anyone in the middle who believes the charges being made; credibility in the political process has sunk to a new low. In recent years, those who win elections under these circumstances have increasingly narrow priorities that differ sharply from the general public. Once elected, these legislators are unwilling to compromise with anyone outside their particular interest group. The result is gridlock as the system grinds to a halt.

Why did this happen? Who is responsible for the growing paralysis that has taken over our politics? Some commentators blame liberals, others blame conservatives. There will be no attempt here to assign blame, but this didn't happen by accident.

As you will see, there are specific groups and individuals who deserve more blame than others. But there won't be an attempt here to point a finger at one group. There's actually enough blame to go around—the responsibility can be shared because the system has been corrupted with the consent of both the left and the right. The best that can be said for old-line Democrats and Republicans is that neither of them ever thought it would come to this. Yet they let it happen, and now both parties are trying to cope with the political wreckage. The focus of this book is where we go from here. Which reforms are absolutely necessary to keep our democratic system afloat?

We've always had ideological conflict in our society, but today's clashes between the left and right have actually paralyzed the law-making process. Factions within our federal and state parties are simply unwilling to work together. Most roll-call votes show almost all Democrats and Republicans lining up against each other. In legislative committees the two sides have basically stopped talking to each other. When one side takes a position, there is a near certainty the other side will put up a wall of opposition. The word "compromise" has become a dirty word in some political circles.

But there was a time in American politics when the government worked. Liberals and conservatives were present in both parties as noted in the approximated illustration below.

Figure 1–1, Overlapping Political Bell Curves

As this figure illustrates, there were some Democrats to the right of some Republicans and there were some Republicans to the left of some Democrats.

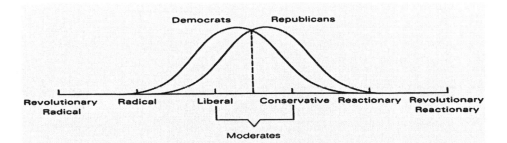

The blending in the center had a moderating effect on American politics. There were personal friendships between conservatives and liberals; they could communicate in a civil manner and work together. The overlapping feature meant that there was a large body of opinion that members shared in common. They were never described as warring tribes that spurned each other.

When I worked in Congress, I remember watching members of opposing parties engage in a sharp debate on the floor, and later walk off the floor and go to lunch together. I attended weekend barbecues that featured family get-togethers with folks from both sides of the aisle.

It wasn't acknowledged at the time as a plus factor, but the overlapping of congressional members may have been the most important characteristic of the political system because both parties had a diversity of viewpoints that made compromise possible. Prime examples of that range of opinion were U.S. Senator Jacob Javits (R) of New York, 1957–81, and U.S. Senator Richard Russell (D) of Georgia, 1933–71. Javits voted with the Democrats more than he did with his own party. Russell, the Democrat, was the founder of the conservative coalition in Congress, and had many strong ties to GOP senators. There were many others with similar characteristics.

But the 1960s changed all that. After a long and bitter national debate, Democratic President Lyndon Johnson persuaded Congress to approve the Civil Rights Act of 1964. Not surprisingly, southern Democrats fought him every step along the way with a filibuster in the Senate that lasted 60 working days. At the end, Johnson won out only because he persuaded a large number of Senate Republicans to support the bill. The President credited Republican Senator Everett Dirksen of Illinois as being the person that broke the Democratic filibuster.

When President Johnson signed the bill, he concluded that the Democrats would lose the Solid South as a consequence. That prediction came true later that year as Johnson won the greatest popular vote in history, but he lost five southern states: Alabama, Georgia, Louisiana, Mississippi, and South Carolina. Since then, these states have become the bastion of the Republican Party. The President knew what he was doing and justified it as the price his political party had to pay to pass the Civil Rights bill of 1964. An advisor told LBJ, "Don't use up your capital on a lost cause." With a touch of anger, Johnson responded, "What the hell's the presidency for if not to fight for causes you believe in?"

The 1960s were also a time when strong-willed conservatives began to intensify their hold over the Republican Party. Former Republican Governor of New York, Nelson Rockefeller, was booed at his own national convention in 1964. After the southern conservatives joined the GOP, Rockefeller-styled liberals no longer felt at home in their own party. The overlapping characteristics of the parties slowly disappeared as officeholders lost their willingness to work together. Now there is little chance that feature will reappear soon, if ever.

Secret Money

The old Hollywood image of political corruption was a sinister character, standing in the shadows, handing out wads of cash to legislators just before a vote was taken. The new version of corruption is a lobbyist, in the open, going to a congressional office to remind a legislator (who received a sizable campaign contribution) that a particular interest group wants to pass or defeat a certain measure on the floor. The style has changed—the effect is the same. The new system is perfectly legal. Big money has divided legislators into opposing camps. Both Democrats and Republicans are awash with huge sums of special-interest money.

A few years ago, most members of Congress actually moved to Washington, D.C., where they and their families socialized across party lines. Now more members return to their home state every weekend to raise money and attend to local interest groups. The "Tuesday to Thursday Club" defines those who leave Washington on Thursday evenings and return just in time to attend meetings on Tuesday mornings. All of this has broken down the communal spirit that was once present in the capitol. For many, going home and raising money has become the most important part of congressional life.

Perhaps the most important thing that destroyed the ability of American parties to compromise and work together was the introduction of unlimited amounts of money to influence the legislative process. Enormous sums of money have been spent to elect both liberal and conservative candidates who are pledged to support specific interests and oppose other points of view. Some lobby groups boost that they never lose because they know how to use money to manipulate the system. Well-funded lobbying groups are bipartisan in that they spread their money around and contribute to both sides. It's a small investment on their part to have dependable elected officials in both political parties because no matter who wins, they win. Interest groups just consider huge political contributions as a cost of doing business. This adds to the supposition that the system is rigged and there's nothing citizens can do about the situation. In the face of big money, it's difficult to encourage public participation because many feel there is no hope to change public policy.

If one looks carefully at the identity of big donors, it becomes clear that both parties are in bed with their own specific lobbying organizations. Neither party is going to shake up the system by bringing forth any real change that is contrary to their largest donors—that's not the way it works.

To a great extent, huge financial interests have sapped the will of the government to accomplish even routine tasks. Important national issues never seem to get on the congressional agenda. The nation's infrastructure is collapsing, but it doesn't concern these groups if Congress ignores the need to repair our roads, bridges, sewers, airports, and railroads. Many members of Congress have no particular interest in passing legislation as long as their subsidies and tax breaks stay in place. All they want is to maintain the status quo and make certain the government doesn't try to regulate them. Big money has rigged the system from the inside, beyond the reach of political party leaders, the president, and regulatory agencies. As long as it takes millions of dollars to win and stay in public office the situation is not likely to change.

There have been times when opinion polls showed that 70 to 90 percent of the people wanted to pass a particular measure, but Congress didn't even bring it up for a vote. Clearly, there is something wrong. There are many responsible members of Congress who would represent us well if the burden of big money were off their backs. Undisclosed campaign contributions are a contamination in the democratic process.

Yet there are many honest and good people serving in Congress, the state legislatures and city government. They understand much better than we do how the system is rigged, and how individuals find themselves powerless to act independently of certain interests that dominate their states. One former member of Congress made this point dramatically when he told me that every time he got off the phone after raising money, he found himself unconsciously going to the washroom to wash his hands with soap—he felt "unclean." He finally retired because of his disdain for the people he had to deal with when raising re-election funds.

But that was a couple of years ago. Election fundraising today takes up even more of a member's time. Campaigns are now going on every day, 12 months a year, always with an eye on the opinion polls. Officeholders are engaged in never-ending fundraising of several thousand dollars each day to make sure they are ready for the next election. Lobbyists who hold the purse strings expect loyalty from those who receive their campaign funds. It's become *legalized bribery*—pure and simple. There is a "pay-to-play" system where a wealthy minority can frustrate a larger majority. We still call it a democracy, but more and more it is dominated by dark money and faceless people far beyond public view.

A friend of mine (with a sense of humor) said she thought politicians should wear uniforms so voters could tell which special interest they represented. But of course that will never happen; there is an effort to hide the association with big money so voters will think these elected officials are still primarily interested in "the people."

In 2010, the Supreme Court held that giving an unlimited amount of money is an expression of their freedom of speech protected by the First Amendment. How about low-income people who don't have millions to give? Who protects their interests if they don't give any money? Then there's the question of the corrupting influence of big contributions.

Former U.S. Senator Dick Neuberger of Oregon used to tell the story of two situations that could occur in his senate office. First, he said, a lobbyist could come to his office and say, "Senator, here's $10,000, I want you to vote for Senate Bill 123." Neuberger said that would be attempted bribery and wouldn't be tolerated. But at another time a lobbyist could come by his office and say, "I want to make a $10,000 contribution to your reelection campaign, and by the way I expect you will vote for Senate Bill 123." Neuberger said the second situation would be "perfectly legal," but then, with a thoughtful look on his face he said, "Is there any real difference?"

Sometimes it may be difficult to put your finger on real corruption. I remember having an elected county judge speak before one of my political science classes. A student asked whether the judge "remembered particular campaign contributions" when making a decision involving someone who was a contributor. The judge said he made it a practice of "never looking at the list of donors." The classroom broke into laughter—no one believed him. Did the judge have a normal level of curiosity of wanting to know who gave him money? Or did he just naturally bend his decision a bit toward those who made large donations? Was this a borderline case of corruption? How about the members of elected bodies at the local, state, and federal levels? How important is money in making local decisions? How can the public believe their representatives and elected judges are independent voices when billions of dollars are spent by those who want to influence them?

There are 537 elected officeholders at the federal level (president, vice president, 435 members in the house, and 100 senators). There are about 87,000 state and local governments with scores of officeholders in each. This includes officials from approximately 3,000 counties, 19,000 municipalities and an untold number of special districts such as school boards and zoning commissions.

All of this is a maze to the average voter who has not even heard the names of most people on the local ballot. Because of this web of elected offices, those who win elections are often those who can put up the most billboards or run the most 30 second ads on television. Many candidates try to build their own name ID while avoiding an association with either political party. Every effort is made to hide behind slogans and win votes without indicating important policy positions. No one really knows what most of these candidates will do if elected.

In theory each voter should search out the qualifications of every candidate, but in practice it doesn't work that way. Individual voters have their own lives and they simply don't have the time or inclination to find out if a city judge or county coroner is doing a good job. The result is that many leave that portion of the ballot blank—or worse—they vote for someone simply because they heard the name or because the candidate had more TV spots.

Some say it's the genius of American government that there are so many imputes for policy-making from so many sources on so many issues. However, it also presents a chance for single interests to stack the deck at a particular point that is most important to the donor.

If the number of elected officials were reduced, voters would have fewer but more informed choices to make. The public would then have a better chance of holding officials responsible for what goes on throughout the entire structure. Right now, we vote for too many officials without knowing what they intend to do if elected. Long ballots with all those choices for unimportant offices can cause voter apathy. Election Day at the local level can be very boring—voting for people you've never heard of.

In my neighborhood we have several orchards and berry fields that border our housing areas. My neighbors assume that agricultural zoning will guard against more houses being built. I always tell them it's just a matter of time before developers will funnel money into electing officials who can change the zoning laws and turn the farmland into a housing development. It's all legal and can happen without anyone taking notice. It's not hard to imagine that my neighbors may wake up some day and find out it's too late to hold anyone responsible.

Financial influences in politics are largely hidden from public view. Most of it is spent to keep friends in office and to maintain access for future contact. Business corporations and labor unions see it as a political investment that will come in handy when the need arises. The problem, however, is that ordinary people are left out of the equation.

In the face of all this, both of our political parties are fundamentally dishonest in how they present themselves to the voters. Democrats, of course, still set out an agenda with all the unfinished reforms to excite their rank and file. Republicans do much the same for the conservative camp. But neither party has the courage to do anything that might be unpopular with those who make huge financial donations to their political campaigns. Those who bankroll candidates expect something in return. Suspicions have grown across the land that many elected officials have been bought off legally. Few people want to talk about it because it sounds like the United States has become a banana republic where unseen hands run everything in the shadows.

Liberals and conservatives in Congress are both dishonest about who wields the power; they claim that the majority party is in control, but that's not really true. Big money wrote the checks that elected them, and it can write checks that will take them out. The average voter may be attracted to politicians promising to take the money out of politics, but the public should not expect officeholders to change the system that made their election possible. Look around—those that promise to "drain the swamp" have actually added more swamp-like creatures to the swamp.

Nearly everyone is frustrated and wants to vent their anger toward those responsible for this mess. The cruel hoax is that voter rage has been deflected by the partisan media into blaming particular politicians when, in fact, it is the entire system that has been corrupted. It does no good to demonize the executive branch, congressional leaders or presidential candidates because they are caught in the same circumstances where big money can buy elections on either side. Voters have not yet been perceptive enough to understand this. The country needs to get big money out of our system and permit the left and right to get back to the business of governing instead of perpetually collecting more money to win re-election.

When the question of public funding of campaigns comes up, the general response from voters is that they don't want to waste their tax dollars on politicians running for office. In truth, the present system costs voters much more because government "tax dollars" are used to subsidize private interests that are supported by elected officials who have been legally bought off by huge contributions to their campaigns. It costs a lot of tax money just to reward those who make the huge campaign contributions.

Undermining the Electorate

The political process is also skewed by how representative districts are designed. In many parts of the country, political district boundaries have been drawn shamelessly so only the favored party has a chance to win. Gerrymandering is the method of drawing district boundary lines in a manner that results in over-representing a favored political party or group and under-represents the opposition. The process was named after Governor Elbridge Gerry of Massachusetts who proposed a set of distorted legislative district boundaries in 1812 that resembled a salamander, a lizard-like animal with claws and a long tail. The name "gerrymandering" stuck to a process that has been used by both political parties to over-represent themselves and under-represent their opponents. It is tailor-made for American elections.

District boundaries with irregular borders are deliberately designed to either include or exclude specific groups of voters. Often these district boundaries look like they were drawn by a madman, but in fact they are the work of political statisticians who pore over computer data so they can underrepresent the opposition. (*Google* "gerrymandering" and you will see examples). The result is that winning and losing candidates can be predicted accurately even before elections occur. Both political parties do it whenever they get the chance to stack the deck, but neither will admit it to the public. The process is designed to violate the will of the people.

In earlier times, voters were able to choose their representatives, but now representatives are able to choose their voters. These noncompetitive districts are so lopsided politically that they often produce candidates with narrow and/or extreme points of view. Once elected, these members of legislative bodies are uncompromising to any and all who may challenge them. In some of these "safe districts," elected representatives view moderates of either party as the enemy. The result is a sizable number of these members refuse to compromise and share power with anyone, even leaders of their own political party.

Because these legislative districts are basically noncompetitive, there is a greater chance that these representatives will be reelected repeatedly, ultimately rising through the seniority system to chair the very committee that has jurisdiction over their particular special interest. The whole arrangement is designed to subsidize and over-represent legislative districts that are the least representative of a nationwide or state-wide point of view. Both political parties are playing the same game—it's an anti-democratic secret that has undermined the representative process at several levels of government.

There is often a cozy relationship between these elected officials and the promotion of a particular economic, political, religious, social, or racial point of view—these representatives know what is expected of them. Literally, the victim in this situation is the taxpayer who has to pay the bill for over-representing single interests. No wonder the national debt grows every year. It is a sad commentary on our electoral process that there are few districts in the U.S. House of Representatives that are truly competitive, where both parties have a chance of winning.

And to add to the situation, we see thinly veiled attempts to fix elections even more by changing voting laws to reduce voter turnout. *When the right to vote is at risk, everything is at risk.* Several states have passed laws that require certain types of photo identification before voting. The nonpartisan U.S. Government Accountability Office (GAO) has published an empirical study concluding voter ID laws are designed to suppress the vote, especially for African-Americans, Hispanics, young people, newly registered voters, and the poor. It is well known that these kinds of voters are much less likely to have picture ID. The Supreme Court struck down sections of the Voting Rights Act of 1965, making it possible for states to enact rules to restrict the right to vote. These new local laws are designed to tip the balance in favor of one political party. To add to this strategy, the number of polling locations and hours of operation have both been reduced, which keeps voter turnout low. Some voters stand in lines for more than eight hours to cast their ballot. People around the world are shocked by the extreme partisanship and misrepresentation in the United States. Americans are shocked, too. What do you think?

Why It Happened

It's interesting to trace the roots of this ideological conflict back a few years and find out why this happened. First of all, there was intense racial unrest between blacks and whites in the 1950s when the Civil Rights Movement began to succeed. White segregationists in the South never forgave northern white liberals and black civil rights workers for imposing racial integration on the country. What had been the Solid South for Democrats has now become the Solid South for Republicans. New efforts have been made to disenfranchise blacks and to underrepresent them. White folks in many southern states are doing all they can to stay in power.

In addition, there have been an almost endless number of national conflicts that have created more division. The Vietnam War of the 1960s and 70s separated the left and right across the entire country. The effort to impeach Richard Nixon in 1974 upset conservative Republicans, and the GOP attempt to drive Bill Clinton from office in 1998 infuriated liberal Democrats. There was even more anger when the Supreme Court decided George W. Bush would be president after the election of 2000. Large numbers of folks were furious when Barack Obama was elected as the first African-American president in 2008. And to top it off, the election of Donald Trump in 2016 divided the country like never before.

Then there was the widespread fear of terrorism that followed 9/11. Connected to this was the concern about foreign terrorists entering the country, the use of torture against our enemies, and a series of unending wars in the Middle East. There was also widespread public outrage when the bankers on Wall Street walked free despite the unscrupulous actions that brought on the Great Recession of 2008. Throw in the alarming number of public shootings that have caused people to avoid public places, then add in the anger over the enactment of Obamacare. And in 2010, a highly motivated group of voters elected a wave of uncompromising Tea Party candidates. The election of Donald Trump has sharpened partisanship on both sides.

When put together, it is easy to see why there is more political division, and why many people have lost their faith in the government. Many people feel that the political system just doesn't work anymore, and they are right. Big money and extreme partisanship have brought out an ugly side of American politics, and it seems to be getting worse every day. We are becoming more like the banana republics we joked about in the past.

During the 1980s, pragmatic political leaders, such as the liberal Tip O'Neill and the conservative Ronald Reagan, stood for clearly defined principles and their respective political parties had well-known records. Leaders of this stripe could approach the voters honestly and reach across the divide to work out their differences. But these two famous contending political leaders—and others like them—are long gone, and in their place, are unnamed, faceless individuals who have no interest in compromising.

In today's political atmosphere, crossing the aisle in a legislative body to cooperate with the other side can be hazardous to one's political future. Many hard-core voters see compromising as a sign of weakness and disloyalty. It is safer politically for elected officials to stay within the partisan tribe and avoid the charge that they have worked with the other party.

In the meantime, all of our problems seem to be getting worse. We limp along from crisis to crisis while talk-show hosts and media people on both sides drum up issues that are designed to inflame public sentiment. There are zealots on radio and television who fan public fears on a regular basis. Hard-core partisans believe only what they want to hear. Those who are looking for the worst are given a regular diet of issues to keep them angry and afraid. Think for a moment of the names of television talk-show hosts that are trying to keep you angry and afraid.

Our deep frustration has caused some Americans to become mean-spirited and aggressive. Some profess to "hate" their political rivals. There is a tremendous amount of anger on the faces of those who carry placards and shout slogans. Often there is a racial or religious component woven into issues. It is not uncommon to see some protesters brandishing guns.

There's a gnawing fear that everything is out of control and getting worse. We are looking for a scapegoat. It satisfies a need to blame someone else rather than digging through all the complex reasons that are really responsible for our ills. But no one is willing to take any personal responsibility for all that has gone wrong.

Reformers of the Left and Right

In the 1960s, the voices of reformers were heard across the land. Democrats and Republicans joined together in the three branches of the national government to aid racial minorities, the poor, and the dispossessed. Proposals were designed to help those who had the least. There was a real effort to close the income inequality gap.

It wasn't a unanimous movement, but there was a majority in both political parties willing to move forward. There was idealism of building a more equal society—of setting our sights higher for the future. There was a boundless optimism that raised our expectations.

Now the voices of reform have been muted. The emphasis in the halls of Congress has shifted to protecting the assets of those who have the most. Wealthy folks at the top don't care about those at the bottom. The middle class is shrinking, and the poor and dispossessed are told they are on their own. The reform partnership between the left and right has been dissolved. Income inequality has grown every year. It's a different political and economic world.

Today there is a lot of shouting between the left and the right, but there is little or no understanding of the true position of either. One hears more often about what each side opposes rather than what it favors. Both sides mouth the slogans of the past, but few take them seriously. We all have become so cynical that we no longer believe what we hear. Most of us suspect there is an ulterior motive behind what is being said, and we are probably correct in that assumption. It is as though our American society has forgotten the philosophical foundations of our belief system. What we have become is not the America we idealize.

Our ship of state has been blown far off course and no one seems able to get her back on path. We are now adrift in uncharted waters with no respected leaders at the helm. The values and pronouncements that once united us are now embraced by each side as though they belonged to them alone. In cable news programs, there is a uniformity of opinion that condemns the other side. Ordinary people no longer respect their neighbors who may have a different opinion.

Political leaders still invoke the principles that made us great, but they do so as though they were the only ones who believe in them. Both sides claim to be patriotic, favoring the true American spirit, but we have all become hardened by the rhetoric. Collectively, we shake our heads and conclude, "The system is broken." This may be the only point on which we all agree.

Nowhere Else to Go

So how did all these corrupting influences come together to derail the political process? Why did Donald Trump win the presidency in 2016?

The gerrymandering of legislative districts, the uncontrolled campaign spending, and the enactment of voter suppression laws have played a major role in the democratic process and caused some people to become desperate. The impact of these corrupting factors has helped to create a government that alienated citizens who felt they were not being represented. In 2016, there was a mass of voters who felt they had nowhere else to go except to vote *against* the establishment they thought was ignoring them. They sincerely believed that shaking up the system would somehow make it better. What do you think of that point of view?

Voters were in an angry mood for good reason: trade policies had resulted in manufacturing jobs leaving the country—thousands had lost their homes in bank foreclosures—big banks were bailed out during the recession while regular people lost their life savings and pensions—social issues like abortion and same-sex marriages were dividing society—there was a fear that a lot of illegal immigrants were invading the country—a black man was in the White House—young people couldn't find a job—automation was reducing factory jobs—more unemployed people were going on public assistance—the middle class was disappearing—there were more tax cuts for the wealthy—public colleges were no longer affordable—the rich were getting richer and the poor were being forgotten—many had abandoned any hope for a well-paid job—and the national debt was spiraling out of control. Middle-class voters across the country felt abandoned while upper income groups were doing quite well. Added to this was a gnawing fear that the nation was in decline as a world power.

There was a lot of fear and resentment in 2016 and there will probably be more in the future. Consider how the effects of automation will shape the American labor force down the road. More jobs will be lost permanently. More folks will feel they have "nowhere else to go." How will a growing number of unemployed workers respond on Election Day? What will be the public reaction to guaranteed incomes for those without a job? Who will the rest of us blame? It's not hard to imagine more Trump-like figures on the horizon. Who would you blame?

In the early part of 2016, public opinion surveys showed that the people had the least confidence in the Congress, big business, and television news. Voters no longer trusted leaders in either political party. The alarm bells were going off, but few in the political establishment seemed to be paying any attention.

If enlightened liberals and conservatives (not tied to big money) had been in control of the American political system, they would have closed ranks and stepped in to show some progress on many fronts. But both political parties were being guided by big money interests and big money didn't care. Distressed voters sensed this disconnect and were attracted to a strong voice that promised to disrupt the system. There was a feeling out there: "If I can't have a chance at the 'American Dream' I'm going to vote for someone who is ready to tear down the system." There was an element of revenge in the minds of some voters.

In an earlier era, both the left and the right would have recognized this as a dangerous situation when people felt they had nowhere else to go. But in 2016, regular Republicans and Democrats ignored the warning signs. There should be an inscription above the door of every decision-maker in commerce and government saying: "Never permit a situation to develop that makes arbitrary change the only reasonable alternative." And right under it another statement written in stone: "If the working class loses its dignity, it will rise up and try to destroy the establishment."

Wrecking the system should never have been viewed as a reasonable alternative. But looking back, it was at this basic level that American leaders failed the country. In the primary elections of 2016, people were angry and they were turning to Donald Trump on the right and to U.S. Senator Bernie Sanders on the left. Voters on both sides were swept into a change agenda without knowing where it would lead. Folks on both sides were giving the middle finger to the establishment, and the party leaders in Washington D.C didn't even notice.

In reflecting on the Great Depression of the 1930s, Supreme Court Justice Louis D. Brandeis wrote, "We can have democracy in this country, or we can have wealth concentrated in the hands of a few, but we can't have both." Brandeis would have rolled over in his grave if he could have seen that in 2016, those with great wealth were using uncontrolled campaign spending, gerrymandering, voter suppression laws, and the increased power of Wall Street banks. It was all legal and it all happened out in the open. Why didn't the establishment act?

Congressional Republicans were too busy blocking Obama to take notice of this growing emergency. GOP leaders were geared up to reward their own interest groups while ignoring their middle-class constituents on Main Street. Leaders on the Democratic side weren't tuned into the situation either—they were in the process of abandoning their blue-collar electoral base in favor of white-color professionals and new entrepreneurs. Both parties assumed that their regular bloc of voters would stay in the coalition. They were wrong.

It is now apparent that the two major political parties may be going through an historic realignment. The dominant face of both parties is changing, and many voters are seeking a new home. It's not yet clear how this process will develop in the future.

The Republican Party, which had always been the party of the country-club set, now was becoming the party of the country as it attracted more alienated rural voters. Joining in were Tea Party supporters and evangelical Christians. In addition, the GOP included many folks who felt that they were being ignored by both parties. It was ready-made situation for Donald Trump.

On the Democratic side there was an increased number of upper income people and urban voters coming from both coastal areas. In increasing numbers,

Democrats were coming from big cities and the coastal areas. Rural voters were feeling left behind. Young professionals and entrepreneurs were also moving toward the left. Many of these voters came from traditional suburban Republican families that had been the backbone of the GOP. But there were thousands of unemployed working-class voters who were looking for a new home. Again, Trump would have a field day!

Added to this political turmoil was the fact that Donald Trump and Hillary Clinton had the lowest approval ratings of presidential candidates in modern times. The campaign was further complicated by another fact: the Russian government used the Internet to convince voters to support Donald Trump. We shall not soon forget the anomalies of 2016.

On election night, TV maps of the nation were colored either blue or red illustrating more areas were dominated by only one party—it was the era of one-party states. The nation was becoming more clearly divided almost like opposing religious crusaders. Republicans and Democrats had become two warring tribes that could not meet and work together. Gridlock became the new normal in the political process.

In this era, it also became more fashionable politically for both parties to go it alone and to discourage bipartisan action. Democrats enacted a major health care law (Obamacare) in 2010 (with no Republican votes) and Republicans attempted to repeal it in 2017 (with no Democratic votes). Republicans passed a very one-sided tax bill in 2017 (with no Democratic support). Both parties saw the other as the enemy rather than a possible ally. Both blamed the other for not reaching out to participate in a joint effort. The most strident voices inside each party resisted any efforts toward bipartisanship. These true believers relished the position of being pure, of not cooperating with the opposition. Much of the country looked on with utter disgust.

The Republican and Democratic parties in 2016 left a segment of their voters behind with "nowhere else to go." These angry voters were convinced that the political and economic system was "rigged" against them. They felt betrayed by the old establishment and were attracted to a new outrageous figure that ridiculed the old leadership who had the audacity to promise to "Make America Great Again." In an important sense, the Trump rallies became a refuge for those who were cast adrift by both parties. They weren't certain where it would lead, but they seemed to enjoy the ride.

It is ironic that the intense partisanship in both parties paved the way for a president that was neither a Democrat nor a Republican. He had no apparent ideology that placed him on either the left or right. The election of Donald Trump in 2016 was a shock to nearly everyone, especially the leaders of both political parties. Neither party understood the depth of anger that was running through the electorate. Democratic leaders thought the old Obama coalition would carry Hillary Clinton to victory—they were wrong.

The GOP thought they could control the bombastic Donald Trump—they were wrong.

Most pundits in the establishment believed that the erratic behavior of Trump would be so offensive that Hillary might make a clean sweep on election night. It turned out to be the opposite; it was the "establishment" that was on trial. Voters found *it* to be more offensive than Trump. Both parties were responsible for the electorate going off the rails and electing a president who had never held a political office. Everyone was surprised.

As we look back to 2016, it is apparent that nearly everyone was smug about the future—they thought they knew how to keep the government going. Now, those same folks have no idea of what will come next. Since then, both sides have spent an inordinate amount of time blaming each other for the rise of Trump. But if we look back a few years, it seems clear that some deserve more blame than others.

The widespread public anger that aided Trump had its roots in an overall Republican strategy voiced by U.S. Senate leader Republican Mitch McConnell of Kentucky. Early in Obama's first term, McConnell announced, "My number one priority is making sure that President Obama is a one-term president." To that end, congressional Republicans refused to cooperate or support President Obama's economic recovery proposals. There was a racial component in the conflict that some didn't talk about publicly. Obama was the first black president and many refused to work with him on any domestic and foreign policies. They wanted him to fail. Perhaps they didn't realize that their bigotry would undermine American politics.

Trump took advantage of the situation—he recognized that he could blame both parties as he belittled and bullied anyone who dared to speak out against him. Donald Trump seemed to comprehend the depth of the public rage against the "establishment" and rode to victory as the outsider that would fix the problem. He delighted in giving the middle finger to both political parties. His supporters were delighted—they loved it.

President Trump delivered a stinging, accusative inaugural address by focusing the blame for the country's woes on current and past leaders of both parties. Whoever wrote his opening address had an understanding of why some voters felt left behind.

Trump surprised everyone as he castigated four former presidents of both political parties who were seated on the inaugural platform behind him—Jimmy Carter, George W. Bush, Bill Clinton, and Barack Obama. (George H. W. Bush was in the hospital and was unable to attend.)

Never before had an incoming president chose to insult all the past chief executives on national television. The new President Donald Trump painted a bleak picture of both Democrats and Republicans as he promised to give power back to the people when he said:

For too long, a small group in our nation's capital has reaped the rewards of government while the people have borne the cost. Washington flourished, but the people did not share in its wealth. Politicians prospered but the jobs left and the factories closed.

The establishment protected itself, but not the citizens of our country. Their victories have not been your victories. Their triumphs have not been your triumphs. And while they celebrated in our nation's capital, there was little to celebrate for struggling families across the land.

Donald Trump won the presidency in 2016 because a large part of the electorate had "nowhere else to go." In winning the presidency, Trump stimulated a segment of the population that felt it had been taken for granted. He unabashedly focused on dividing the nation along political, racial, cultural and ethnic lines. It is no accident that the first black president was followed by the whitest president in modern history—an ugly part of the American past was unearthed again.

White Supremacists

When black people move up in the world, it bothers some white folks who feel they've been left behind. Upsetting the status quo causes anger to flare and sometimes crosses to burn. This has been true throughout our history. There has been a recurring pattern of conflict that begins when emerging minority groups challenge the power structure by pressing for equality. It's a time when some people want to remind themselves that they are superior to those they look down on.

There have always been waves of discrimination, cross burnings, and lynchings that followed black people as they moved up from the absolute bottom of society. "Keeping blacks in their place" has been the ultimate goal of whites on the fringes who felt insecure about their own positions in society. The process has been going on since the beginning of American history, but it really became a pattern after the Civil War ended in the 1865.

The Ku Klux Klan was formed in 1866 in an attempt to restore white supremacy after the Civil War and the reconstruction period. There were waves of localized violence to intimidate and punish any former slaves who dared to act as equals to whites. Jim Crow laws were passed that required segregation in public places. Informal rules of this kind were observed in many regions of the country outside the South. It was a time when black folks kept their heads down. The color line was everywhere. Laws requiring segregation of the races in public places was upheld by the United States Supreme Court as recently as 1896.

During and after World War I, thousands of African-Americans left the rural South and moved into industrial cities in the North, Midwest and West.

A reaction to this change was met with a resurgence of the Klan as it moved out of the shadows and marched down the main streets of American cities, especially in Washington, D.C. There were members of the Klan in Congress, the Supreme Court, city halls, and state legislatures across America. It was a time when President Woodrow Wilson showed a film in the White House, *Birth of a Nation*. The movie glorified the Klan as the defender of white womanhood.

After World War II, the Klan came back strong again in response to the visible movement of black folks into better jobs and some measure of equality. There was renewed anger when President Truman announced the end of segregation in the armed forces in 1948. The National Association for the Advancement of Colored People (NAACP) argued and won cases before the Supreme Court that declared racial segregation in public schools to be unconstitutional.

The Civil Rights Movement in the post–World War II era and the action of federal courts intensified the opposition from the Klan and other groups. Presidents Eisenhower and Kennedy called in the U.S. Army to enforce court-ordered integration in schools and universities. Alabama Governor George Wallace made a popular stand as he stood in the schoolhouse door and declared, "Segregation today, segregation tomorrow, segregation forever." Klan membership spiked again.

The passage of the Civil Rights Act of 1964 and the Voting Rights Act of 1965, during President Johnson's term of office, provided white nationalists with more motivation to engage in clandestine activities, including the assassination of Martin Luther King, Jr., and several other black leaders. In the aftermath of the King assassination, there were riots across the nation. African-Americans were becoming more assertive and so were the hooded members of the Klan.

The relationship between black progress and white resistance was apparent again when the first black president, Barrack Obama, entered the White House. The election of Obama enraged right-wing fringe groups across the country. Opponents of Obama rarely mentioned his race in public, but everyone knew some folks *hated* the first black president. There was a thinly veiled racist effort led by Donald Trump to question Obama's citizenship, and a concerted plan in Congress to oppose Obama in everything he proposed. It had been 150 years since the Civil War, but there were many who still felt threatened because black people were moving too far, too fast. Everyone knew that race was a factor, but only some had the honesty to admit it. Donald Trump denied that his campaign in 2016 had racial overtones, but his disdain for Obama was very apparent to everyone.

There's always been a psychological need to hold black folks down so insecure white folks had someone beneath them. White supremacists focus on separating the races as a means of elevating themselves. The phrase: "I ain't much, but I'm better than them" says it clearly.

The Klan has spent more than 150 years elevating the white race and demonizing black people. The myth of black inferiority declared that African-Americans were child-like and immoral—that they must never be permitted to marry white folks. The Klan and neo–Nazis have built their organizations around the myth of white supremacy—that white people are the backbone of civilization, and that in order to save civilization, the white race must remain pure.

* * *

I have been a political science professor for many years, and in that capacity I invited many speakers on campus (from both sides) who had diverse, sometimes violent points of view. I brought in members of the Ku Klux Klan and the leader of the American Nazi Party and gave them the opportunity to make their case. As expected, they fulfilled everyone's expectation, defending the "white race" against blacks and Jews. Those were wild evenings, but free speech won out and democratic beliefs prevailed. The campus community congratulated itself for exercising freedom of speech and rejecting racist beliefs.

In retrospect, I wondered if I would have welcomed the Klan and Nazis leaders with such open arms if I had been African-American or Jewish. From my academic perspective, these guest speakers were racist and anti-democratic, but they weren't a threat to me personally. How would I have reacted to introducing them to the student body if my brother had been lynched by the Klan, or if my grandparents had perished in a Nazi death camp? It would have been very difficult for me to welcome them on stage to advocate ideas that were personally threatening to me and my family. I would not be able to ignore what they have done, and would do again.

Society doesn't expect black people to be objective about racism nor Jews to be open to the views of Nazis. Yet it is vitally important to hear the views of those who advocate killing and maiming others, and it is even more important to remember what they have done. Everyone should read the story of Ann Frank (a Jewish child who died in 1945 at the age of 15 in the Nazi's Bergen-Belsen death camp) and Emmett Till (a 14-year-old black child from Michigan who visited the South in 1955 and was beaten to death by two white men in Mississippi for allegedly flirting with a white woman). Countless innocent people have been killed because of the Klan and the Nazi Party. There are lessons there for each of us.

The great majority of Americans reject the actions of white supremacists, but without realizing that these kinds of atrocities cannot exist without some complicity of non-violent citizens who maintain a polite silence when hostile remarks are made or racist jokes are told. The values of white supremacy are passed on not only by what some people say, but also by what others don't say.

There wouldn't be a Ku Klux Klan or Nazi Party without the informal backing of a huge segment of the population that supplies its unspoken consent. In ideologies of this kind, there is a violent tip at the top of a giant pyramid that is built on millions of silent people who supply passive approval. Clearly, those who say nothing are an important part of their political base.

People at the lower level of the pyramid may disclaim an association with those at the top who are involved in targeting minorities, but brutal acts occur because of the majority is silent. Bystanders at a violent demonstration provide cover for those who perform the illegal acts. There are many photos of crowds that gathered to watch the Klan lynching of a black victim, and accounts of those who watched quietly as Nazi storm troopers attacked a synagogue. Doing nothing, or not speaking up, is itself giving some comfort to those who target minority groups. We may not like to hear it, but in a democracy where public opinion decides public policy—opting out is taking a side. Those who commit the violent acts do so with the tacit support of those who offer no objection. It was Edmund Burke who said, "All that is necessary for the triumph of evil is that good people do nothing." This should be the watchword for liberals and conservatives alike.

Necessary Reforms

Racism is difficult to deal with. Laws can change behavior, but (in the short run) governmental rules can't change the way people think. But there is something governmental leaders can do—they can create a public atmosphere by condemning racism with a loud voice—and they can serve as examples of racial tolerance. If, for example, the President of the United States does not strongly reject the Klan or Nazis, these extremist groups see it as encouragement to act out their racism on the streets. Years of progress can be undermined in a day.

The same dynamic is at work if political leaders do not take a stand on divisive cultural issues. People who harbor discriminatory or homophobic attitudes are always looking for a notable person who doesn't speak out against exclusionary practices. Much of the cultural division in the United States today comes from those who are looking to public leaders for cover. There's some truth to the maxim, "racism will grow if it is ignored."

* * *

To continue on the subject of reform, there is a pressing need to change the way we finance political campaigns. Big money and honest politics have never fit well together. It is a fact of life that people with money will try to buy political influence if they can. Corruption is creeping into American politics from both the left and the right. We need to recognize that even honest elected officials will likely *remember* the goals of their largest donors. Money and special interests go hand in hand. Large contributions are made with a clear purpose and everyone knows it. There have been recent cases where campaign donors appeared to be more important than public opinion in determining a congressional vote that favored large corporate interests. In 2017, two-thirds of the people disapproved of a tax cut for the very rich, but Congress passed the law and the president signed it. The high-income donors got what they wanted. In 2018, nearly three-fourths of the people wanted a ban on assault-style rifles. You know how that has gone.

Campaign finance reform is not a liberal issue or a conservative issue: it is an issue that affects democracy. There is an abiding principle that government should represent people rather than wealthy special interests. Huge sums of undisclosed and uncontrolled financial donations have corrupted American politics. It is naïve to think otherwise.

The threat of corruption increased sharply when the Supreme Court handed down its decision in the *Citizens United* case in 2010. The court declared that political spending is a form of protected speech under the First Amendment, and that the federal and state governments may not restrict individuals, corporations, or labor unions from spending as much money as they please to support or denounce political candidates. Since then there is no limit on how much money can be spent and there is no requirement to disclose where the money comes from. An enterprising donor can easily circumvent the laws that were meant to control the flow of money.

That decision opened the financial floodgates while ignoring the arguments that it will contribute to corruption at all levels of government. Those who oppose the Supreme Court decision see this issue as an institutional reform. Reformers argue that taking big money out of the equation would make the system more accountable to everyone. But because the Supreme Court has made this decision, it may take a constitutional amendment to overturn the *Citizens United* decision.

There are many other ways to control money in politics and make the process more transparent so secret money does not subvert government decision-making. Each state has the legal authority to determine how campaigns are to be conducted. There have been three basic approaches applied at the state and federal levels:

- Imposing deadlines for contributions and spending reports during the campaign so the public is aware of how much is being spent and who is giving money to specific campaigns.

- Establishing financial limits of how much can be spent on specific offices and enforceable limits on how much an individual can give to each candidate.
- Providing some form of public financing of campaigns whereby small contributions from individuals are matched by larger sums from the government.

The above methods have been combined in various forms at the city, state, and federal level. At the time of the *Citizens United* decision in 2010, 24 of the 50 states had some laws that regulated how money could be contributed or spent in campaigns. Since then, several states have repealed or changed their laws, but a few states have not complied with the new doctrine. The question of campaign financing regulations is still an open question.

In addition to campaign finance reform, there is an equally important issue of restoring voting rights to minorities that were taken away when the Supreme Court gutted the Voting Rights Act of 1965. This long-standing federal law was aimed at overcoming various barriers to voting in selected states that had a history of preventing African-Americans from voting. A key provision of the law prohibited certain jurisdictions from making changes in voting laws without approval of the U.S. Attorney General or the U.S. District Court in the District of Columbia. The Supreme Court invalidated that section of the law by a 5 to 4 vote in *Shelby v. Holder* (2013). The decision made it possible for states to pass a series of laws that are designed to suppress the right to vote. In the long run, this judicial decision could change the outcome of elections.

Within two hours of this Supreme Court decision, the Attorney General of Texas announced a voter identification law that would make it more difficult to vote. Several other states (mostly in the South) quickly passed laws that ended same-day voter registration, shortened early voting, closed some polling places, purged the voting rolls of persons who did not vote at the last election and moved the polling places to remote areas. In 2018, there was only one polling place provided for the 13,000 people of Dodge City, Kansas, and it was located one-half mile outside the city limits on a lonely country road with no public bus service. Dodge City is 60 percent Hispanic. It was not admitted by those in power, but the goal of the election rules in Kansas, and elsewhere, was clearly aimed at suppressing the vote of a targeted group.

According to a Pew Research study, the United States was ranked 31 out of 34 developed countries in the world on voter turnout. Typically, slightly more than one-half of the registered voters actually turn out to vote in presidential election years. Sometimes that percentage drops to below one-third of the voters during a midterm election. The real effect of the *Shelby* case is that it is making it even more difficult for some voters to cast their ballots.

There are several reforms that would increase voter turnout:

- Automatic registration of voters when they reach the minimum voting age.
- Provide voter registration material when securing a drivers' license.
- Declare Election Day as a holiday or hold it on a weekend when more people can vote.
- Enable people to vote by mail, thereby eliminating the expense of polling places.
- Schedule early voting so people wouldn't have time-conflicts with work.
- Issue state ID cards to all citizens so everyone had an equal chance to vote.

All of these ideas have been implemented in some developed countries around the world. The United States is one of few countries where a low voter turnout is intentionally sought for political reasons.

The third recommended reform concerns the method used to decide the boundary lines for legislative districts. The national census is used to determine the total population of specific states and the results are used to reapportion how many seats each state will have in the U.S. House of Representatives. The next step is that the state legislatures and governors in each state are given the task of drawing the district boundary lines that will remain in place until the next census, ten years later. How the district lines are drawn, however, determines the type of candidate who can win seats in the state legislatures and the Congress. Leaders of both political parties spend a tremendous amount of time and energy in drawing districts that will produce the maximum number of election victories for their particular group.

As noted earlier, the process of gerrymandering is the drawing legislative district boundaries in a manner that over-represents a political party or group. It works especially well in the United States with the winner-take-all system, where the candidate with the most votes gets 100 percent of the representation (the entire position) while those that come in second or third place get nothing.

It is not uncommon for a party with slightly more than half of the population to win nearly all of the seats. And this is how it's done: Let's assume that Party A has a majority in the state legislature, and therefore has the privilege of drawing the district boundaries in a manner that will benefit its own members. The tactic is to analyze the population in specific areas and shift the boundaries around until there is a clear advantage for Party A in nearly all of the districts. Party B may have a substantial number of voters in the state but, when gerrymandering is applied, Party A will gain more seats than it deserves and build a majority in the legislature that can't be easily overcome. The overall result is that Party A will increase the total number of seats in the local, state, and federal legislatures and have a deciding voice in nearly all areas of public policies. It results is a gross overrepresentation of one party in the government.

This process is achieved by drawing district lines using two well-worn techniques:

- Create irregularly-shaped districts by including Party A voters and excluding Party B voters in specific districts, thereby giving Party A most of the election victories.
- Dilute the power of Party B by splitting their voters into several districts thereby denying Party B a chance to concentrate their voters in one area and win an election.

Gerrymandering is also used to underrepresent racial and ethnic groups. An example of this occurred in 2018, when the campus of The North Carolina Agricultural and Technical State University was split into two congressional districts, thereby denying the predominantly black student body a chance to combine their total voting power. Before the boundary changes there had been one black candidate elected. After the split, however, the new district boundaries paved the way for the election of two white candidates in districts with dependable white majorities.

Gerrymandering may not only change election outcomes, it tends to encourage hardcore partisan candidates to run in districts that are noncompetitive because they are beyond reach of the other party. These so-called "safe districts" discourage challengers from running against firmly entrenched incumbents. These districts are so one-sided in composition that it is not uncommon for these legislators to run unopposed with a free ride to repeated victories.

The widespread use of gerrymandering is one of the reasons why long-standing incumbents in the U.S. House of Representatives and state legislatures have become so unwilling to compromise. For all practical purposes they are a power unto themselves. The seniority system in legislative chambers provides them with near absolute power to represent specific interests in their districts. These members are in a position to subsidize special interests, thereby adding to the national debt. This is also one of the main reasons why the leadership of Congress is so out of step with average people who feel alienated by the system.

As stated earlier, both American political parties have perfected the art by using population data creatively to tilt the balance of voter composition in key districts. The process employs techniques of computerized science designed to misrepresent the people in various states across the nation. It is an open secret that both parties will try to underrepresent the opposition. State legislatures are partisan bodies and they are motivated to use anti-democratic means to gain a partisan advantage if they can get away with it.

For this reason, there is a need to take the redistricting process out of the hands of Democrats and Republicans and have the task completed by a nonpartisan commission or a judicial tribunal. The process can be done fairly if district boundaries are drawn in a sensible manner that can be reviewed by the courts. Computers can draw district boundaries more fairly than humans—it's not rocket science. There will always be a motive to cheat in the process, so the goal should be to minimize the input from those who can benefit from gerrymandering.

* * *

These proposed reforms are institutional, not partisan. They don't just favor Democrats or Republicans—they are designed to make the system more accountable to everyone. All of these reforms are aimed at enhancing the democratic process. Increasing public participation is a cardinal rule of democracies. The present anti-democratic features cause citizen alienation which is one of the reasons for the current political division. Many leaders on the left and right, including the League of Women Voters, Common Cause and other so-called "good government" groups have argued in favor of these changes. These topics have also been discussed in countless newspaper editorials that have pointed out the need to represent everyone in government, not just the few who can afford to spend millions of dollars to represent their particular interests.

It should be noted that these present practices of using big money, voter suppression and gerrymandering for political gain are aimed at undermining the voice of those without political power. Low-income folks, blue-color workers, and racial minorities are outmaneuvered easily by those who benefit from these practices. Some of them were the alienated voters who had "nowhere else to go" in 2016 and voted for Donald Trump out of a sense of desperation. Racism, big money, voter suppression, and gerrymandering are not friends of 21st century American democracy. We seldom think about it, but there is a limit in how much a system can be abused before it breaks. None of us want to find out what happens when we lose our capacity to govern.

It is tempting to blame President Donald Trump for all that has gone wrong. But Trump didn't create this state of affairs—he just knew how to exploit the dysfunction to his own advantage. As stated earlier, "he ripped the scab off of political and cultural sores that had been festering for years." This situation will not get better automatically when he leaves.

Questions for You

1. In what way did the passage of the Civil Rights Act of 1964 begin the eradication of the overlapping political bell curve? How did the events of the 1960s change the conduct of American politics? How do you feel about that?

2. What has been the effect of uncontrolled amounts of campaign contributions in American politics? How did you interpret the story of US Senator Dick Neuberger and the $10,000 political contribution? Do you think the story is relevant to the real effect of political contributions?

3. How can voter suppression laws change the outcome of American elections? What do you think the author meant when he wrote, "When the right to vote is at risk, everything is at risk?"

4. From your own experiences, how have partisan TV and radio hosts caused the American public to become more polarized? What do you think is their ultimate objective? Why or why not are you concerned about this situation?

5. What did the author mean in discussing the 2016 election by the point that voters had "nowhere else to go?" Do you agree or disagree? What have your friends and family said about their voting choices in 2016?

6. What is your reaction to the allegation that both political parties share the responsibility for the election of Donald Trump? In your judgment, how has each party changed as a result of that election?

7. What is your reaction to the quotation: "Obama was the first black president, and many refused to work with him on any domestic or foreign policies? They wanted him to fail." Do you agree or disagree? How do you feel about the Obama presidency?

8. How do you react to the author's statement, "It is though American society has forgotten the foundations of its belief system?" Do you agree or disagree? Why?

9. What do you think of the statement that in race and politics, "opting out is taking a side?" What do you do or say when you hear a racist comment or joke?

10. Do you agree that the proposed reforms outlined in this chapter are "institutional, not partisan?" If that is so, why haven't regular Democrats and Republicans taken steps to reform the process?

11. Google the term "gerrymandering" and look at the shape of some legislative districts on the Internet. How do you think American politics

would change if legislative districts were drawn to more accurately reflect the balance of the two parties? How might this reform influence the type of candidates who could win across the country, and change the way members interact with each other?

12. Why do you think the United States government has become so dysfunctional? In your judgment, why has the process of polarization spread to so many areas of life? What steps do you think should be taken to reverse the process?

2

Left and Right

The left and right in politics are nearly as old as the American Republic. Legend has it that the terms were first used to describe opposing political points of view at a French political meeting in 1791 as a group of contending leaders was meeting to lay plans for a new constitution. Those favoring a greater opportunity for the emerging forces of democracy were grouped together at the left side of the gathering, while those on the right side defended the established power of the monarchy and the church.

The classical descriptions from that meeting are as follows:

- The extreme left side was the position of the revolutionary radicals who wanted a complete destruction of the traditional system, including the monarchy, the church, and all governing authority. These were the violent revolutionaries of France.
- On the far left were the socialists who wanted all land and other property to be seized by the state and used for the common good. These were the non-violent radicals of 1791.
- Those sitting on the middle left wished to create democratic institutions in France; they favored a greater voice for the middle and lower classes. These were the classical liberals of the era.
- On the middle right side were those who sought more stability and protection of private property and business interests. Conservatives of this kind have voiced this position throughout human history.
- Those on the far right spoke of a new monarchy and retention of the church and nobles in society. A reactionary point of view has always favored the return of a once glorious bygone era.
- Those on the extreme right were ready to use violence to reinstate the king. In France, and elsewhere, revolutionary reactionaries have pressed hard for absolute power in an authoritarian state, and are willing to use physical force to reach that goal.

While the specific description of the left and right have developed from a variety of sources over the years, modern Western political philosophy still reflects the core attitudes found in that meeting of French political leaders. These positions on the political spectrum may not fit every contentious topic, but these terms are used daily to describe national and international issues. The political continuum presented sets out a contrasting scale of positions that are commonly used to label political ideas and people around the world.

FIGURE 2–1, THE POLITICAL SPECTRUM

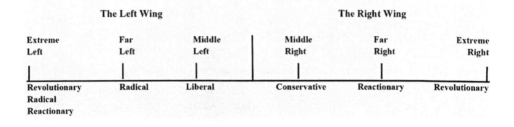

Persons on the extreme left and far left are the utopians of politics. They have a very optimistic view of human nature and the ability of people to improve themselves and live in society with few restraints. There is a greater faith in the individual to use freedom constructively and an expectation that the average person will not infringe on the rights of others. People in this category are usually secular in their outlook.

Those in the middle left are those we have come to call liberals and progressives. They are somewhat less optimistic about the human condition, yet they, too, focus on equality and individual rights as a means of improving society. Because a sense of hopefulness prevails among liberals, there is little fear of disrupting present institutions because there is a belief that better forms can be devised.

Continuing from the center and moving to the right, the term conservative has been used to characterize the middle right because they favor conserving and maintaining present institutions as a means of stabilizing society. Here the view of human nature is more doubtful. As they look around, conservatives see ample evidence of people who cannot be trusted, and they also are aware that people will probably continue to abuse the rights of others.

On the far right and extreme right, pessimism of human nature is at its highest. The term reactionary is applied here to describe those who are reacting in opposition to the present situation, and who believe that civilization has deteriorated because humanity has gone astray.

Revolutionaries on the right are sometimes influenced by a particular brand of religion, ranging from an evangelical version to extreme forms that may involve the use of terror to eliminate enemies of their faith. Revolutionaries on the left, however, almost never believe in a god of any kind. These competing characteristics are especially noteworthy when confronting international terrorism in all parts of the world. A belief in a god is often found with people on the right, but less frequently on the left.

Revolutionaries at both extremes are distinguished from all others on the spectrum because these two smaller groups (at opposite ends of the spectrum) advocate a violent overthrow of the present system. On the extreme left, revolutionaries wish to bring forth a bold, new system where there are no long-term restraints on people, where everyone lives in international harmony with no governments or political boundaries (Marxism). On the extreme right, revolutionaries advocate a resurrection of elements from the past (Fascism). Here the effort is to build a nationalistic, authoritarian society where people support a strong leader.

Revolutionaries of the extreme left and on the extreme right may have a similarity of intensity in belief, but have profoundly different views of human nature. In practice they are bitter enemies, and they are pledged to annihilate each other. The extreme tips of the spectrum are reserved for those dedicated to a violent revolution whereas the center portions are devoted to a non-violent approach. It is helpful to view the political spectrum as a political thermometer with moderate temperatures in the middle and boiling points at both ends.

In real life, however, each of us is spread out on the political spectrum in a unique way; we are all a combination of views unique to us alone. For this reason, positions on the political continuum can be labeled as a particular perspective, but it is difficult—if not impossible—to label individual people with any precision. A person cannot be a perfect representation of a position on the spectrum in much the same way as they cannot represent all the characteristics of a political party, an economic system, or a world religion.

The real value of comparing the left and right is to note there are ideological clusters on each side of spectrum not unlike the concentration of certain opinions in each of our political parties. There is still a lot of variety among individual liberals and conservatives, but it is helpful to notice the general continuity of values that are common in each group.

There are also many practical problems when classifying people as being on the left or right. Some, for example, consider themselves to be on the left in respect to social policy, but they favor fiscal policies from the right. In reverse, there are people who see themselves as having right-wing views on foreign policy, but they cling to left-wing ideas on some aspect of domestic affairs. Others have such divergent points of view that they don't seem to fit into any particular political group.

Donald Trump may be the most notable example of someone who does not fit neatly on the political spectrum. In the past he was registered as a Democratic, and later became a Republican. His critics contend that he changes his point of view depending on how issues affect him personally— he is also driven by the need to take a position in opposition to his political enemies. Trump sees himself as a "counter-puncher" that always strikes back against his critics. He admitted in an interview in 2018 that his targeting of the press as "the enemy of the people" was just his "way of fighting back." Trump is erratic in politics. Even his supporters do not embrace many of his policies because his views run counter to traditional conservative doctrine.

Trump's unpredictable positions illustrate how much Americans depend on the regular, traditional views of the right and left. Yet Trump's unusual combination of ideology is attractive to many who are not consistently liberal or conservative.

Since there are no widely accepted definitions of the key positions on the political spectrum, we often hear people stating examples when identifying a particular point of view. They may say, "When I say liberal, I mean someone who favors civil rights for minorities," or "A conservative is one who favors reducing the size of government." While both of these examples may be essentially correct, they offer only a vague idea of the terms we use daily to describe both our friends and foes in politics, and no analysis as to why they feel that way.

Most people have no working definition of these terms, yet they use them daily to describe their foes in politics. A trade union member might say, "Sure, I know what a conservative is—he's the guy who doesn't care about the working man." A retired farmer offers this comment, "All liberals do is raise our taxes and pour money into the big cities." From a critic of the military comes the charge, "The generals are a bunch of reactionaries who love war." And finally, from a businessman, "Radicals have burned our flag, insulted our honor, and tried to destroy the free-enterprise system."

Fixing Society

It is interesting when we consider how quickly people jump to political conclusions when they hear disturbing information. Many of us have a pre-programmed reaction to the news. For example, what would be your first thought if you heard anyone of the following announcements on an evening TV newscast? Think about each one of these topics for a moment.

- There's been another mass shooting today in the United States.
- Unemployment in minority neighborhoods has increased to record levels.

- Organized prayers in public schools have been held to be unconstitutional.

Some people would have this reaction to the comments above:

"I need to buy more ammunition to defend myself."
"I have a job—they can find one if they really go out and look."
"Children should have prayer time in school no matter what the court says."

There is a strong strain of individualism in the above statements, seeing the issues through the eyes of someone who takes sole responsibility for themselves. In addition, there is a message here that each of us is on our own to defend ourselves, and to be responsible for our own employment, and that we can worship as we please. There is a certain personal strength in each of these statements with little or no mention or concern for those who may feel otherwise.

But another group would have a different reaction to the same announcements on the evening news about mass shootings, unemployment, or prayer in school:

"It's high time we have background checks on all gun purchases."
"The government should set up a jobs program for the unemployed."
"Children have a constitutional right to not engage in religious activities."

The above reaction reflects a strong collectivist and secular theme. There is a strong sensitivity as to how these issues will affect the entire community. The focus is on everyone rather than individuals. There is an effort to settle the issues of guns, unemployment, and religion in a format that would include the entire public by setting out policy requirements that may or may not be acceptable to everyone. Without realizing it, we often respond to issues in an automatic manner. We jump to conclusions without thinking it through completely. There is an inclination to fall back on a pattern of thinking that reflects our political values. Many of us engage in ideological thinking without a giving it much thought.

People with a conservative approach to politics usually have a more personalized view of the world. They are ready to defend themselves individually in a situation where there is a threat; they have a greater sense of economic independence, and they have their own individual feelings about religious liberty. They feel less responsible for the welfare of people outside their group.

Liberals usually see these challenges from a more inclusive perspective involving the entire community. Their first thought is how this problem can be dealt with in a manner that will protect everyone's safety with firearms, job security, and the rights of non-religious people. Their orientation is more reflective of the entire country.

People of the left often feel the need to defend the role of government to deal with critical issues. Progressives generally believe in a collectivist approach. They view government as a positive instrument that can promote everyone's welfare. There is often an emphasis on helping those who can't help themselves. Government is a friend to people on the left. Without it they would not be able to build the kind of society they envision.

People of the right, however, have a different relationship with government. Much of their agenda is aimed at eliminating some government action. Conservatives would rather "go it alone" without restrictions. There is a built-in suspicion among some conservatives with any proposal that involves government action. The view from the right is often that government is a necessary evil that usually subtracts from human freedom. Their continuous message is that government doesn't work very well.

Liberals generally believe that there are some things that are good for all of us, such as environmental standards. Conservatives often disagree with this approach because they resist being controlled by any agencies that might limit them. This factor was apparent as right-wing groups generally supported disassembling of the Environmental Protection Agency and the Trump Administration's withdrawal from the Paris Climate Change Agreement in 2017. There continues to be a strong preference on the right to be free from cumbersome rules, not being held back by restrictions or regulations. This yearning for independence will become even more important as the climate change issue becomes more critical to human survival.

* * *

Both conservatives and liberals have a prescribed view of how to fix society. It is as though each has an opposing pair of ideological glasses that determines how they see a particular problem and how they think the problems should be resolved. Each, of course, believes strongly that their general approach to policy-making is best.

On the right, there is a conviction that individuals should be responsible for their own welfare. Society has no particular obligation to subsidize or provide special services to those who are in distress just because they made poor choices in the past. Each person is free to act on their own, to abide by their own decisions, and not expect any government aid to rescue them from their own personal problems:

- Those who don't want to work hard don't deserve a good-paying job.
- Individuals who don't save part of their income will not be able to retire.
- Personal health care is an individual concern, not a government responsibility.

Conservatives generally believe that we must live by our own choices and not expect to be bailed out by society. If we don't work hard, save our money, or provide for our own health care, we should not expect any special treatment by the rest of society. If a person wants to be lazy, spend all their money and not take care of themselves—they must accept the consequences of their choices.

In addition, people on the right opt for freedom and oppose most government regulations, subsidies and protection because it upsets the laws of supply and demand that govern human interaction in the natural world. The assumption is that individuals live in a natural state and they should be free of artificial rules set up by some public bureau or agency. Whenever conservatives think of a good society, they automatically think of a free society where individualism is valued and prized. They concede that life has a few rough edges, but that we are all better people when we take full responsibility for our own actions.

On the left the focus is on the whole of society enhancing the life of individuals by providing critical services everyone needs for the good life. The focus here is to make it possible for people to prosper without the fear of economic chaos, physical harm, or a spiritually numbing life. The goal is to minimize the sharp edges of human existence with public services such as free health care, a minimum wage, and a clean environment. For example, there is a belief that government should step in to:

- Prohibit discrimination based on race, gender, ethnicity, or national origin.
- Establish and enforce environmental standards for clean air and water.
- Protect individual choices as it relates to family planning or sexual preference.

There is also an assumption on the left that everyone deserves a second chance even when they've squandered past opportunities. There is an egalitarian mentality that the needs of society must be addressed so all gain an equal benefit. The most important follow-up question for liberals is how to apply a solution that solves the problem for the greatest number of people.

But there are classical criticisms of both the left and right that seem to be everlasting. Throughout history the following comments have been made again and again.

Criticisms of the Left

When Bernie Sanders ran for President in 2016, the scariest thing that Fox TV News could say about him was that he was a "socialist." They didn't analyze his position on issues; they just gave viewers the impression that he was probably a politically dangerous man. Fox News knew (as we all know) the word "socialist" is packed with negative emotions for many Americans. It is out of step with our view of who we are and what we believe. What is there about that word that sends political shivers down the spine? Why do many in the United States view socialism as an idea that would weaken us all from the inside? Why do some voters automatically vote against anyone who they think is a socialist?

In the United States, we talk about "creeping socialism" as though it were a disease that sneaks into a country without warning and saps all of its economic, social, and political energy. Not long ago I heard a person on television talk about "religious socialism" with the warning that it could cause people to lose their spiritual way as well. The TV personality criticized socialists for having faith in humanity instead of God. It is not uncommon to link words together such as "Socialist/Communist," suggesting all these unfavorable labels can be lumped together.

There is a not too subtle "dog whistle" that tells the public that the left can't be trusted to run the United States because this kind of leftist ideology is tied in with European socialism. One of the scariest things is to charge that "liberal reformers" are trying to make the United States into another Sweden or Denmark. Scandinavian socialism is made to appear as impractical, foreign, un–American and probably dangerous to our way of life.

We can look through nearly any part of American history and note that the left has always been presented by its critics as being outside the experience of good, God-fearing, Americans. Somehow the left has always been suspected of having covert ties with underground Marxist-types who want to radicalize and seduce people by giving them free stuff such as college tuition and health care. The fear is that capitalism, private property and democracy itself would be eroded until it finally slipped from our grasp. We are told by the right that we must always remain vigilant so we don't squander our freedom by following a socialist ideology.

That position makes many U.S. citizens feel like they are living in a lone fortress where freedom still prevails, but it is hanging by a thread. This belief in intense individualism makes many conservatives feel they must fight off threatening ideologies that are being advocated by outsiders. There is a general belief that socialism has infected many countries around the world— that we are surrounded by socialist countries that are creeping in our direction.

There is also a feeling that progressives mislead people into thinking they can gain benefits without putting in the hard work or paying for it. Conservatives are fond of saying, "There is no such thing as a free lunch." The implication is that Obamacare, food stamps and free education are all a cover-up that draws people into an expensive trap—one where taxes are sky-high and people give up their birthright of freedom. There is a real fear on the right that America will be overcome by collectivist thinking and individual initiative will soon disappear.

Conservatives warn that the liberal rhetoric reflects weakness and soft-headed thinking. The charge is made that the left doesn't understand that society should reward those who work, not those who wait for a hand-out. Perhaps the most often heard criticism of the left is that it has an excessive faith in human nature. Liberals are often accused of having their "heads in the clouds," of launching expensive social programs that won't work. The charge is made that these idealistic, experimental ideas will just end up raising everyone's taxes. Critics of the left are fond of pointing out that many of these programs are well-meaning but completely lacking in any understanding of reality. Right-wing opponents have a field day pointing out all inconsistencies and glitches in new programs. When a new idea is launched, there is a litany of predictions about all the things that will probably go wrong.

Perhaps the most important social program implemented by the left in recent years has been Obamacare, which was designed to provide health insurance for some 20 million Americans who were not already covered. The left had been trying to pass some form of universal health care for decades. The point was made repeatedly that the U.S. stands alone among Western nations in not providing health care for everyone. The underlying theme was that poor people faced more expensive health charges because they couldn't afford health insurance. Progressives felt a special obligation to help those who couldn't help themselves.

But the right focused on any and all reasons why the program wouldn't work. Conservatives said there was no need for universal health care, and that it would "bankrupt" the country. Since Obamacare was put into operation, right-wing groups have taken great delight in pointing out individual examples where monthly premiums have gone up by some outlandish percent. Obama was criticized repeatedly for his pledge that individuals would always be able to keep their own doctors after the plan was launched, when in fact that wasn't always possible. Conservatives compelled the Supreme Court to review the measure twice, and there were more than 50 attempts from conservatives in Congress to repeal it. But despite the widespread disagreement that swirled around the legislation, the Affordable Care Act of 2010 (at this writing) remains as one of best examples of how the left attempted to aid the less fortunate segment of society. But some on the right say that it was aimed at aiding those who were the least responsible because they didn't provide insurance for themselves. Thoughtful conservatives would add, "I bought health insurance for myself, you had the same chance, but decided to not take responsibility for your own life. Why should I bail you out with my tax dollars?"

There have been endless attempts to get rid of the Social Security, Medicare, Medicaid, food stamps, school lunch programs, unemployment insurance, bilingual schools, and early childhood education. In the years to come, it is likely that the left will continue to be faulted for spending too much on those who have the least. Progressives seem destined to constantly explain why they persist in pursuing such humanistic goals in the face of rising costs and only limited success.

In a sense, people on the left can't help themselves. They seem to have their eyes fixed constantly on what needs to be done for those left behind. Their agenda is inspired by what a good society "might be" if government was mobilized to help those who have the least. The cry of the powerless is always heard on the left. The most important factor from their perspective is to cultivate a sense of compassion and empathy—to gear up for the sake of those who are destitute. There is a belief among progressives that everyone should have the essentials of life as a basic right before anyone has more than is necessary. Leftists see a good society as one that is dedicated to promoting equality and basic human needs in every walk of life. They argue that it is only then that the full potential of society can be realized. But it's hard to put that message on a bumper sticker.

Liberals are often regarded as the "do-gooders" of society, and almost never known as the best fighters in a political battle. Some liberals are rather non-competitive in personal affairs; they don't seem to have the stomach for a good fight when compared with conservatives. Leftists are by nature, caregivers, not warriors. There aren't that many liberals who are military generals, police officers, or prize fighters. In a political knock-down, drag-out fight, leftists are more inclined to look for a compromise rather than go for an all-out victory.

The concern for the general welfare on the left sounds a bit weak when compared to the rugged individualism of the right. Liberals are less likely to appeal to the masculine side of public opinion. John Wayne and Charlton Heston are not their heroes. They seldom appear to be tough politicians who are out to destroy their opponents.

Wanting to help the powerless naturally puts liberals in a different mode. They don't speak with the confidence of the wealthy and the well-connected. Their message is often based on conciliation, cooperation, and sharing. Their appeal to public generosity sounds noble, but there isn't a natural public audience for that position. Redistributing the wealth is not a popular idea on Main Street America, especially from those who have succeeded in business.

People on the left seldom attack their opponents directly. They spend too much time explaining themselves, and too little time displaying their strength. It takes time and energy to outline a new program that helps everyone. Their goals are often idealistic and they expect the other side will be idealistic also, which is seldom the case. The liberal lofty view of human nature makes them feel good, but it doesn't help them win a political fight.

Criticisms of the Right

When Donald Trump ran for President in 2016, he said many times, "I am the law-and- order candidate." Despite the simplicity of his statement, it had two very different meanings that were heard loud and clear by two different sets of voters. For his potential supporters, the meaning was that he would crack down on terrorism, illegal immigration, civil rights demonstrations, and violent street crime. But the other meaning of "law and order" was heard by his detractors as an indication that he didn't care much about the plight of the poor and the powerless. The message heard by minorities was that he was backing the police when it came to fighting crime. Some African-Americans, Latinos, Muslims and other minorities came to understand that he wasn't in their corner. He polarized the electorate every time he made that statement, but it attracted thousands, perhaps millions, to his candidacy.

Trump's law and order declaration served a useful purpose on both fronts. First, he could tell his admirers what they wanted to hear, and at the same time, he could strengthen his hand by coming down hard on those he viewed as trouble-makers. In a dramatic fashion, Trump showed his "tough guy" role when he encouraged his supporters to attack protestors inside his own campaign rallies. Some folks cheered him, others jeered him. It was political theater.

Conservatives have long appealed to the American sense of good citizenship where everyone minds the rules of the game and waits for reforms to be made through regular channels. It is an old story of those in power saying to dissidents that they should "work through the system." In the past that admonition was observed by most, but now people are becoming more aware that the system may be "rigged." Folks at the bottom are saying that they are the only ones who were expected to play by the rules—those at the top were making their own rules.

On a related topic, right-wing leaders have spent a lot of time denying a governmental obligation to address problems at the bottom of the social/political structure. They reject race, income, and social class as contributing factors that hold people back in life. The right starts out with the assumption that everyone has an equal chance to succeed in life. They emphasize the lesson that personal success comes through high individual standards, self-discipline, and hard work. The right focuses on individual identity rather than group identity. They argue that every person can make it if they work hard and do not depend on others. Right-wing leaders like to draw attention to those who pulled themselves up by their bootstraps. They talk about the feeling of pride people get when they win in a competitive situation. It's like having your own sporting contest in which you fight hard and come out on top. The underlying belief is that people are responsible for their own success or poverty, and that they should not expect any help from those at the top. What might be seen as a lack of empathy by the left is seen as policy of personal responsibility by the right. But conservative leaders are often criticized for their lack of sensitivity to those who need help from the government.

When former General Motors head Charlie Wilson became Secretary of Defense in the Eisenhower cabinet, he spoke candidly about welfare recipients. Wilson said he always preferred hunting dogs to kennel dogs because they could take care of themselves by hunting and not sit on their rear-end waiting to be feed. The story of poor people being compared to dogs was repeated many times by liberals who claimed that Wilson was insensitive to the causes of poverty.

It is not uncommon for conservatives to contend that they are liberating welfare recipients by requiring them to work. Folks on the right say we all feel better when we compete for the valuable things in life—that when welfare programs are cut, folks learn to look out for themselves. They see hunger as a motivator—as something that makes people work hard.

The right is frequently accused of satisfying its own economic self-interest by claiming to favor more freedom for everyone else. The left contends that conservatives cut social programs because they don't want to pay the bill for helping the downtrodden. The allegation is made that upper income groups just don't feel any responsibility to help the poor. In a similar vein, the right is often criticized for reducing the political bargaining power of consumers and working-class people so that business groups have a free rein to avoid any regulation that may hinder their operations. Liberal critics argue that making money and avoiding taxation are the main motivations for conservatives.

In response to that charge, right-wing groups try to change the emphases of their policies by providing more choices for the individual. One of the most successful proposals from the right has been to increase personal freedom by undercutting the power of labor unions. Approximately one-half of the states have enacted Right to Work laws which are strongly favored by conservatives. The central purpose of this legislation is to promote the right to work without joining a union or paying union dues. In practice, when union dues and membership are made voluntary, the effect is to drastically cut the amount paid into the union and ultimately to weaken the entire labor movement.

Right to Work laws are extremely popular with business groups because the real effect is to weaken unions and make it possible for management to set hours, wages, working conditions, and overturn job security rules without going through collective bargaining. These laws are also popular with some disgruntled union members because individually they don't want to pay union dues. An additional benefit to business in these laws is that financially depleted unions have less to spend in funding candidates who are unfriendly to business. Union leaders regard Right to Work laws as the most detrimental measures that can be used against the trade union movement. AFL-CIO leaders have said they would "mortgage the kitchen sink" to stop a right to work law in their state.

As a rule, folks on the right resent most kinds of controls—governmental or otherwise. There is a general feeling that individuals should be free to act without the heavy hand of government, and that raising taxes only slows down the economic engine that benefits everyone. Accordingly, when conservatives came to power in 2017, their first order of business was to slash environmental controls, reduce the role of consumer affairs, decrease the number of public employees, and give upper income folks a massive tax cut. After all the rhetoric about free enterprise, the underlying goal was to roll back governmental regulations, reduce social programs, and provide tax cuts for the wealthy. The charge is made from the left that conservatives only care about themselves, that they are insensitive about the needs of the less fortunate.

Earlier, the point was made that liberals are driven to fund a new program when they see a social need that wasn't being met; it is also true that conservatives are driven to act when they see an opportunity to cut their taxes. The result in both cases is that their policies raise the national debt to a dangerous level. For liberals it is spending more—for conservatives it is paying in less.

Liberals are silent about overspending for social programs that adds to the debt—conservatives are quiet about tax cuts for the rich that reduce revenues and add to the debt. They both absolve themselves while ignoring their own fiscal mismanagement.

It is interesting how few people seem to recognize or remember the covert mission of the left and right. As a rule, right-leaning administration in recent history have all focused on reducing government regulations that benefit business interests, and left-wing governments have been eager to expand the role of government for the benefit of those at the bottom of the economic/social structure. It's what we call American politics.

Charges and Counter Charges

Liberals are often accused of trying to enact a "nanny state" where everyone is protected from everything. The charge is made that the left thinks they are more compassionate than anyone else, and therefore think they know "what's good for everyone else." Governments with liberal majorities usually enact regulations that take away what conservatives regard as important personal freedoms. The right contends that this reduction of personal choice is an insidious process that creeps into every part of life until the individual wakes up some day in a dreary society where everyone is forced to live in a stifling, brain-numbing sameness where individuals lose their will to be creative and no longer take responsibility for their own welfare.

As expected, the left rejects the "nanny state scenario" as completely false. Progressives argue that rules and regulations are absolutely necessary in real life to maintain a fair society where individuals can be free to interact in an open environment. Leaders of the left contend that it's absolutely necessary for governments to act in the public interest. They assert, for example, that it is entirely proper to break up monopolies, to provide for bridges that are safe to cross, and to have a public water supply that is safe to drink. Liberals contend that governmental rules are absolutely necessary in a civilized society where everyone has a chance for the good life. Conservatives don't necessarily deny that point, but they do stress that the "welfare state" can be excessive in protecting everyone from competition in life.

As stated before, leaders on the left think they are the only ones with a *heart* because they want to help the least fortunate. Conservatives think they are the only ones with a *head* because they want people to help themselves so they can be a vigorous asset to society.

The response from conservatives is that they care enough about average people that they want to see them able to use their abilities in a free and open society where individual initiative reigns. They are irritated by the constant charge that "conservative don't care about the poor." The point is made repeatedly that human beings are happier and more productive when they are free to be creative and act on their own behalf.

The right contends that lasting human progress has only come about when private entrepreneurs had the freedom to apply their talents without unnecessary government regulations. For example, Alexander Graham Bell invented the telephone, Thomas Edison, the durable light bulb, and George Eastman developed photographic film. These and scores of other inventors made breakthroughs on their own without government help. Opinion leaders on the right contend that they want to liberate the human spirit because the accomplishments of entrepreneurs improve everyone's lives. Real human progress, they contend, has come about through individual freedom and private inventiveness. Government controls, they charged, have only slowed human progress.

And so it is that the main division between the left and right boils down to each side claiming that the other does not understand what brings out the best in humanity. Conservatives see liberals as being hopeless idealists who don't understand that people work best when they are hungry for success. In return, liberals see conservatives as being insensitive and cold-hearted because they don't care about people who need a hand up when they are down. Both are stuck in their views of what is wrong with the other.

When conservatives talk about what's wrong with society, they almost always focus on big, expensive government programs that seem to stumble along in an ineffective manner. They mention the U.S. Post Office with its huge deficits and rising postal rates. They point to private mail carriers such as United Parcel Service (UPS) and Federal Express Service (FedEx) as examples of private businesses that are more efficient and provide better service. In opposing universal health care, conservatives maintain that free enterprise medicine is not only better, but more wholesome. The American Medical Association ran an emotional photo of an older, country-doctor type with a concerned look, leaning over a bed to take the temperature of a child who obviously had a high fever. The caption read, "Do you want government in this picture?"

But, on the other side, when progressives talk about what's wrong with society, they also focus on human emotion where poor people are denied health care because it is expensive, where children go to bed hungry, where people of color are denied a chance to live with dignity. Liberals shine the spotlight on the declining middle-class and the huge incomes of Wall Street bankers, hedge-fund managers, and the spiraling cost of prescription drugs. The underlying message is that only government can step in to level the playing field. It is interesting how often government is the underlying issue. The right usually sees government as an enemy of progress, while the left views it as the agency that gives everyone a chance. Liberals ask the emotional question: "Should a person face bankruptcy just because they get cancer?" Conservatives answer the question by saying everyone has an opportunity and obligation to buy health insurance on their own before they become sick. What do you think?

When hardcore conservatives and liberals have a conversation, they seldom talk about the same subject—they only deal with topics that suit their particular political needs. They each try to change the subject to one that better fits their preconceived ideas. Both of them ignore what the other person is saying, and focus only on how they will change the topic to something else. Listening to them is like watching a tennis match with both players trying to score points by surprise moves for which the other player is unprepared. No one really listens.

In today's world, there is no real communication between diehard members of the left and right. It is the classic orientation of true believers who simplify complex issues and sometimes make up facts to suit their needs.

Many of us have gone through painful Thanksgiving or Christmas dinners as know-it-all members of the family trade ideological comments back and forth while the rest of us shuffle our feet under the table. The food on the table may be good, but everyone gets indigestion because of the political tensions in the air. Conservatives and liberals are at their worst when they are related by blood. Long-standing issues between siblings are compounded by information each of them got yesterday from watching cable news programs. In recent years, family dinners have often turned into free-for-alls where family members try to shout each other down.

TV cable news shows with an ideological slant have actually started supplying their faithful viewers with stock answers they can use against an arrogant uncle from the other side. The format goes as follows: "If he says this, you can say that," or if she brings up this example, you can undercut it by discrediting that source.

The left and right approach problem-solving differently. Liberals are forever probing to find an inner reason why certain problems exist. For example, there is the question of why some students fail in school. Progressives go beyond the test scores to find out if the ills of society have hard-wired some children to fail; they point out that some kids have been traumatized by poverty, neighborhood violence, and the absence of positive mentors. Conservatives take a deep breath, brush off all those negatives, and point out that *some* children succeed under these circumstances, thereby proving that kids can make it if they really try. Right-wing leaders in education say it's all about individual effort. Each child has an equal chance and society shouldn't "slow down success" in schools by propping up some students while holding back the others. Conservatives favor public funding of private education and charter schools that end up leaving schools in the ghetto with less public funding.

The right focuses on individual ability to win out in the world and always has stories that exemplify dedicated folks who rise from the bottom. People on the left don't deny that it's possible to swim against the current, but they take notice of the correlation between those who fail and the high incidences of poverty, crime, community drug use, and broken homes.

The two groups might think they are talking about the same subject, but they're not. It's the old story of individualism verses the collective needs of society. It's almost like the two are seeing a different reality, and in fact they are. Each begins the process from an opposing perspective and proceeds to move quickly in the opposite direction. It's not surprising that Republicans and Democrats can't decide how to design the public schools. Their opposing visions of how to foster educational success causes them to have different educational visions. Liberals are forever putting themselves in the shoes of a failing child while conservatives are thinking, "It's not that complicated—just quit whining and get to work."

Most of the media appear to favor the liberal practice of digging into the reasons why there is a particular problem. Major TV networks (NBC,

CBS, ABC, and CNN) and many national magazines are also eager to find out why some people are falling behind in school. In doing their stories, mainstream journalists often focus their research on the social and economic reasons why children can't read, why youths are attracted to drugs, and why many minority group members end up in jail. It's no wonder that conservatives think the press has a left-wing bias on education and social issues. What do you think?

Blind Spots

Persons on the right and left believe they understand each other, but neither does. Each lacks the insight to understand what the other really believes. There are liberals who get angry just hearing what conservatives are advocating on Fox News. On the other side, some conservatives make it a practice of never watching MSNBC or CNN because they believe it is owned and operated by left-wing people. Both have blind spots that make it impossible for them personally to understand the opposing side. Hardcore people on both sides act in a manner that is remindful of a cult or narrow-thinking religious sect—they have made up their minds, and don't want to even consider another point of view.

For example, secular liberals have a blind spot on the issue of religious convictions in politics. The left has separated church and state so completely in their heads they cannot appreciate how and why some people have merged the two into one inseparable whole. The problem comes up every time evangelical Christians speak of God-given rights, declaring that God has declared that certain rights are guaranteed to every citizen despite any restriction set by society. Right-wing groups don't think that Congress or the Supreme Court has any authority to legalize abortions, allow same-sex marriage, or permit the teaching of evolution in public schools. From a Christian perspective, these practices are contrary to God's word. God won't change his mind just because man has passed a new law.

Liberals are not known for having strong religious convictions, and they generally don't think theology has a constructive role in a political dialogue. That means drawing a clear line between the two, and opposing the introduction of any religious principles into public affairs. Liberals don't bring religion into political discussions, and they don't think anyone else should either. Whenever Christians bring up religious issues or public funding for religious schools, people on the left contend that it should be a private, not public matter.

Leaders on the left believe that most disagreements can be settled with compromises. They argue that capable, reasonable politicians can always make a deal and work out any differences—each side should get a part of what it wanted. Liberals don't understand that "deals" cannot be made on issues involving God. Left-wing leaders are not even in the same ballpark when dealing with those who stand on the Bible as their source of authority. It never occurs to progressives that certain issues will always be beyond the reach of human dealmakers. The two sides are worlds apart when they discuss religion. Many liberals believe in God, but they seldom, if ever, evoke the Deity in arguing a political cause. It really comes down to the question of whether religious beliefs should ever shape public policies. Many conservatives believe there is a role for religion in public affairs—most liberals do not.

On this subject, the two sides have no awareness or insight as to how the other thinks. Some right-wing leaders think that liberals are "doing the work of the Devil." Liberals don't even take that charge seriously, but they do think the other side has a lot of "religious bigots." Neither side appreciates the legitimacy of the other. It is an issue that may never be resolved.

Evangelical Christians believe there is a higher moral law that is above anything human beings might promulgate through government; they will never approve of something they believe is morally wrong just because it's been declared to be the law of the land. On the other hand, secular liberals can't accept the belief that religious doctrines should overrule public policy. Because of these mindsets, it's clear today that the separation of church and state may never be a settled matter. There is an impasse here that threatens to divide the country even more in the future. Neither side shows any sign of giving up or backing down. What is your view on this subject?

On a comparable matter, orthodox conservatives have a blind spot on the matter of economic issues, especially as it relates to government regulation. They generally believe in a person's right to operate without restraint within the free-market system without government intrusion. There is a conviction here that the market forces will reward or punish, and that government should stay out of the process. Many right-wing leaders ignore the consequences inherent in an unregulated system that may result in members of the public being victimized by unscrupulous capitalists. Many believers in the free-market want to abolish a long list of public agencies with any regulatory or rule-making powers such as the Department of Labor, the Environmental Protection Agency (EPA), the Department of Commerce, the Securities and Exchange Commission, the Department of Education, the Federal Trade Commission and the Consumer Financial Protection Bureau. This kind of thinking promotes an open season on shutting down large parts of the government. This became the agenda for right-wing members of the Trump Administration when they came into office in 2017.

The banking crisis that began in 2007 caused the greatest economic recession since the Great Depression of 1929. It was caused by major U.S.

banks taking unsecured risks in volatile markets, and the failure of regulatory agencies to step in and halt these dangerous practices. The result was that people panicked and the economy went into free-fall mode. It was necessary for the federal government to bail out the banks with a loan of $700 billion of taxpayers' money.

Not only was Wall Street rife with irresponsible behavior, the U.S. Justice Department lacked the will to pursue anyone personally to make sure it wouldn't happen again. Since 2007, major Wall Street banks have grown in size and many reformers conclude that little has been learned by the Great Recession that destabilized economies around the world.

There is still a belief that government should not "kill the goose that lays the golden eggs." Despite the disastrous results in 2007–08, there is still a reluctance to do anything that might hinder Wall Street. The few reforms that were made have been watered down since Donald Trump came into power in 2017.

In closely related areas, inflexible free-market thinkers also have turned a blind eye to controls on air and water pollution, promotion of federal standards in the workplace, consumer protection, and unsafe or deceptive trade practices. Here again they have faith that the market will correct any excesses. At this same level of thought, they don't want to talk about economic monopolies that eliminate competition. Faith in the marketplace is nearly absolute on the right, with little acknowledgment that the economy can be dominated by predatory forces that reduce the freedom of others and promote a situation where another economic collapse can occur. One conservative I know says the same thing over and over: "The only thing the government should do is direct the US Army. Everything else should be unregulated." What do you think?

Business conservatives are driven by the profit motive—they believe it should not be restrained. They think individuals have the right to take as much as they can with little thought about the impact on the public. The rationalization is that pure competition will balance out excesses through a natural process. But the ultimate business plan is to monopolize the market as much as possible. Frequently, the end result is disastrous.

Looking back over history, it is apparent that the builders of great economic empires of each era were their own worst enemy because they didn't seem to understand that being completely self-centered was not a wise business model. They could not conceive of the idea that prosperity is the most durable when it is widespread. Right-wing conservatives—then and now—fail to appreciate the thinking of Henry Ford, who believed that workers should get a fair wage so they could buy the Ford cars that were coming off the assembly line. Government regulation can promote a healthy economy with reasonable rewards across the board, for both producers and consumers, but it is a blind spot for many on the right.

Free-market thinkers have little concern for the "other side." Typically they will take as much as they can get without considering what will happen as a result. The tax cuts of 2017 were a case in point. Critics pointed out that 83 percent of the tax cut benefits went to the upper 1 percent of income earners. The result was more income inequality plus an increase in the national debt.

Conservatives have a real blind spot on government regulations. In the long-run, unrestrained economic activity gravitates to greedy behavior, greater income inequality, and ultimately a national crisis. The resulting crashes bring new economic controls that are, of course, the opposite of what is desired by economic elites. But some right-wing leaders can't seem to stop before they go off the cliff. The temptation is too great: low wages, monopolistic practices, unrestrained profits, and a deregulated economy cause irrational behavior for free-market conservatives. They can't seem to recognize that just because something looks tempting, doesn't mean it won't blow up in their faces.

But not all blind spots are singular; most of them are operating simultaneously. Virtually all the hot-button issues of today have caused both the left and right (at the same time) to lack any appreciation for the other side. Gun control verses gun rights is a case in point. Seemingly the only curiosity either of them has is the question, "Why can't they see that they're wrong?"

As a group, liberals have few insights as to why some people must own firearms. Leaders on the left don't understand that gun owners have a special attachment to their weapons that is very personal. Gun enthusiasts like the way guns look and feel. The gun cabinet is an important feature in their home. Both young and old have a real fascination for shooting at both stationary and moving targets. It is not uncommon to give a child their first gun as a Christmas present. Teaching gun safety and owning several rifles is a fundamental part of their lives. Also, there is a belief that the Second Amendment to the Constitution testifies to the proposition that every citizen has a birthright to provide for their own self-defense.

Self-styled militia members go a step further—they see weapons as the last means of survival if all else fails. There is a profound sense of fearing the worst as they store up guns and ammunition with the thought that someday their continued existence may depend on their personal arsenal. Right-wing talk show hosts report stories that promote fear—they are forever encouraging people to be prepared with a gun at your side. They contend that America was founded on the ability to fight back, and that we would not be complete as a people if there were any limits on the right to buy, own, or carry a gun.

The conflict comes to a head with a wide variety of gun enthusiasts after every mass shooting as new efforts are launched to control guns. The types of measures vary in design, but the public relations conflict is basically the same. The question is asked, "Won't more controls on guns promote public safety?" The answer from the left is a strong "yes," but on the right it is a resounding "no."

Regular television and radio schedules and commercials are set aside when a mass shooting occurs. The focus is on the number and ages of the victims, the background of the shooters, the type of guns used, and whether the weapons were purchased legally. Gun owners brace themselves for a new rash of gun control measures that are proposed after each shooting. The whole country gets involved as the stories are rolled out in great detail.

Despite the loud debate, the two sides do not hear each other. No matter how much the claim is made that it's only about public safety, a persistent number of gun owners on the right fear that the government is "coming to take our guns." On the left there is a belief that gun owners don't really care about innocent people being killed as long as they can keep their guns.

The level of fear is raised frequently by organizations like the National Rifle Association (NRA) that warns that keeping records of firearm purchases and background checks is the first step in setting up a list of gun owners so the government can "take away our guns." Many think it would have happened long ago if it hadn't been for the NRA and right-wing militia groups.

Some firearms owners see themselves as the last line of defense; they have a fierce sense of independence and are not willing to depend on anyone else if they are under attack. There is always the fear that federal agencies or local law enforcement officials will come to get your guns. For that reason, many prefer to own semi-automatic assault rifles (such as the AR-15) on the expectation that someday they may have to fight the police or the U.S. Army.

But what the right does not appreciate is that the public effort to regulate guns has been initiated by regular citizens, not by the government, and that the effort to control guns will not diminish soon, if ever. The spontaneous student movement after the 2018 school shooting in Florida is a case in point. Thousands of young people and parents turned out to demonstrate in major cities, in front of state capitols and in Washington, D.C. It was a citizen-driven movement; the government did not take a stand.

While both sides in the controversy have blind spots for each other, it should be noted that they are nearly equal in numbers on both sides across the nation. There seems to be little hope that either side will acknowledge that they have a blind spot on the issue. In some quarters, asking someone to change their views on guns is not unlike asking a devout religious person to change their religion. It ain't going to happen now, if ever. What do you think?

Illegal Politics

Breaking the law is as American as cherry pie. Both the left and the right have advocated the idea that is alright to violate the rules of the game if it improves the situation. Illegal Politics has been the friend of American pathfinders on the right and left who sort of made up the law as they went along; those pioneers and others made this country into a mighty nation. Discontented people were attracted from every culture and every corner of the globe. They built a coast-to-coast empire that became the envy the world. Disregarding the law, when necessary, became an important part of the American character.

But the practice of breaking the law has come back to haunt us. The frontier is winding down, and the old rugged individualism does not fit well into modern 21st century life. We have created a freewheeling mindset that may be partially responsible for our disrupted politics and uncivil society. The Trump phenomenon is the latest example of a "shoot from the hip" approach in our politics. Voters in 2016 wanted someone who would shake up the system. They got their wish. Now what do we do next?

Despite the present circumstances, we are fond of saying, "everyone must obey the law," and that we are a "nation of laws, not men." But it is really more accurate to say obey the law if you're satisfied with the status quo—if you're not satisfied, break it to bring on a change. Some of our most celebrated moments for the left and the right have occurred when we acted illegally. In reality, we have always been ready to break the law if there was a need to start anew. The movers and shakers in the U.S. have never been bothered by legal obstacles.

Americans have a built-in justification to make up the rules as they go along. The westward movement is a case in point. Just ask Native-Americans. Pioneers and settlers broke the law anytime it was to their advantage, and the government usually backed them up. Treaties with Native-Americans lasted only as long as they suited settlers' needs. The whole idea of Manifest Destiny was based on assumptions that the United States had a right to expand in every way possible, and to disregard everyone in its way. Ask the Mexicans and Canadians about our willingness to move the borders when it was in our interest.

Americans are quite content to live on the cutting edge. They love to feel they are unique and special. There's even a name for it: "American Exceptionalism." Unlike people on distant continents, folks in the U.S. feel that they can break the rules while the rest of the world will just have to accept it. Waiting your turn and minding your manners have never been strong characteristics in the fifty states. Check out the way Americans crowd in when getting on a public bus. There is seldom an orderly line as there is in Britain.

Despite our public misbehaving, there is a myth that we've always been the good guys that followed the legal path. But reality is just the reverse. When the stakes were high, Americans were always ready to break the law. Both the left and right have a long history of success while violating the law. In fact, illegal politics and behavior has been the handmaiden of most of the major changes in American history. Much of what we regard as progress has come about through illegal means.

Great wealth and power were accumulated by American businesspeople of the right while ignoring clearly written, anti-trust regulations. Captains of industry made great strides as they bought off politicians and built giant monopolies across the country. These tycoons used private armies and brutal tactics to come out on top. Great economic empires have been built by breaking the law—illegal politics paid off big time.

The response from the left was also based on widespread disobedience of the law. The early American labor movement launched illegal strikes that often resulted in widespread violence and destruction of property. They matched the Robber Barons every step along the way with aggressive picket lines and violent strikes. There were notable examples of leftist revolutionaries who were willing to use any means to win the day, including the assassination of public officials. It's pretty clear that illegal politics opened many doors for the labor movement.

Add in the experience of Prohibition laws of the 1920s which spawned criminal empires in most parts of the country. Normal, law-abiding people openly broke the law on a regular basis every time they purchased illegal alcohol. Organized crime figures were admired and emulated by the public. Americans followed the criminal careers of Bonnie and Clyde as the pair outwitted the law. It was not uncommon for the public to root for the law breakers.

In more recent times, the Civil Rights movement used civil disobedience as the most notable tactic to demonstrate that the laws were unjust and discriminatory. Black and white protestors became national heroes as they intentionally violated the law. Protests to end the war in Vietnam threatened to shut down the country as disobeying the law became a badge of honor. Recently we have had a multitude of lawless riots, as well as the continuous violation of immigration regulations, the declarations of sanctuary cities, and laws governing the use of marijuana and other drugs. Americans have perfected law-breaking into a political art.

It is not uncommon for law-breakers to be regarded as political heroes. In 1967, the *New York Times* and *Washington Post* published the Pentagon Papers, which was a secret account of American involvement in Vietnam from 1945 through 1967. The government ordered the *New York Times* to stop publishing, but the *Washington Post* and other newspapers continued publication in violation of the law. Later the Supreme Court sided with the lawbreakers, stating there was a First Amendment right to publish the material, even though it was illegal at the time.

But getting approval from the courts doesn't really matter. If Americans feel the cause is just, virtually anyone can become a law breaker in the United States without feeling guilty. A positive way of saying this is that one of the great reasons the U.S. has done so well is that the people have built a political culture around thinking for themselves and not minding the rules of the game. It's a very "non–European" way of viewing life. We're different and we know it.

A famous international relations professor, Hans Morgenthau, argued that nations have different behavior patterns based on their national character. Morgenthau cited a classic study of allied troops in World War I armies, in his book, *Politics Among Nations*. French troops on the battlefield were considered best when charging across an open field under heavy fire; the British prided themselves on holding a position to the last man; Russians could be depended on to obey commands even when it no longer seemed sensible; but the American troops excelled in sizing up an unexpected development and deciding to take an entirely new approach contrary to earlier orders. Clearly there is something in these divergent behaviors that is akin to a national character. One reason why Americans were good at changing the rules to fit the circumstances was because that trait has been enshrined in American history. That's how we see ourselves and (deep down) that's how we think we are expected to act.

Facing new, unexpected situations successfully is the signature of the American character, and early arrivals from the old world were the first to act independently. There were extreme challenges in building small outposts and settlements along the eastern seaboard in the 17th century. Later colonists from the thirteen states faced long odds when they took on the military might of the British army in the Revolutionary War of the 18th century. A totally new type of nation was launched when the Constitution of 1787 was promulgated. Following that unusual event, the westward movement of the 19th century was a continuous struggle against nature and indigenous people. All of these examples illustrated what Americans could do when their backs were up against the wall.

But there was also a dark side to the story. Americans on the move into uncharted territory were often a lawless lot. Frontier justice was often heartless—many were executed without a proper trial. The Ku Klux Klan was illegal, but hundreds of African-Americans were lynched with the support of the local sheriff. There was a time when every major American city had an organized-crime boss. Breaking laws became popular in every part of the country. We still lead the world in the number of gun deaths each year and the per capita number of people in prison. There is an excessive character in our culture. But despite those negative statistics, Americans are rather proud of their law-breaking tradition.

People around the world know the United States through Hollywood movies. There were the Westerns with John Wayne, the gangster movies with James Cagney, and more recently the characters of Rocky and Rambo. No other nation has produced more rugged individualists who could think for themselves under pressure. Hollywood has built an expectation that the U.S. always comes out top in the final reel; and many of us have decided to play out the roles we saw on the screen. American heroes break the law in grand style.

Movies in the United States reflect something that was and is still real today. There is a strong strain of ignoring propriety and striking out on your own. There have been times when there were few rules in remote areas and everyone was really on their own. It always was a bit risky, but it became the American way of setting up "a new society" to fit the situation.

Americans have some reservations about what the Donner Party did in 1846 when they were trapped by an early snow storm while crossing the Sierra Nevada. But rather than perishing in the harsh winter, they broke the rules of civilization as they became cannibals to avoid starvation. These accounts weren't pretty, but they were part of the American story: "Damn the rules of a civilized society, we did what we had to do." Americans have always been survivors despite the rules of the game.

Americans had opportunities that did not exist in other parts of the world; folks could leave their modest dwellings and move westward. They could leave behind the old ways and build a whole new way of life. An independent spirit propelled those who were dissatisfied. Some wanted wealth; others wanted land; others wanted freedom from discrimination, and perhaps most just wanted to be left alone so they could live as they pleased. In all cases they were willing to bend the rules or make new ones to achieve their goals. *The Grapes of Wrath* wasn't just a story of the 1930s—it had happened many times before, and it continues to happen today.

The American character can also be illustrated by tracing the long-range migration trends of history. Most of the immigrants who came to North America were from areas around the world where they had nothing to lose. They would have stayed where they were in Europe if they had land or an important position. But if they had no future, they set sail for the New World. Those who settled on the East Coast stayed if they were doing well, but if they weren't, there was an incentive to move to the Midwest. The same circumstances came into play in the Midwest as the most dissatisfied folks moved to the mountainous West or as far as the Pacific Coast. For some there was the hope that things would improve if they went out on their own, and they usually took their guns with them. An armed people with nothing to lose became an important image of how Americans saw themselves.

There was a saying on the frontier, "God created men but Sam Colt made them equal." Colt invented the first semi-automatic six-shooter pistol which was wildly popular during the westward movement, and the motto is still repeated today by those who see firearms as the great equalizer in their lives. Guns have always been a part of the American mystique. Large numbers of Americans idealize the gun culture. Owning, handling, and firing weapons are an important part of the national character. The very idea of the government (or anyone else) taking away our guns would send a wave of indignant anger across the country.

Perhaps the westward movement (which is still in progress) gave us one of the strongest characteristics of the American spirit. There is still a willingness to do the unexpected, to strike out into uncharted territory. Americans like to think they can always land on their feet, no matter what the challenges. They have a reputation around the world for being resourceful, and also for taking the law into their own hands.

In 1893, a University of Wisconsin historian, Fredrick Jackson Turner, proposed the "Frontier Thesis" in which he argued that the wide-open spaces of the American frontier had liberated people in the new world from the old ways of European life. It gave these traveling people a sense of independence, a chance to experiment, and an opportunity to make great contributions while rejecting the tradition-bound ways of the past.

But what happens when the frontier is gone? What will happen when the wild areas are settled and these rugged individualists are crowded into cities across the country? Will the "go it alone" mentality operate smoothly in a sprawling urban environment like 21st century Los Angeles? How about armed, angry folks out on the freeway? Is it a good idea that guns are plentiful and people can carry them openly in any public place wherever they please? Will the idea of rugged individualism become toxic in American politics and society? Why are there so many mass shootings? What lessons can we draw from the increasing number of deaths from firearms? Some argue that the idea of the anything goes mindset has brought out a form of social disorganization that threatens our modern lifestyles.

Both liberals and conservatives acknowledge that there is a certain recklessness in American politics today that is alarming. Neither the left nor the right can hold back the destructive behavior so prominent in political campaigns and the governing process. Civility has disappeared in public affairs. But Americans are still attracted to the John Wayne approach to settling disputes.

The 2016 Donald Trump voters were a case in point. They threw their support behind a bold, untested, charismatic, sometimes profane figure.

Trump thumbed his nose at the establishment, he promised to keep out foreigners, abolish government regulations, and bring back lost jobs. He had the audacity to tell black voters that they "had nothing to lose" in voting for him. His cabinet was made up of people who pledged to dismantle a political system built by old-line conservatives and liberals. Strangely, a New York billionaire activated a new brand of American pioneers who are still looking for the "promised land."

Americans are evolving into a different kind of people. There is a growing degree of extremism creeping into the mainstream of politics and culture. In the Western vernacular, people are more likely to "shoot from the hip" and say anything that will defeat the opposition. Winning is the only thing that is important for some.

It no longer seems to matter if political leaders tell lies. Televised versions of gross distortions of the truth have been heard over and over, around the world. When these statements are proven false, hardcore supporters of the liar don't even take notice. There is now a polarized political culture that is impervious to the truth.

It is not uncommon for old friends to cut off their relationships because of political disagreements; some people can no longer work together on a common project because there is so much distrust and anger. People of opposing political parties are less likely to marry and stay together. There is tribal warfare going on. This whole situation doesn't feel right to moderates on the left or the right, but they are unable to do anything to stem the tide of destructive behavior that is tearing the country apart. While the present situation is worrying, many expect things to get worse; there is little appetite to reach out to those on the "other side" to heal the wounds that seem to be getting deeper. Illegal politics are here to stay, at least for the foreseeable future.

Questions for You

1. If all of us are unique in respect to political views, what is the value of using a political spectrum? Why do you think the media labels people as being either on the left or right?

2. Compare and contrast the statements made by the left and right in the "Fixing Society" section. Which side is closest to your views? Why?

3. Why, in your judgment, is the concept of socialism so unpopular with a large segment of Americans? Cite an example of a person or group that has a negative view of socialism.

4. In what way does Obamacare fit into liberal values? What is your personal response to liberals defense of the Affordable Care Act?

5. Compare and contrast the way liberals and conservatives compete in an open political conflict. Why, according to the author, do liberals lose many political fights?

6. How does the right dismiss the importance of race as a reason why some folks have lower incomes and endure hardcore poverty? What do you think about that point of view?

7. *Google* Right to Work laws. Why do people on the right argue that these laws promote the freedom of workers? Why do these laws decrease the political power of labor unions?

8. What are the classic differences between conservatives and liberals on the role of government promoting education in impoverished areas? How do those differing points of view illustrate the basic philosophy of each group? Which position, do you think, brings out the best characteristics of humanity?

9. Why are the issues of "God-given rights" and "government regulation of business" blind spots for many Americans? Do you have a blind spot on either of these issues? Why or why not?

10. Why is the author doubtful that there will ever be a workable agreement on gun control versus gun rights? Do you have an answer to this controversy?

11. What conclusions did Hans Morgenthau make on comparing military troops in World War I? Do you think there is such a thing as the "American national character?" Why or why not?

12. To what extent has "the American character" brought reckless behavior and disruption into US culture? Are you concerned about this apparent direction of the country? Why or why not?

Why Do People Engage in Ideological Thinking?

Cite an example of a friend or member of your family that "jumps to ideological conclusions" on a particular political topic. Why do you think that many people, including yourself, react emotionally and ideologically to political or social issues?

3

Foundations of Politics

What we call ourselves politically and what we call others has always been revealing. While the words "liberal" and "conservative" are preferred, but some people avoid either identity and use the term "moderate" instead. Still others dilute the labels further by qualifying themselves as "moderately liberal" or "moderately conservative." And finally, some want to reject all the labels, claiming that they don't fit into those old categories.

Those on the right are more careful than anyone else of what they call themselves; they seem to want everyone to know their specific identity. Often there is an attempt to associate with favorable symbols by saying, "I'm a Reagan Conservative." Left-wing folks don't have any comparable phrase they still use. Years ago, some called themselves "New Deal Liberals," but that was a long time ago, and that era is no longer relevant to describing people today.

In foreign affairs the terms are stretched further to fit a particular mold. Sometimes we try to identify our friends and foes using the left and right context despite the fact that some foreign situations are way outside the American experience. Some right-wing dictatorship regimes in the Middle East, for example, are referred to as being "strongly conservative." Some left-wing dictatorships in Asia are said to have "emerging liberal tendencies." And finally, in Syria, violent revolutionaries (favorable to the U.S.) were described by one very creative talk-show host as being "moderate revolutionaries."

In recent years the term "independent" has become very popular, especially among those who are turned off by partisan politics. But the word is losing some of its middle-of-the-road meaning because it is being used to cover up groups or individuals who have a very clear agenda identified with either the right or left. There seem to be fewer than ever who consider themselves to be neutral and truly willing to agree with either side based on the merits of an idea.

Then we go to an even smaller group who claim the name "radical." Almost always, these folks are focused on the problems of the poor and dispossessed. The Occupy Wall Street or 99 Percent Movement were well-known examples. The goal here was to illustrate the wide gap between the very wealthy one percent and the rest of the population. Leftists camped out in the commercial centers around the world and carried placards to dramatize income inequality. A similar example dealing with race was the Civil Rights Movement and the more recent group, "Black Lives Matter." In both cases, the term "radical" was used with pride by people who were willing to put their bodies on the line, but opposed the use of lethal force.

There is a comparable degree of intensity of personal involvement on the extreme right, but people in this category do not want to appear to be outside the mainstream. No one wants to be called reactionary even though it is clear that some people on the right are activated because they are *reacting* to a perceived threat. The Ku Klux Klan came into being as a reaction to the growing prominence of African-Americans, Jews and Catholics. The American Nazi Party and other nativist organizations are reacting in much the same way.

But both the Klan and the Nazis like to call themselves "conservatives" for two reasons. First, they wish to associate with a term that has traditional respectability, and second, they regard their principles and beliefs as being so self-evident and correct, that a moderate terminology seems to be wholly appropriate. Today there's a multitude of armed people who call themselves "conservatives" because it is considered to be respectable. Some of these folks have multiple weapons and promise to use them if necessary.

The revolutionary reactionary right is also home to various movements that seem to have little in common with each other except that they want to destroy present institutions. This place on the spectrum includes such diverse groups as the Islamic State of Iraq and Syria (ISIS) and the Jewish Defense League (JDL). Some are religious fundamentalists (Christian, Jewish, and Islam), while others like the Nazis and other super-nationalist groups are opposed to all religions. Some of these reactionary groups have strong positions on race, religion, ethnicity or nationality—others don't seem to care.

Then there are some right-wing revolutionaries in the Northern Ireland Protestant community who favor the British Monarch. They call themselves "political Protestants" because they define their politics as a part of their religion, but they don't believe in God. Many members of the opposing left-wing Irish Republican Army (IRA) claim to be Catholics even though they are atheists as well. They call themselves "Protestants" and "Catholics," but neither side ever argues about religion—it's really about nationalism. Politics can be complicated.

Many reactionaries were attracted to Donald Trump's message "Make America Great Again." The word "Again" was heard by some as a promise to turn back the clock to a time when abortion was illegal, gay people were afraid to come out of the closet, and white people could use lethal force to keep people in "their place." There are also many on the right that are convinced that the United States has been infiltrated by inferior racial or religious groups, and others who don't care about religion or race. In addition, there are armed, military-style factions prepared to fight the federal government, especially the Bureau of Alcohol, Firearms and Tobacco (AFT) because they fear that their guns will be confiscated, and also the Bureau of Land Management (BLM) because the federal agency sets grazing fees for Western ranchers. The one characteristic that links all these reactionary groups together is that they are *reacting* to a situation that they believe has threatened their way of life; they want to repeal present policies and substitute practices that benefits their own group.

I know several folks in this category who swear they will shoot on sight any government official who comes on their property. One man constructed 12 homemade, anti-personnel land mines and buried them around his farm, but first he got rid of his farm animals that would detonate the mines. This man defends this practice by claiming that he has a constitutional right to target anyone who comes on his private property. By his own admission, he hates all federal officials and most state officials. He said he wouldn't hesitate to shoot agents from the Internal Revenue Service (IRS) or the Bureau of Alcohol, Tobacco and Firearms (ATF). One time, he said, he almost shot a travelling salesman who was dressed up in a suit like a federal agent. He and others like him are ready to kill intruders on their property. There are growing numbers of people who believe they have every right to defend themselves against a government that (they believe) is preparing to take away their guns. There are folks I know in rural areas that just naturally unlock the gun cabinet when they see a strange car drive in from the road. Most of us have no idea how many people are prepared to fight in order to keep their guns.

In this world of clandestine politics, the word "radical" has come to have varied meaning. In the American lexicon, journalists and political leaders often use the term to describe extremes at both ends of the political continuum. Media people commonly refer to the "radical left" or the "radical right," suggesting that the word fits on both sides of the spectrum. There is usually no mention of the fact that the extreme right and left despise each other, and there is also no discussion of how differently the two see the world.

Many think of radicals and extremists as being one of the same. Both words are used to discredit or undermine an idea. When something is branded as a "radical" or "extremist" notion, it is sorted into a category of being foolish or ill-conceived.

Along these same lines, the word "extremism" has also become a weapon word in politics. It is regularly used to defame groups, individuals, and ideas. One effective way to dismiss a passionate speaker is to label them as an "extremist." Former Arizona U.S. Senator Barry Goldwater is remembered most of all for a comment he made in his presidential nomination acceptance speech at the Republican Convention of 1964. He said: "Extremism in the defense of liberty is no vice, and moderation in the pursuit of liberty is no virtue." The recorded statement was repeated over and over by his opponent Lyndon Johnson to make Goldwater appear dangerous. Goldwater lost his presidential bid in a landslide election in which the entire Republican Party lost legislative seats at the federal, state, and local level. The word "extremism" evoked fear among voters of both parties who imagined that if elected, Goldwater might start World War III.

While the American people have an aversion to anything described as "extremist," this type of behavior has deep roots in our history. During times of political tension or economic dislocation, extremists have always risen to prominence. After the Civil War, former right-wing members of the Confederacy formed the Ku Klux Klan that was famous for lynching black people. During hard economic times, the left spawned anarchists and Marxist factions that assassinated their enemies. Throughout American history there have been pitched battles between various labor groups and private armies hired by management. To repeat the phrase coined by the African-American activist H. Rap Brown, "Violence is as American as cherry pie."

It's not difficult to understand why right-wing people take violent actions because change is occurring too quickly. But the reverse can happen as well. There have been notable movements that took to the streets because change was occurring too slowly: the struggle for civil rights and ending the war in Vietnam are prime examples. Protest activities on these two issues started out with people speaking in opposition to government policy; the movements moved to the street protests, and finally to violence and widespread disobedience of the law.

Police attempts to suppress street demonstrations often create unintended consequences. Television viewers are shocked as they watch the police using excessive force against protesters. In this day and age, it doesn't work well to try to beat people into submission while everyone else at home is looking on through their TV sets. This has been true in conflicts around the world, including the British army in Northern Ireland and the Israeli army in Palestine. Right-wing governments have been slow to recognize this factor as they fall into the trap of beating people with clubs in full view of a television audience. In recent years, there have been unsuccessful attempts by governments to ban TV cameras in political protest situations. Television watchers wince when they see men, women and children bitten by attack dogs or knocked down by high-pressure fire hoses.

Police agencies and other armed governmental personnel often charge there is a left-wing bias in the news coverage because television pictures (of people being beaten) have a way of favoring the protesters. The overwhelming fire power on the side of the government causes the public to see it as an unfair fight with the CS gas, riot-squad officers in black combat uniforms all on one side while protesters are just in street clothes. In recent years, military attack vehicles have been given to police agencies. These huge armored vehicles add to the appearance of an overreaction by the police. Police commanders and military juntas have been slow to recognize that television has a way of favoring David over Goliath. In a real sense, mobile television crews and the video capabilities of smart phones have created a technology that favors street protestors.

Street protest leaders know this, and they are usually very articulate on camera in terms of describing a conflict in terms of powerless people who cannot defend themselves. With few exceptions, media coverage has a way of politicizing their story. For this reason, left-wing protest groups have usually viewed TV cameras as their friend.

In Northern Ireland, the IRA (Irish Republican Army) had a special group of young women in the front row of demonstration for two reasons. The first was because the police were reluctant to beat women in full view of the TV cameras, and secondly, because the IRA was proud of gender equality in their operations. For a time, I worked with a television crew in Belfast. We were often informed before a riot began so the crews could be ready to shoot footage for the evening news. The IRA was fully aware of media deadlines and did their best to cause disturbances early enough in the day so it could appear on the evening news. We, in the television crew, were always treated as special guests by the IRA. I found the same was true in Israel where Palestinians knew the telephone numbers of media people so they could get "proper coverage" as well. Left-wing revolutionaries know the value of the press.

When discussing political violence, there's also a bit of confusion in how we use the word "revolution." Those who fought and died hundreds of years ago in the American Revolution are placed on a political pedestal—but they are admired only in the past. School children revere and honor the fathers of their country (such as George Washington) as "revolutionaries" but they are never taught to respect those who advocate a new revolution. It is one of those contradictions not discussed by those who develop the school curriculum. Political violence in the past is respected, but in the present it is considered completely unjustifiable.

Then add in the irregularities in word usage. We have widely different meanings of these words in our everyday vocabulary. Consider the unique meanings in the following sentences:

- She is far too liberal in her morals.
- You should wear something a bit more conservative.
- That's a radical car you have.
- Please add a liberal amount of cream to my coffee.
- Our football coach has a very conservative running game.

When one considers the unusual meanings of words above, it is small wonder that our political vocabulary is so complex and confusing. Then add in the fact that some words are going out of style. For example, right-wing groups have devoted a good deal of time and effort to demonize the word "liberal" to the point that it is seldom used anymore by people on the left-wing. In response, old liberals now call themselves "progressive" instead. There are also new labels that have been coined to load in a special meaning. Each generation seems to resent some of the memories attached to old labels, and some insist their beliefs are so unique that they require a new name.

The terms used to describe political movements are really code words used to identify one group as worthy and respectable, and to suggest other designations are somehow wrong or out of touch with reality. The coded words have a tendency to change with each new generation.

New Words for Old Ideas

Left	Right
Liberal	Conservative
Old and New left	Old and New right
Progressive	Traditionalist
Neoliberal	Neoconservative
Social liberal	Fiscal conservative
New Deal liberal	Reagan conservative
Radical liberal	Christian conservative
Manchester liberal	Thatcher conservative
Moderate liberal	Ultra conservative
Independent liberal	Moderate conservative
Anarchist	Independent conservative
Democratic socialist	Libertarian
Labor populist	Democratic capitalist
Marxist	Fascist
Anti-fascist	Alternative right
(Antifa)	(Alt-right)

Many of the preceding terms are packed with emotion, and persons identified with them claim an exclusive insight. Members of some of these groups refuse to be categorized on a comparative political spectrum because they contend that their philosophy contains a new truth that defies analysis and is based on a wholly new view of politics. Everyone feels they are special in a political sense, and no one wants to be a cast in the role of just opposing someone else. Some groups such as Libertarians, Neoliberals, Christian Conservatives, and Anarchists insist they don't fit on the political spectrum. They maintain that they are neither left nor right, while a few of them claim to be both.

Eternal Questions

Yet regardless of the contrasting terminologies, there are legitimate differences that separate the political philosophies of the left and the right. Despite the many new variations and shades of opinion, the distinction between the two opposing sides can be classified when individuals are examined carefully in how they respond to three fundamental questions that must be addressed in every political doctrine. How a group or individual reacts to these queries determines both the direction (right or left) and degree (moderate or extreme) on the spectrum.

1. **What is the nature of humanity?** Are people inherently good or bad? Is it possible to improve the human condition substantially or are individuals always flawed by inborn characteristics that cause them to be irresponsible and non-cooperative? Can people be trusted to live in a state of greater freedom? Will most people squander their freedom or will they use it wisely and prudently? An answer to these questions is built in to every political doctrine.

The overall view on the worth of the average person has been quite unfavorable over the centuries. Historically, there was almost no faith in the wisdom of common folks. Authoritarian figures throughout the world propagated the belief that one's individual status was determined by birth, gender, race, or ethnic membership. There was little or no expectation that human beings had any potential to govern themselves. Those in power always had a vested interest in maintaining their exclusive right to rule. Their use of mythology, rank, title, royal birth order and traditional procedures insulated the top elites from any outside scrutiny. In both Eastern and Western civilizations there was a strong belief that most people were not worthy to judge the policies of the church or state. Those at the bottom of the structure were politically expendable, and had no separate rights of their own.

But Christianity and other world religions had more complex views of human nature. According to some religions, humans were born in sin and most of them would likely be condemned to eternal suffering in Hell. Yet it was also possible that humans had the capacity to be rewarded with an eternal paradise and complete happiness. The political implications of these two views are enormous. If people are regarded as basically sinful and inclined toward evil deeds, then certainly the political system would reflect the need to keep them under control. If, on the other hand, the assumption is that individual persons are basically good, and could be made better, then that belief will also be important in shaping the political system. Yet the bottom line in early history was that the masses would always be ruled from above.

Opposing assumptions on the potential of humanity have been inter-twined in political and religious philosophy from prehistory to the present. Contrasting views on human nature have been the points of departure for every major philosopher from the Greeks to modern times. Underlying every political and religious doctrine have been many gradations of optimism or pessimism about whether human beings have any inherent qualities or abil-ities to participate and improve their own condition on earth. The following is an example of the range of responses to that question:

FIGURE 3–1, INHERENT FAITH IN HUMANITY

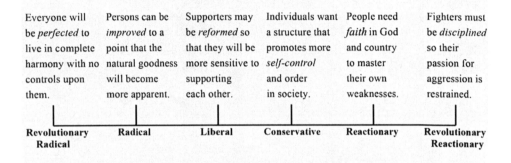

Everyone will be *perfected* to live in complete harmony with no controls upon them.	Persons can be *improved* to a point that the natural goodness will become more apparent.	Supporters may be *reformed* so that they will be more sensitive to supporting each other.	Individuals want a structure that promotes more *self-control* and order in society.	People need *faith* in God and country to master their own weaknesses.	Fighters must be *disciplined* so their passion for aggression is restrained.
Revolutionary Radical	**Radical**	**Liberal**	**Conservative**	**Reactionary**	**Revolutionary Reactionary**

Directly or indirectly, this question has been asked or assumed: Are peo-ple inherently good? On the political left the answer has been shades of "yes." On the right the answer has been various degrees of "no."

Perhaps the two most important political questions are: How much can we trust the average person? How much should society help individuals to live a better life? As would be expected, the degree of faith in humanity varies tremendously between the left and right. The gradations on the political spec-trum are characterized by the statements in the above figure. On the left there is an expectation that humans have a genuine potential to live in some degree of harmony, and society has an obligation to aid everyone to live a more rewarding life. On the right, however, there is less optimism about humanity, and there is a greater emphasis on well-developed structures to promote the welfare of all the people.

Note the italicized words below which move from left to right on the spectrum:

- Revolutionary radicals are dedicated to the belief that humans can be *perfected.*
- Radicals are inspired by the proposition that people can be *improved.*

- Liberals are motivated by the promise that the human condition can be *reformed.*
- Conservatives belief that people are at their best when they show more *self-control.*
- Reactionaries want a nation where individuals are inspired by their *faith.*
- Revolutionary reactionaries demand a state in which people are *disciplined.*

It is clear that one's point of view on human nature supplies the single most important belief in a political philosophy. The expectations of how people will act and react in an open setting are crucial because the design of the institutions will be based on their anticipated conduct. It follows closely that if individuals are expected to be trustworthy and wise, then the various institutions may be more flexible—but if the average person is driven only by self-interest and greed, then the general structure of society will reflect a more restrictive view.

A basic optimism or pessimism about the human condition is intertwined also with the second question to be asked. The two enquiries are interdependent, but they must be pursued in order because assumptions about human nature are always the first and most important factor in determining how the institutions of society should be designed.

2. Given the nature of humanity, what are the best forms of institutions for society?

Should there be fewer or more societal restraints on people's behavior? Is there a need to design the institutions with a definite structure and orderly design? How important is it to provide an atmosphere of stability and predictable order? What will be the probable outcome if there is wider latitude of choice? Will greater freedom improve society, or will folks abuse that situation by harming others?

The nature of humanity is first established in the minds of every revolutionary and constitution writer before a new system is imagined or proposed. It is only then that the next important question can be considered: how to organize the institutions of society?

The theoretical structures of society vary greatly on the political spectrum. But these gradations from left to right are very important because that are implemented when establishing an ideal system for human beings. Moreover, these beliefs about humanity's role in society are used on a daily basis to socialize people as to how they are expected to behave. In some nations, individuals are taught the absolute need for strict rules to live by. But in other countries, the socialization process provides for much greater diversity as to beliefs and rules of conduct.

FIGURE 3–2, MOST DESIRABLE FORMS OF INSTITUTIONS

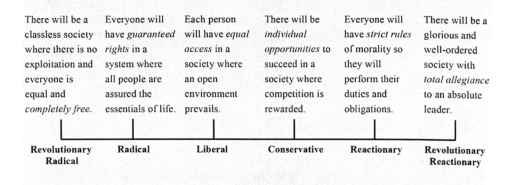

There will be a classless society where there is no exploitation and everyone is equal and *completely free.*	Everyone will have *guaranteed rights* in a system where all people are assured the essentials of life.	Each person will have *equal access* in a society where an open environment prevails.	There will be *individual opportunities* to succeed in a society where competition is rewarded.	Everyone will have *strict rules* of morality so they will perform their duties and obligations.	There will be a glorious and well-ordered society with *total allegiance* to an absolute leader.
Revolutionary Radical	**Radical**	**Liberal**	**Conservative**	**Reactionary**	**Revolutionary Reactionary**

Again, note the italicized phrases. On the left end of the spectrum, the institutions are designed to focus on humanistic goals with the expectation that people will not abuse the benefits provided. But on the right side of continuum, however, institutions are geared more to controlling the disruptive qualities of people, and to maintaining the advantages of those who hold authority, wealth, or power. Life in these various societies would be dramatically different as noted by these political philosophers:

- Revolutionary radicals visualize a totally *classless society* in a model prophesized by Karl Marx (1818–1883).
- Radicals accept the idea of a rational, *community-wide consciousness* that was once imagined by Jean-Jacques Rousseau (1712–1778).
- Liberals propose a series of *guaranteed personal rights* that were inspired by John Locke (1632–1704).
- Conservatives wish to preserve *individual opportunity* in a society that was described by Edmund Burke (1729–1797).
- Reactionaries hope to restrain humanity under *harsh rules* and restrictions advocated by Thomas Hobbes (1588–1679).
- Revolutionary Reactionaries demand a glorious system of *complete allegiance* in a regime established by Adolf Hitler (1889–1945).

After the questions of expectations for humans and the proper institutions for them have been established, one more issue needs to be addressed: what means are justifiable to attain the goals of society. As was the case with the first two philosophical inquires, this question also must be asked in order because the justification for particular strategies arises only after the designs for a society have been set.

3. **Given the nature of humanity and the design of institutions, which political strategies should be employed in society?**

To what extent are democratic procedures: freedom of expression, elections, lobbying, legislative bodies, and competing political parties useful in deciding the conduct of politics? Will individuals cooperate peacefully through the political system? Can they be trusted to decide important matters of policy, or must there be checks on popular rule? What rights should be enjoyed by minorities and those who may disagree with those in power? How are internal dissenters and enemies of the state to be treated? Should the death penalty be used to punish serious dissent? Are force, violence, and terrorism legitimate strategies to use against internal opponents? Which tactics or enforcement systems are necessary to create the ideal society?

Political strategies to be used in society are determined in part by one's position in politics and also by an awareness of which tactics are appropriate to reach a particular set of goals. For example, most of the objectives for liberals and conservatives can be achieved through bargaining, compromising, and other strategies within the system. Indeed, if there are common values these two shares, it is the preservation of the political system through mutual accommodation. Both have considerable influence in society as it is presently constituted. They not only prefer moderation in tactics, they depend upon it because their entire strategy in politics is designed to function in a situation where the political system is orderly and stable. Moderates get nervous if people raise their voices in anger or take to the streets. But it is noteworthy that persons at the far ends of the spectrum are more inclined to use more assertive tactics, and in some cases, they are willing to use violence.

It is a logical step in politics to design one's strategies to fit one's political goals. Normally, goals and strategies are closely linked. If a moderate goal is sought, it is likely that a fairly moderate strategy will be appropriate. But if the goal is to overthrow the system, then certainly the strategy will be more aggressive. For example, persons on the extreme left and right want to dismantle the present system and start anew. The enormity of this task and expected resistance from others often cause these revolutionaries to feel a sense of desperation; their deep sense of anguish and discontent quite naturally justifies tactics in their minds that would not be considered by the more moderate element in society.

But the most important dividing line on the entire spectrum is whether to use violence against the opposition. All other factors shade together as matters of degree and intensity. But the conscious plan to use lethal force against opponents on a prolonged basis separates the revolutionary from all others in politics.

Revolutionaries on both sides have a violent mindset that sets them apart from all others. The continued use of force colors their entire view of life. In many cases it is literally a matter of killing off the opposition. It is noteworthy that the death penalty is usually supported by folks at the both tips of the political continuum. This political spectrum illustrates that political strategies range all the way from democratic procedures in the center to more assertive tactics on the far sides, and finally to the use of planned violent revolution on the extremes. As noted earlier, the spectrum is like a political thermometer, with a cool area in the middle range, warmer temperatures on the far sides, and boiling points on both ends.

FIGURE 3–3, JUSTIFIED POLITICAL STRATEGIES

A violent revolution to overthrow and crush the exploitive imperialist system.	A confrontation to restructure society by imposing a new humanistic model for the future.	A reform of the system through policies to provide equality in all areas of life.	A movement to preserve a free enterprise system in an open and competitive society.	A crusade to repeal all decadence by restoring the patriotism and purity of an earlier era.	A violent counterrevolution to execute and destroy the subhuman traitors in the present, rotten, evil system
Revolutionary Radical	**Radical**	**Liberal**	**Conservative**	**Reactionary**	**Revolutionary Reactionary**

Competition is an important theme on the right side of the spectrum. Right-wing folks generally believe that it's a tough world out there, everybody is pretty much on their own, and it's important to defend yourself and your own group. Conservatives and reactionaries share the admonition that the wise person needs to compete vigorously against others for the scarce resources available, and then defend those holdings against all others. This view of human nature is very pessimistic on the right, and therefore people are likely to band together to use weapons against outsiders. There is an expectation that the first order of life is to guard your own possessions, and not depend on anyone you don't know. Perhaps the difference between the left and right is the sharpest when it comes down to the question of trusting people outside of the immediate group. On the right there is always a view that some sinister force is lurking outside, while people on the left people are generally more willing to trust a new group or idea.

In a new situation, the liberal strategy is to immediately come up with a plan of sharing resources so that all would be given equal treatment. The left shows an almost automatic inclination toward building a democratic-styled government based on equality. Socialism fits well into this kind of society where critical services are offered freely to all citizens; there is a feeling of empathy for everyone and a sort of idealistic faith that everyone can work together.

Conservatives have a negative reaction to the "let's share everything" proposal. There is an inherent belief in the right that their inequality is a fact of life, and there is no particular reason to share resources. It follows that there is less interest on the right in designing a democratically elected body where the essentials of life are shared. Capitalism fits well into this temperament. Folks on the right would generally agree with these thoughts:

- No one else has a right to what I've earned, and I have no right to other's possessions.
- Government should not require one person to subsidize another.
- Political fairness is getting what you deserve, not what you need.
- Poor people have no special entitlement to financial support.
- Social Security and Medicare rob people of the freedom to take care of themselves.
- High taxes punish the most creative, hard-working people in society.

As stated earlier, the unifying conviction on the left is that human beings are burdened down by exploitation and suffering. The strategy on this side of the spectrum is to take action to improve the situation. The left always has a plan to redistribute the wealth. A predictable strategy is to use government to lift the burden from the dispossessed and to dismantle the structures they believe are causing human exploitation. Again, the trust factor comes into play.

When liberals and radicals see wars, segregation, poverty or inequality, they are motivated by a collective call to action—they want to put an end to the destructive struggle. To help others, leftists carry placards out on the street, write letters to the newspaper, sign petitions, or run for public office. Their strategy is born out of a shared conscience based on a strong sense of empathy. They just naturally put themselves in the shoes of others. In their political campaigns, they appeal to a sense of justice—to right the wrongs they see around them. The left can't rest until something has been done to ease the plight of the downtrodden.

As expected, the right has a different view. They not only disagree, but conclude that the overactive policies of liberalism make things worse instead of better. Conservatives and reactionaries are careful not to promise anyone a rose garden—they don't want to raise expectations of help where none is deserved—they believe "do-gooders" and "idealists" cause less-motivated people to become dependent on government. Leaders on the right see human suffering, wars, injustice, and poverty as unfortunate facts of life that will always be there. There is a loud silence from conservatives when liberals talk about what needs to be done to take care of all these problems. Conservatives are fond of saying, "Just because there's a problem doesn't mean we should create another government agency to look for a solution." Often there is the additional warning that the government will probably make it worse instead of better. Those on the right side of the spectrum have the firm conviction that individuals are responsible for their own welfare—there is no collective responsibility to try to cure all the ills of society.

Outside Threats

Throughout history the American people have spent a lot of time creating a defense against real or imagined threatening situations inside and outside their country. In addition to the actual wars, there have been several cases of widespread fears that bordered on hysteria. Some of our most dramatic moments have occurred when we felt threatened by some malevolent force.

After World War I, there was a Red Scare of internal subversion. Early morning raids rounded up leftists with the plan to deport them. During World War II, selected Japanese citizens on the West Coast were thought to be disloyal. Internment camps were established to house thousands of innocent U.S. citizens of Japanese ancestry. During the Cold War there was an obsessive fear of Communists who were thought to be lurking everywhere. Thousands of U.S. citizens were compelled to sign loyalty oaths. But Communists today are no longer considered to be a threat, so the threat has shifted recently to Muslim terrorists and Central America refugees. The Trump Administration moved to deport people over the southern border, and to bar migration from selected Middle East countries. There is a never-ending story of being endangered by real or imagined threats.

Today the situation in the United States is even more complicated by the fact that an ever-increasing number of Americans feel threatened by each other. Additional reasons to be afraid come daily from specific cable-news outlets. Thousands, perhaps millions, are fearful about their futures, and it's getting worse. Folks on both sides of the spectrum feel threatened. Here are 20 identifiable groups that feel varying degrees of fear from their fellow citizens:

- Blacks have a fear of aggressive police treatment and the prospect of being killed.
- Whites feel threatened by a growing number of non-whites and people of other cultures.
- Muslims face continued marginalization by a large segment of the American public.
- Hispanics live in fear of deportation and widespread public discrimination.

- Factory workers are fearful of industrial automation and jobs leaving the country.
- Women are threatened by sexual abuse, mistreatment and economic discrimination.
- LBGT folks feel vulnerable in a political system that may strip them of their rights.
- Moderates are alarmed by the recent actions that undermine the rule of law.
- First Amendment supporters have a growing fear that the free press is being minimized.
- Right-wing media broadcasters are angered by the dominance of the mainstream media.
- Gun owners are fighting government restrictions on buying and carrying of firearms.
- Evangelical church groups feel threatened by anti-religious policies and secularism.
- Children have a daily fear that they may be targeted in mass school shootings.
- Environmentalists are worried about the dangers of pollution and climate change.
- College students feel angry about rising tuition costs and fewer career opportunities.
- Younger wage-earners have a real fear that the Social Security System may go broke.
- Elderly people feel powerless about rising crime rates and increased living costs.
- Military leaders fear that the US is losing its defense capabilities in the world.
- Veterans are discouraged by the marginal treatment of injured military service personnel.
- Hard-core right-wing voters are angered by the lack of support from the "establishment."

It is surprising how many different kinds of groups in the United States feel genuinely threatened by a variety of situations. Fear, threat, anger, and personal loss are words that describe how many Americans feel about their future. These and other topics of concern are some of the main reasons why the politics of hope have been replaced by the politics of fear in some quarters. When people feel threatened and fearful, they become anxious and combative. There is an expectation that "our group" is pitted against another, that we are losing ground, that we may have to use stronger tactics against our enemies. The present situation is bringing out all the worst features of tribalism. It has developed into a zero-sum game—the fear that if someone wins, "we" will automatically lose. This is the kind of political environment that a Man on Horseback could rise to power and promise to "Make America Great Again."

Added to this is the feeling that people are isolated into competing groups, and they think their particular group is under some threat. They are divided into subcategories that are Democrats or Republicans—liberals or conservatives—white or black—Hispanic or Anglo—rural or urban—rich or poor—male or female—gay or straight—Wall Street or Main Street—young or old—union or non-union—religious or secular, and a whole host of other divisions that relate to guns, cultural issues, income inequality, health care, climate change, gender roles, abortions, taxes, immigration, and the environment. Identity politics goes hand in hand with fears and threats, and cable news shows stoke the fires on a daily basis. When people feel threatened, they start blaming each other. Does this sound familiar?

The difference between the left and right on this topic has a lot to do with the general orientation each has on the world. There is a persistent feeling on the right that we are under attack and that we had better fight back because the situation is getting worse. Folks on the right feel victimized even when they win. On the left, there is a feeling that our democratic values are being diminished by the threatening tactics from the president.

The right-wing response to threatening situations is predictable and understandable. Those who want to defend society have a natural interest in being on the lookout for anyone who wants to overturn the current institutions. Heroes on the right are leaders like the John Wayne character who warns everyone, "It's time to circle the wagons and fight off the invaders."

Perhaps the best examples of these kinds of folks are found in Northern Ireland, where right-wing Protestants have had "their wagons in a circle" for hundreds of years. Ulster Protestants are actually proud that they've always lived in a garrison state. They are constantly aware of the majority of Catholics in Ireland who seemingly surround them every day. They call themselves "loyalists" because they are loyal to the British State—they have been defending the Crown for hundreds of years. Since the 17th century, they've been living with the threat of being overrun. Living under siege has been their signature in life. Building real walled cities became a part of who they were. Today they feel fulfilled by standing firm. In a strange way, they seem more content when the odds are stacked against them. There is a saying in Northern Ireland that "the way to make an Ulster Protestant happy is to make them unhappy." A Catholic Irish friend exaggerated a bit when he told me it was impossible to know whether Protestants were happy or sad because they never smile.

The example of northern Irish Protestants illustrates what threat can do to a people and how it can influence their political posture. During my 11 years in Northern Ireland, I was reminded often of how threat can amplify activity on the right side of the political spectrum and how it could choke off left-wing thinking. When folks feel they are fighting for survival, it's difficult to be optimistic about the nature of humanity. Conservativism and right-wing thinking are natural outgrowths of living under siege. There aren't that many liberals who are career combat military officers or border guards. Being under a real, constant threat changes a person and makes them less trustful toward others outside their circle of supporters.

The situation in Israel is not unlike Northern Ireland in terms of being surrounded by threatening circumstances. Defending the country has made a deep imprint on Israeli citizens, especially those who have experienced military combat. I had dinner one evening in Jerusalem with a young Israeli soldier named Amos. The most noticeable feature about him was a black patch over his right eye. It turned out that the loss of his eye had changed him politically.

Amos had been raised in the United States in Milwaukee, Wisconsin, but had immigrated to Israel as a young man. By his own admission, his family had raised Amos to believe in the goodness of humanity. "We were," he said, "liberal to the core." But all of that changed when Amos and another Israeli soldier were surrounded one night by young Palestinians who were using slingshots to shoot ball bearings at them. The other soldier fired back and kept the Palestinians at a distance, but Amos hesitated. He said he just couldn't shoot at another person. The result was that the attackers got close enough to hit Amos in the eye. With a look of anger, he looked at me and said, "Liberalism was my weakness." Since then, he said he has come to recognize there are a lot of bad people out there who will hurt you if given a chance. Amos said he was converted to a new political point of view out on the battlefield in an instant. He said he "thinks differently about a lot of things" since his injury. The political hazards of life have transformed the way he thinks. He has a very different view of human nature. In a matter of minutes, he moved from the far left to the extreme right. Amos said he is raising his children to fight back and defend the family. His story may have application to many families who live in a war zone.

What happened to Amos reflected the experiences of many Israelis who were raised in a leftist environment with an emphasis on humanistic values and culture. It is difficult, if not impossible, for them to support human rights in their homeland while fighting an indigenous people who also claim that same homeland. Some contradictions are too much to bear. It's hard to be a liberal while carrying an AK-47 for personal protection.

The next story is an example how a classical liberal in the United States might respond to a threatening situation. I had friends who were unlike any other married couple I knew. Harlan was a retired army colonel, and his wife

Marie was a left-wing activist who organized peace marches all of her life. He was a decorated combat field officer; she was a dedicated advocate for world peace.

During the Cold War era their dinner conversations were a continuous debate on how the United States should respond to the threat of international Communism. Her idealism and his combat experience made them equals. The dialogue was always the same: it was military preparedness versus peaceful diplomacy. As far as I know, neither of them ever backed down.

The retired colonel was predictable in his role. He was a soldier and took the military point of view in combating Communism all over the globe. Marie, on the other hand, was a left-wing activist who believed in organizing people to support the United Nations. The most important theme in her life was her belief in the *goodness* of people. She sincerely believed that contending groups could be brought together. But until then, she marched in every "ban the bomb" demonstration, and read everything she could find about how to promote world peace through cooperation. Her ideology was made stronger by her commitment to the United Nations.

Marie was a great example of how many left-wing persons responds to a threat. On her desk there were piles of letters she had written and received about the Vietnam War. She had clippings from the *New York Times* and the *Washington Post* and many local newspapers. The bumper stickers on her car were, Give Peace a Chance, and End the War Now. On the wall was a framed picture of Marie's mentor, Eleanor Roosevelt. By her own admission, Marie was a feminist and a "peacenik." Under the photo was Marie's favorite quotation:

> A woman is like a tea bag—
> you can't tell how strong she is
> until you put her in hot water.

When Marie spoke in my political science classes, my students were enthralled by her commitment. Despite her advanced age, she always had the most idealistic view in the room. She never stopped speaking out and she never agreed that force was necessary. Her retreating position was always the same: "Just think of how much good we could do if we would all work together for peace."

Her husband, Harlan, had a very different view of how to respond to threatening situations. Harlan was a believer of military collective security pacts and maintaining a strong military posture in the world. His favorite saying was, "When the good guys have overwhelming power, we'll have peace, and not before." The two of them never stopped quarrelling, but I always thought their arguments were more interesting than other couples I knew.

Sometimes we can learn the most about ourselves by simulating a conflict. How we respond to a threat reveals a lot about each one of us. In the next section the focus is on how we might react in a threatening situation where violence could occur.

A Poor People's Conference

Perhaps the questions of expanding the so-called welfare state and the threat of political violence are two of the most volatile issues in American politics. Nearly everyone has a strong reaction to these topics. When the two are combined, there is the potential to activate a broad range of division between the left and the right.

Imagine you are the governor of one of the fifty American states and that the following scenario has unfolded on a Saturday evening: welfare recipients from throughout the state have converged on the state capitol for a weekend of meetings and discussions concerning proposed reduced welfare payments in the government budget. Groups of several thousand men and women are being housed in local school gymnasiums on cots. Their transportation to the capitol has been paid by local governments.

Leaders of the welfare group contend that public assistance payments have been cut by massive amounts. All of their discussion centers on the proposed welfare payment schedule, which was announced two weeks ago. Standard monthly grants for the coming year have been cut by ten percent. After these reductions have been made, the state will have one of the lowest public assistance schedules in the nation.

The delegation of welfare recipients argues that they cannot maintain their families on this proposed schedule. They charge that the state is taking food from their children's mouths to balance the budget. Most have come to the conference in an angry mood to protest and to find some means to restore the payments to the previous level, which was considered by some to be below the poverty level. Accountants in state government estimate that the budget would be substantially out of balance if the cuts were restored. Federal welfare funds have been exhausted for the year. The question has been reduced to two choices:

1. restoring welfare payments to the previous schedule at the expense of many other basic programs in the state, or

2. holding the line on ten percent budget cuts in all state departments, including the Department of Public Assistance.

Leaders of the state legislature and the governor have sympathized on many occasions with the welfare clients, but have stood firm on the position that all budgets in the state must be trimmed to accommodate the loss of anticipated revenue for the coming year. According to one veteran legislator:

> We all have to tighten our belts during a recession to balance the budget. All state employees are unhappy with the outlook for next year, but they just have to bear with us. Just yesterday, representatives from the Highway Department contended that they really needed an increase to maintain our highways at present safety standards. Members of the State Board of Higher Education came in last week and said they feared nearly irreparable harm to every university in the state. The list goes on and on, but we can't play favorites. If we restore welfare payments to their previous levels, many state employees would receive drastic cuts in their salaries, and over 200 jobs would be eliminated so the budget could be balanced. I know it will be difficult to live on the reduced sums. We may be able to do something about it later if revenues pick up during the year. Presently, we are looking into the possibility of shifting some of the welfare costs to local churches and civic groups. Perhaps it might be better if local charities could help solve some of their own community problems.

This past month, the state legislature acted on a new tax package which would cut personal income taxes and corporate taxes in an effort to stimulate the sagging economy. The entire tax plan will be referred to the people for a vote next month. Most major economic groups have endorsed the tax reform—it is expected to pass by a wide margin.

Spokespersons at the Poor People's Conference are well aware of the economic situation, but they maintain that the new welfare schedule is unacceptable. This is the second downward revision of welfare payments in recent months. The general feeling in the group is that the present level is far below poverty standards, and the new lower level of payments would endanger the health of thousands of children across the state.

A welfare mother from the largest city in the state brought the conference to a standing ovation when she asserted:

> I will not stand still while the state reduces my family to the status of a public liability and an economic problem to be resolved by local handouts. We cannot exist on crumbs thrown to the poor and still maintain a decent home for our children. Why should you and I go home quietly and accept this starvation status when there are public employees at the upper level in the state who are making $250,000 a year? If the state needs more money, why don't they raise income taxes on those people who ride around in big cars? We have a right to live just like everyone else. Other people in the state receive payments and subsidies from the public treasury without a stigma. Why do we have to beg to receive money to feed and clothe our families? I will not let my children go to bed hungry just so this state can balance their damn budget. This is serious! If we don't get a restoration of just and equitable payments, I say we should go down fighting. If the governor and legislature don't answer our plea in the next hour, let's move into the area around the buildings and break every window we can find!

At this point several thousand welfare recipients begin milling around the many state buildings on the capitol mall. The mood of the crowd is angry.

Undercover members of the state police on the scene conclude that loss of life and property is imminent if a solution is not found in the next hour. The first question that comes to your mind is how you can resolve this conflict without allowing events to get out of control.

As governor you must work quickly, because in less than one hour there may well be a violent confrontation in the center of the capitol mall. Everyone is looking to you. Are you ready to take action immediately? Maybe you should talk it over with someone before you act—but who is available? Remember this is a Saturday evening (a lot of political crises occur on Saturdays and Sundays). Your regular advisors are not in town; the legislature is not in session. Who could you contact during the next hour? As far as you know, nothing like this has ever happened before in your state.

To add to your problem, you are also facing re-election in less than three months. What you say and do will certainly become an issue. Whatever you do will probably become a campaign issue. This could be the topic that decides your political future. If this situation gets out of control, your political career may be over. You have to make the right decision and be able to defend it. It's times like this when you feel really alone.

It won't be long before the media finds out about this situation. They'll bring in TV cameras and the welfare receipts will make a statement and you will be asked to respond.

Your press secretary comes into the office and reminds you that there are four members of the legislature (2 Democrats and 2 Republicans) who happen to be in a meeting across the capitol mall. In the absence of any other state official, you decide to call them to your office for their advice.

The four legislators have been outside on the mall and they understand the issue that is threatening public order. You invite them to sit down around a conference table and offer their advice. Which recommendation sounds the best to you: Legislator 1, 2, 3, or 4?

> **Legislator 1.** Governor, you have human beings out there who need your help. If they cannot exist on the new schedule of welfare payments, then we must find the money to restore the cuts. The highways and state buildings can go without maintenance for one more year, but a child can't go without food. You have no choice but to walk out there and give them a solemn pledge that you will take the budget back to the legislature and restore those cuts. Just because they are on welfare doesn't mean that they have no rights! They are people; they shouldn't have to beg for handouts—they have dignity! We have the resources to feed and clothe them; we have a moral obligation to find a solution that will provide them with their basic human needs.
>
> **Legislator 2.** Governor, this problem has been growing more severe in recent years and I was afraid it would come to this. But now that we have this situation, we must respond in an equitable manner so that the problem is resolved and no one is injured. I see this as a three-step process. First, you must convince them that nothing can be done right now because the legislature is not in session. Second, they must recognize that violence will hurt their cause because the public and the legislature

will surely turn against them. And third, tell them that you will call a special session of the legislature for next Wednesday morning, and that you will devote your full energies to finding a solution to the problem. If that is agreeable, I recommend that you appoint their leader as a spokesperson to address the special session of the legislature on Wednesday.

Legislator 3. Governor, you have no choice but to deploy the State Police and National Guard as quickly as possible to protect property and lives. Inform the leaders of the welfare group that you will take their concerns under advisement, but that no decision can be made under the threat of violence. If you don't act resolutely today you will lose control over the entire situation, including the state legislature. In all likelihood, there is little or nothing that can be done to help these people, but right now you must defuse this situation and let these people know that they cannot riot for the purpose of altering the state budget. There is an election coming up in three months; the proper channel for this group is to take the issue to the people. Right now, tell them to disperse and go home.

Legislator 4. Those people don't deserve a response from you any more than a street gang that was trying to overturn the government. They've been living off this state for years; some of those people don't want to work and they think the threat of violence will make us raise their monthly dole. If they really wanted to help their families they could get a job. I say send the State Police and National Guard out there with a warning to get off state property in 15 minutes or get arrested. You can't be soft on a group like that—they're dangerous people! This is a good chance to round them up and put them away. If you don't get tough with these people, other radicals will hear about it and they'll storm the capitol. You and I both know that terrorists must be behind this—you have to stop them now!

Which of the four statements would you accept if you were governor: 1, 2, 3, or 4?

Read the four choices again and consider each of the points raised by the four legislators. Choose the one statement that comes closest to your opinion. Remember those are real people out there that will affected by your decision. Also keep in mind that you will need to defend your choice during your re-election campaign. Whatever happens out there will reflect on you. It's entirely possible that the state police may get carried away and fire at the protesters. Someone could get wounded or even killed. But you are the governor and you alone can decide how to resolve this problem.

Stop reading and indicate your choice of advice from the legislators— 1, 2, 3, or 4?

Rank order your choices with the first being the most acceptable and the last being the least acceptable. In the space below, write down your reasons for making those choices.

———
———
———
———

Keep in mind that you want to avoid violence but you also need to defend your decision. In your mind, jot down the points you will make in a brief statement that you will make on television this evening to explain your actions as governor in this crisis. You will have to address the question of whether the state should respond to the threat of violence. Your reasons should be defensible to the citizens of your state. Stop for a moment and think of what you will say.

As you may have guessed by now, the choices that were presented to you as governor were classic examples of opposing opinions of the left and right. The major purpose of this simulation was to provide an opportunity for you to evaluate your own political attitudes and to decide where you might fit on the political spectrum.

In real life there is often a need to act under pressure. That's when your basic values surface and cause you to act. Did you feel any pressure? Were you surprised by your reaction?

After reading through the recommendations of the four legislators, it should be apparent that all four major non-revolutionary views were represented. Consider how each responded to the three fundamental questions stated earlier:

- What is the nature of humanity?
- How should the institutions of society be constructed?
- Which political strategies should be employed?

Pause and reflect; search through your memory of the four opinions and through your own mind. Where does each of the legislators stand on the political spectrum? Which of the four is closest to your political orientation?

Legislator 1. Here is the radical who is primarily concerned with human needs first. There is a great faith in humanity, but a lack of patience for the political system that has placed the poor at such a great disadvantage. The radical takes the side of the poor people against the welfare system and the state leaders.

Legislator 2. The liberal wants to help the poor, but is also concerned about maintaining the integrity of the system. There is an effort to resolve the problem within the law by bringing the poor people into the regular political process. The liberal hopes to help the poor people within the system without a physical confrontation.

Legislator 3. The conservative has definite priorities: defending public property and maintaining order. There is an insistence that the poor people will never succeed until they go through proper channels as other citizens have done. The conservative defends the system against a group who has the potential to cause disorder.

Legislator 4. The reactionary is angry that the poor people would even try this approach because it violates the traditional procedures of law and order. There is a lack of patience for the poor as individuals and as a group. They are seen as lazy people who are trying to get something they don't deserve. The only answer is to teach them a lesson in law and order. The reactionary sees the conflict as an assault on the governmental system that must be repelled.

If you are wondering what the revolutionaries would have done in the situation, consider the following:

- Revolutionary radicals would have armed the poor people and led them in a violent revolution against the state government.
- Revolutionary reactionaries would have fired on the poor people and used the violent situation as a rationale to impose martial law.

The Poor People's Conference and its aftermath illustrates that the political spectrum can be an important tool for understanding the many dimensions of politics. Real political situations do, in fact, have some predictable, philosophical choices. Not only does the spectrum help us to categorize political philosophy, but more importantly, it gives us some understanding as to why people have such different orientations in politics. And in this case, it may have given you additional understanding of your own point of view.

Take a moment to remember how you reacted to the simulation. Did your views reflect the ideology of your friends, family, or ethnic background? Do you feel good about your choice of action? How do you think the public would respond to your actions?

Was there anything special about your particular views on this subject? How do you feel about folks who receive welfare payments from the state? Is it ever justifiable to use violence to change public policy? Have any of your family or friends ever been on welfare? Which factor was most important in determining your choice?

Questions for You

1 Why do you think people use political labels to categorize each other? Do you use the words "liberal" or "conservative" often? Which terms are perceived as being the most favorable in your particular group? Which words would you not use to classify your own point of view? Why?

2. To what extent does television coverage often favor the protestor's cause? Do you know of any specific recent cases where TV coverage was restricted by the police or the army? Why do you think there was an effort to suppress press coverage?

3. Read through the *New Words for Old Ideas*. Which of these groups would you most likely associate with if given the choice? Why? How about your family? Which terms would they avoid? Why?

4. Why does the author feel that defining the nature of humanity is at the heart of every political doctrine? Historically, what was the earlier view of human nature in most parts of the world? Why was that view held? Which parts of the world are those views still held?

5. Survey the various positions on the Inherent Faith in Humanity spectrum. Why do you think there is so much disagreement between these competing positions? Do you agree that this question is one that every constitution writer must answer before writing the document? Why or why not?

6. To what extent does the design of American political institutions reflect a wide section of the political spectrum? (Think the three branches of government and the length of office for members of the House and Senate, the President, and the life terms for members of the Supreme Court.) Do you think the writers of the Declaration of Independence or the American Constitution were radicals, liberals, conservatives, or reactionaries? Be sure to look at each document separately and consider the political events of the time.

7. Interpret the following statement: "It is a logical step in politics to design one's strategies to fit one's political goals." Do you see any examples in current politics where the strategies and goals of moderates, activists, and extremists have been matched inappropriately? If so, what are they?

8. Why is competition such an important theme on the right side of the spectrum? How does this reflect the perceived nature of humanity, and the probable reaction of other people in conflict situations?

9. Why do you think liberals are willing to share scarce resources and aid those who are in need? What would be the likely conservative response to the "Let's share everything" proposal from liberals? What would be your overall reaction to the liberal's proposal? Why?

10. What did the stories from Northern Ireland, Israel, and the United States tell you about how perceived threats can shape personal ideologies? What does the author mean in the statement, "Identity politics goes hand and hand with fears and threats, and cable news shows stoke the fires on a daily basis?"

11. Which of the four legislators' recommendations would come closest to your decision if you had been the governor during the Poor People's Conference? Why did you choose that response? Do you think that your views would be acceptable to the citizens of your state? Why is it so difficult to find a solution in this type of situation?

12. As governor, what particular points would you make in your prepared television remarks? After considering the theme of your speech, do you think you would have improved your chances for re-election? Why or why not?

Where Do You Fit on the Political Spectrum?

After you have reviewed the three eternal questions in this chapter search out your own response to each of the philosophical enquires. In each case, cite examples from your own life to support your general conclusion. Write down your answers to the following three sets of questions.

1. How much faith do you have in humanity? Do you usually trust people to do the right thing most of the time? Are most people generally good or bad? How strongly to you feel about the general nature of humanity? How much do these values guide your political actions?

2. Given the nature of humanity, how would your design our political, economic, religious, educational or social institutions? Should we provide more or fewer choices for people in their daily lives? Which changes would you make in our government, economy, churches, educational or social structure? What major changes would you make in how individuals are treated in society?

3. Which political strategies would you justify in society? Are democracies generally the best form of government? Is there ever any excuse to use force against individuals who do not obey the law? Are there ever any justifications for disobeying the law? Is revolution ever justified?

After reviewing the three "eternal questions," where would you place yourself on the political spectrum? Do these questions help you analyze your own political values? In your judgment, what other factors should be considered in your particular case?

4

Personal Experiences

I recall watching television with my six-year-old son one evening. A paid 30-second ad came on advocating a new tax on business gross receipts. He turned to me and said, "Do we favor that tax?" My first thought was positive because I thought he wanted to know more about different kinds of taxation. Then I realized that he just wanted to know what he *should* believe. He wanted the security of being in step with the family. Many adults do the same thing with their political group—they want to know "what they *should* believe."

This same process reoccurs every day as people try to stay in tune with their political mentors. It's amazing how many folks listen to opinion-makers daily so they can find out what they *should* believe. Have you ever wondered why there is such a similarity in what the leaders and followers are saying? It's pretty clear that a lot of folks copy what they hear on cable news. In reality they are not unlike my six-year-old son who wanted to know the family position on something as obscure as a tax on business gross receipts.

One time I interviewed a Marxist and a Nazi on the same day—the Marxist in the afternoon, the Nazi in the evening. They were worlds apart in what they believed, but I was struck by the fact that both had swallowed the "whole thing." Each had a complete, preprogrammed set of answers for every question. Neither one of them had any doubts.

A ready-made belief system offers a real sense of security—a person doesn't have to think through all the nuances of a problem. Accepting a doctrine or political ideology completely absolves a person from thinking anew. When challenging issue arises, an individual *knows* how to respond—they *know* what to say. It is helpful to compare political ideologies to religious beliefs—both provide a set of preprogrammed views on the world. Many have no "doubts."

One often hears the comment, "Never argue about religion or politics." Perhaps it is because these two sets of beliefs are based on our personal feelings, and neither is provable in a literal sense. Both of them supply a foundation of beliefs that guide us through a lifetime. In both cases individuals often swallow "the whole thing."

When discussing religion and politics, it is apparent that there are no water-tight doors between our spiritual beliefs and our political ideology. How we acquire our ideological and religious views have a lot in common.

The Function of Ideologies

If a person has their ideological commitment reinforced daily (as many do in mass movements) a single issue or ideological view can become dominant in all aspects of life. Consider the life patterns of those who show up carrying placards in front of the Supreme Court building, or those who go out in the street to protest election results. In both cases, individual thinking becomes less important, and after being out on the street for a while, nothing else matters except the group's position. Ideologies can build up in a person's mind and come to dominate their thinking. It's part of our tribal behavior patterns.

Individuals dedicated to movements of the left and right sometimes cut themselves off from other points of view. It is that isolation that causes them to become obsessive, to concentrate all their attention on one area. There is no room for personal reflection or humor in their daily lives. They act as though they have found a faith that shaped their lives.

Persons driven by a singular ideology are a serious lot who seldom see any humor in life. They almost always stick to the script of what's wrong with society—how to fix it—and an individual's role in the process. These points are highlighted in the three functions served by all ideologies.

1. Ideologies provide an explanation of why a particular problem has developed.

The focus is on why did this happen? What are the real dimensions of the situation? Why is it so important that we act? It is a call to action—to correct something that has gone horribly wrong. Perhaps the best way of clarifying this function of an ideology is to note current statements that define a particular problem as viewed with a right-wing perspective. The following declarations are stated in an absolute form with no room for misunderstanding:

- Abortion is the murder of unborn children.
- Gay activists are trying to convert our children.
- Muslim terrorists want to kill all the Christians.
- New immigrants are diluting American culture.
- Every child has a right to pray in public schools.

- Marriage should be for only one man and one woman.
- Every God-fearing American should be armed.

There are no gray areas in the above positions. These are one-sided declarations that describe a situation that may alarm a segment of the population, but for some, these are the most important propositions of their lives. There is an unspoken assumption that these topics demand an action plan that is included in the second function.

2. Ideologies prescribe a specific path for those who are activated.

It is a solution-oriented doctrine designed to correct the problem. A vision of a better life is basic to all ideologies. There is a call to transform society, to promote a specific set of values, to construct a grand strategy that will resolve the existing problem. This second function can be best understood with corrective examples taken from the American left-wing agenda:

- Abortion should be safe and legal and covered by health insurance.
- There is a need to publicly fund all election campaigns.
- Every citizen has a right to free medical care.
- No corporation should be able to avoid its fair share of taxes.
- Everyone should be free to marry the person they love regardless of gender.
- Background checks should be conducted on every person who buys a gun.
- Every nation on earth should be involved in reducing the effects of climate change.

The idea of defining and resolving the problems are critical, but it is also necessary that individuals have an important role in fighting for the cause. Therefore, the final function of an ideology concerns the enlistment of persons into a movement.

3. Ideologies personalize politics by providing individuals with a key role to play.

Folks get permission to act out their dreams within an organized context. Each believer has a personal obligation to engage in some action. For some, ideologies are a sort of metaphysical foundation for each person's political hereafter—it supplies them with a path to follow that will promote the good life. This third function can be illustrated by encouraging personal involvement of members of the Ku Klux Klan and the neo–Nazis. Each member knows what he or she should do:

- To indoctrinate everyone about the evils of race mixing.
- To eliminate the influence of Jews, Catholics and everyone who isn't an Aryan.

- To promote the beliefs of Christianity and Americanism in our national culture.
- To wear hoods and Stormtrooper clothing to terrorize the opposition.
- To block the border and stop the influx of inferior peoples.
- To burn crosses and otherwise intimidate anyone who doesn't support the white race.
- To personally attack enemies of White America.

Ideologies in this kind of organization can fill out a person's life with important tasks. It not only supplies members with things to do, it excuses personal responsibility because each individual is part of a greater cause. In extreme cases, an ideological commitment can result in a justification for mass murder, as was the case in the following:

- Lenin's Russia after the Revolution in 1917.
- Hitler's Germany after coming to power in 1933.
- Mao's China after winning the Revolution in 1949.
- Pol Pot's Cambodia after seizing power in 1975.

In all these examples an ideological doctrine was used to justify the wholesale killing of millions of people who were thought to stand in the way of specific political goals. In each instance, the level of organized killing shocked the rest of the civilized world.

A political ideology can cause a sort of political madness among people, causing them to perform inhumane acts. But an ideology at a non-violent level may also give some the courage to carry a sign and peacefully protest against the inhumane treatment of people. Ideologies can be the means of achieving human progress *or* a doctrine to promote political evil.

During the 1960s, civil rights workers in the United States risked their lives to win the right for black people to live and vote in a non-segregated society. Both blacks and whites who favored civil rights were willing to stand up to police dogs, high-pressure fire hoses, beatings by mobs, and being thrown into jail. All of this was done to establish a more open society where race would not be used to keep people in a powerless position.

In more recent times, strong ideological positions have been taken by folks on both sides of the abortion question. Many defended women who want to terminate their pregnancy legally, but others were equally certain that abortion clinics should be closed. People on both sides put up with personal abuse from counter-demonstrators who disagreed with them. A belief in an ideology can cause a person to exercise their democratic rights on both sides of the spectrum.

Human beings have a need for consistency in political beliefs. Individuals often go out looking for a justification of their views. The overall picture of the world must fit into some pattern that is logical in each mind. For most of us, there is a political foundation inside our heads that is shaded either left or right. Sometimes we can learn how people formed their ideologies by reading their personal stories.

Learning Political Values

During the Great Depression of the 1930s, many American households did not have indoor bathrooms. "Going to the yard" was a common expression used for trips to an outdoor toilet for families that could not afford indoor facilities. It was especially uncomfortable during the winter months or when it was raining.

But the 1930s was also a time when there were millions of able-bodied men out of work that could dig the trenches necessary to put in the indoor toilets. President Franklin Roosevelt launched the New Deal and the Works Progress Administration (WPA) that put the unemployed to work doing many kinds of jobs, some of which were in small-town America.

During the summer of 1939, a four-year-old boy and his father stood at the edge of a freshly dug trench with black pipes at the bottom all ready to be hooked up to a sewer system. The boy was excited at the prospect of having an indoor toilet and asked his father, "Who did this for us?" The dad brought it down to his son's level and said, "President Roosevelt wanted us to have an indoor toilet." The boy understood that the president had helped his family, and after the sewer line was hooked up, he still remembers thinking "thank you" every time he flushed the toilet. Later that boy transferred his earliest sense of political gratitude to the idea that governments could help the average person. He never forgot his story about who had helped his family. It was the beginning of his political socialization process.

Years later in 1955, a teenage girl had trouble sleeping at night because she was afraid World War III would start and she would be killed by an atom bomb. Her teacher tried to console her and said that the U.S. Air Force was watching over all of us and that they would protect us. The teacher said that President Eisenhower knew how to keep us safe. That made a deep impression on her. A few months later the girl was given an assignment to write a paper on the topic of "Something That Changed My Life." She remembered the conversation about national defense and went on to write a research paper on the topic. She sent for materials on the Cold War, intercontinental missiles and the U.S. military. She also gave a speech in an English class about national defense. Her interest was building.

After college, she was commissioned as a second lieutenant in the U.S. Air Force and went on to a career as a military officer. Throughout her life she had a firm commitment to military preparedness. To this day she credits those two high school teachers with developing an interest that helped shape her life. It changed her life.

These two stories were positive lessons about the government—the first about how the government could help a family, and the second about how the government would defend us. But the lessons could have been the reverse: it could have been a government that refused to help a family, or an irresponsible, war-like leader that jeopardized world peace. Each of us has a multitude of stories that account for our political socialization process. Learning political values is a life-long process. We all are a product of a unique, personalized socialization process.

Our family, schools, churches, and the people we work with all shape our views. Sometimes it is difficult to understand the impact of a particular experience. But as we look back, we can see how we were socialized, how we learned our political values. It could have been a conversation around the family dinner table when a parent said, "Senator Jones is going to destroy everything this country stands for," or a clergy person saying, "Don't vote for Julie Smith, she favors abortion," or later in life when a person becomes aware that everyone in the office agrees about the threat of climate change, so maybe, I should go along too. Sometimes the lessons occur when we are children, other times it happens when we are adults. For many of us, the lessons never end—we are a work-in-progress—we are all becoming a political person.

Political values are learned in ways that are unexpected. Often, we are influenced by people we respect, but sometimes it is the reverse. I remember a friend saying, "My dad always believed in the right to carry a gun; I hated my dad. That's why I'm on the other side."

Sometimes the best way of understanding how our lives can be shaped politically is to review the political developments of actual people. Susan and Scott are two very successful people in their mid 70s. Susan says she is a secular liberal and Scott sees himself as a religious conservative. Here are their separate stories of how each of them became a political person.

Their stories have common geographical roots. Susan's parents moved from Kansas to Southern California just before she was born; Scott was born in Minnesota and moved to California with his parents when he was he was five years old. Susan's first political memory was in 1952 when a playmate told her a political joke: "What happened when the Democratic presidential candidate, Adlia Stevenson, stepped on his dog's tail? The dog yelped, IKE, IKE, IKE." Scott's first memory was also about that campaign. He remembered all the folks in California wearing "I like Ike" buttons. He's pretty sure his parents voted for Dwight Eisenhower.

Neither of their parents were very politically minded, but both said they were born into Republican families. Their views about politics were pretty vague, but they did have a feeling that the Republican Party was somehow more dependable, and like other children, they wanted to follow their family's political affiliations.

The main topic in Susan's household was religion: her father was a Christian minister in a small, fundamentalist church and Susan learned to recite the titles of all 66 books in the Bible. She had perfect attendance in Sunday school for 14 years. Her father was not active in partisan politics, but he did join the John Birch Society, a very conservative political group that was mostly concerned with warning people that Communists were infiltrating America.

Scott can't remember his parents talking about politics, but he's pretty sure they voted on a regular basis. His father worked at several jobs in north Sacramento; the longest job was at a service station. The family lived in a working-class neighborhood that had "a lot of minority groups." Scott had several Mexican-American friends—race was never a "big thing" in his life. As he grew up, Scott was more interested in girls and cars—politics never entered his mind.

As a teenager, Susan remembered her home community having a "sundown law." Black people knew they had to be out of town by sundown. She also remembered the 1960 Election distinctly. Protestant ministers in her neighborhood were praying that the Catholic candidate, John F. Kennedy, would lose to the Protestant, Richard Nixon. In 1964, she recalled supporting the moderate, Nelson Rockefeller, while her mother and father liked the more conservative Republican, Barry Goldwater. Overall, there was an assumption that her family would remain in the GOP. But she remembered that voting was considered to be very important; her father took her to the courthouse to register as a Republican as soon as she was eligible.

A few hundred miles to the north in Sacramento, Scott had only a few memories about coming of age politically; he doesn't remember much about partisan politics or specific candidates; he was too busy taking college courses and earning a living. Scott was looking for a career in accounting, but he also discovered he had a talent as a salesperson. He started a successful career working at an aerospace firm in Sacramento until he had a bad experience with a labor union that changed his political views.

Scott had received regular increases in his wages at his job in Sacramento, until one year, he was told that he would not get a raise because other workers in his category had not done well. The union contract required that all workers in a particular shop would receive the same pay increase. He resented being tied to other workers. Scott felt the union had "held him back." He quit the job at the aerospace firm and never again had anything to do with unions. One of the main reasons why Scott is a Republican today is that he supports the anti-union position of the GOP. He is also opposed to the Democrats because they are "too close" to unions. There was a strong feeling within him that everyone should be rewarded for their individual labors, and that unions were for "freeloaders" who wanted to get "something for nothing." Scott's experience with the union shaped his views about politics in general and unions in particular. By his own admission, it was the most important event in determining his political views.

In the meantime, Susan's life was beginning to move in a different direction. She was 18 years old when she got a job working for a small daily newspaper in her home town. She remembers November 22, 1963, like it was yesterday, when her editor ran through the pressroom shouting that President Kennedy had been shot. The editor told Susan to go to local library to "get all the facts about the President." Susan had just starting to do the research when she heard the church bells begin to toll. She knew the president was dead and she put her head down on her typewriter and cried. She said her sadness surfaced first because he was the president, but even more because of what he stood for. Things had changed dramatically in her life since the local ministers in her hometown were praying to stop JFK from winning the 1960 election. She was beginning to feel independent from her parents. Her feelings about politics were changing.

Scott was well aware of the political events of the 1960s and 70s, but he did not get involved. He watched the campus disturbances from afar and felt it was just a "group of silly college kids" out on the street. His anti-union position remained strong and he recalled that he enjoyed crossing picket lines set up by union members. He became more active in his church and served on a board that helped churches to get started in northern California. He doesn't recall any political leaders of that era that he respected, except President Ronald Reagan, when the president fired 11,000 air traffic controllers in 1981 when they refused a presidential order to go back to work. "I really liked that," he said.

Meanwhile, Susan was going through a transformation that would change her life. She began to feel uncomfortable in her church because she began to doubt the doctrine. Looking back, she said it was because she had left home and started to explore what other people believed. When she was 27 years old, she secured an administrative assistant position at California State University at Bakersfield. There she got involved in working on a political campaign to elect a Mexican-American Democrat to the California State Assembly. After winning the election, she joined the new assemblyman and moved to Sacramento to work in the California State Assembly, and finally she became a trusted staff member of the Democratic Speaker of the Assembly. Susan became even more involved in liberal politics as she witnessed the organizing activities of Cesar Chavez and Dolores Huerta of the United Farm Workers. She was personally impressed by liberal leaders like George Moscone in the California State Senate because he and other Democrats "cared so much for the downtrodden." On her 28th birthday, she actually had a small celebration with her friends as she changed her political registration to become a Democrat.

In his later years, Scott began listening to Rush Limbaugh's radio program every day from 9 a.m. to noon. By his own admission, listening to Limbaugh gave him the strongest political feelings of his life. He said so many of his earlier attitudes now made sense. He followed Limbaugh's thinking in denouncing Bill Clinton, but later he discovered that Obama was "much worse." There is now a strength and certainty in Scott's voice as he talks about the "damage that Obama has done." He blames him for excessive economic regulations, gay rights, same-sex marriage, permitting men to go into women's restrooms and expanding the "liberal agenda" across the nation. He is upset with Obama's appointments to the Supreme Court, the terrible trade deals, and the "phony warnings" about climate change. According to Scott, Obama has given young people a negative example; they no longer know the difference between right and wrong. "Kids today have no boundaries," he said. But most of all, Scott is angry because he believes Obama issued executive orders that violated the Constitution. "And to top it off," he said, "Obama let in a lot of convicted felons from Mexico that have actually killed people in sanctuary cities like San Francisco."

Scott has never given any money to the Republican Party, but he has become a stronger Republican because he listens to Rush Limbaugh. He said, "Limbaugh is a smart guy that knows what's going on." He couldn't think of any area of disagreement he had with Limbaugh. Scott acknowledged that Limbaugh didn't support Donald Trump in the beginning, but finally he "came around." Scott was proud to vote for Trump in 2016, but he disapproved of Trump's crude comments. He paused thoughtfully and said, "Trump is really a jerk." Although he voted for Trump, Scott said, "90 percent of my vote was anti–Hillary."

Susan was an enthusiastic voter for Hillary Clinton and was crushed when Hillary lost. She was appalled by Trump's language in the campaign and couldn't believe American voters would elect him. She has many Mexican-American and gay friends; she is afraid of what Trump will do to minorities. Susan is also nervous about his ability to launch "nuclear weapons without being checked by anyone else." She is very worried about what Trump will do with the Middle East and other hot spots in the world, but she tries to be optimistic, hoping that the press will expose Trump's illegal actions to the American people.

While Susan and Scott are far apart on many issues, they agree on one point that surprised me. Neither of them trusts Donald Trump, and they both said it might be a good thing for the country if Trump were no longer in the White House. When they spoke of Trump being replaced, they each looked away without giving any details.

I asked both of them why they were proud to be an American and they both said basically the same thing. Susan is proud of the freedom of the press and our religious liberties. Scott said the country is the "home of the free." Both of them have faith in the country to prevail and deal with many problems, both at home and abroad, despite President Trump.

When I asked them which political leaders they respect, there was a long pause with both of them. Neither of them came up with a name. Clearly, they have more faith in the country than those who would lead it. Susan is hopeful our freedoms will be preserved. Scott is hopeful that the economy will turn around. But neither of them knows who should lead us.

Susan and Scott are two good examples of Americans who were socialized at different times of their lives under very dissimilar experiences. To a great extent both of them changed as they moved away from their parents: Susan later became a liberal Democrat and Scott deepened his identity as a conservative Republican. They became stronger in their political values as a result of events during their twenties: for Susan it was partisan politics in the California State Legislature; for Scott it was his negative experience with a Sacramento labor union. And finally, both of them are secure in their political values as partisan members of a political party. But they both have a spiritual faith in our destiny. Susan said she hoped, "God would take care of us." Scott looked me straight in the eye and said, "Whatever happens, I know this country is blessed."

An Autobiography of a Liberal

Two friends of the author on opposite ends of the political spectrum volunteered to write companion pieces on their political beliefs. The following autobiography offers a nonfiction account of the origin and development of this person's liberal perspective.

Ever since I was about 15 years old, I wondered why I was drawn to people in trouble. In books or movies, I always worried about those left behind. The word "empathize" was not yet in my vocabulary, yet I was a walking example of someone who always put himself in someone else's shoes. To this day I have little interest in books and movies unless they have a social, political, or racial message. It's usually about helping the downtrodden—targets of discrimination—the outcasts of society.

I remember thinking I was different than a lot of guys in school that made fun of other children. There were incidents in grade school and high school when a group of boys would shame or ridicule someone who couldn't defend himself. Everyone laughed except me. I didn't do anything heroic like defend the kid physically, but I would speak up and say, "Why did you guys do that? He wasn't bothering you." Then, within a few minutes, I would go over and stand by the person who had been the target of the jokes.

One of my proudest moments was years later, when a young man named Edward told me that I was the one child who "stood up for him in grade school." He said he nearly quit school because the bullies taunted him on a daily basis. To this day, tears come to my eyes when I remember the names the other people I've known like Edward, who just didn't fit in. Later it dawned on me that my whole life has been becoming aware of the *Edwards of the World*. These folks were drawn from different races, religions, nationalities, and belief systems. So why was I drawn to them? What made me tune into the cries of the dispossessed? Why did I always think about the little guy? Was there something wrong with a young man who didn't identify with the rich and powerful?

Those questions are difficult to answer, but I can see some connection to my mother. I didn't realize it at the time, but my mother had a soft touch for every homeless person who came through my hometown. She never spoke about why she fed the hungry, but I suspect it was because of her strong religious beliefs. There was no lecture for me, but I learned by example. In family conversations, she was the only one who defended the less fortunate. We had a string of relatives who needed help. There were uncles and aunts who didn't have enough for the essentials of life. She could always find extra clothing, food or a little money. It was important for her to share. She didn't say much about her feelings for the less fortunate, but I know she believed in that it was important to be kind. By nature, she believed in sharing with others.

Other members of the family may have regarded her as a pushover because she sometimes gave away too much. But she was my quiet example. She didn't realize that she was raising a little liberal that would someday flirt with radicalism. She had no idea that her little boy would spend his entire life working for left-wing candidates and speaking out in favor of government programs to help the poor. Neither did she consider that her son would be driven by the desire to find out why people disagreed so much on the topic of aiding the underprivileged. She was the teacher and I was her student.

When I was younger, it bothered me a lot to hear persons who were insensitive to the poor, but then I came to realize that it also was part of my education. I encountered people who seemed to enjoy showing off their wealth. There were others who profited by exploiting those who were poor, and there were even some who discriminated against others for racial or religious reasons. All these things upset me, but those experiences added to the depth of my political socialization. I began to understand why some people were different.

By the time I was 18 years old, I began to see life as one big research project. Everywhere I went I asked questions and I soon discovered that people loved to talk about themselves and what they believed in. My rule was: don't argue—just ask why.

I remember learning early on that tempers would flair when discussing politics or religion. I wondered why until I realized that these two sets of beliefs have a lot in common. You can't prove either one because they are basic beliefs all wrapped up in how we are socialized and who we respect. Both religion and politics have the added quality of providing an answer to the most important questions of life: Why are we here and what should we do to make this a better world? I also learned that I could separate people by hearing them talk about those two topics. Some people cared about others, while other folks just cared about themselves. I was surprised to see how quickly people would tip their hand—they seldom kept it secret. It came up every time they talked about religion or politics.

I had always been a supporter of Hubert Humphrey—first as Mayor of Minneapolis and then as a U.S. Senator representing Minnesota. One of my favorite quotes from Humphrey was a speech he gave before the Democratic National Convention of 1948. He brought liberals to their feet with his ringing proclamation: "The time has come for the Democratic Party to come out of the shadow of states' rights and walk forthrightly into the bright sunshine of human rights." That was the year the Dixiecrats walked out of the Democratic Convention in opposition to the civil rights plank favoring integration of the races. Humphrey, known as the "Happy Warrior," was the essence of liberalism. I always admired him as a person, and I wished I could be like him.

I was stirred by Humphrey's call for equality. Just thinking about him made liberals like me smile. He always believed that average people could have a better life if we acted collectively to promote economic justice. In many ways, Humphrey was the conscience of America. He had the courage to point the finger at the forces of inequality and discrimination and to propose solutions that were fair to everyone. He gave everyone an opportunity to be a better person.

The last time I saw Hubert Humphrey was in Washington, D.C. It was in a congressional conference committee meeting between the House and Senate conferees. A group of young Republican House members was trying to weaken a civil rights amendment by cutting out the enforcement provisions. Humphrey sat at the end of the table watching and listening. He was suffering from cancer and was bent over and gaunt, but then he stood up straight and lectured everyone (in a booming voice) about how the government could act as a positive force to preserve the civil rights of everyone, especially the poor. His old, high-pitched voice was still there along with his idealism from his early days. Humphrey shook his finger at the young Republican members of Congress as he scolded them for trying to "rip the guts" out of the bill. When he finished, everyone in the committee room (including the Republicans) stood up and cheered. The committee adjourned with the bill intact. It was his parting shot. He died the next year in Minnesota.

Looking back, I remember feeling like a traitor in 1960 when John F. Kennedy ran against Humphrey in the Wisconsin Primary Election. Kennedy needed to win in Wisconsin to prove he could beat Humphrey in his own backyard. I was torn between my heartfelt support for Humphrey versus the magnetism of Kennedy.

The turning point came in April of 1960 when Kennedy came to speak at the University of Wisconsin. As the representative of the Young Democrats, I met briefly with Kennedy along with two professors. We were in a small room off the stage of the auditorium, waiting for the crowd to settle in. It was my first personal contact with a presidential candidate. I stood back and watched the young senator from Massachusetts who seemed so ill at ease. He kept touching his hair and straightening his tie. I was surprised because he seemed so unsure of himself. He didn't really hold up his end of the conversation in that small room with three other people. I wondered whether he was really prepared to address the students.

But when the auditorium filled, Kennedy was transformed: he stood up straight as he strode out on the stage to a roaring crowd. Within the first minute, hundreds of people were cheering. He rose to the occasion—he had the crowd in the palm of his hand. For the first time in my life, I understood the word *charisma*. He had a political charm that defied description. Somehow, I stumbled through introducing him that morning, and I knew my loyalties had changed. I was, from that day forward, a Kennedy supporter and went to work in his campaign as a volunteer. My political activism had taken a new form.

Liberalism flowered in the 1960s. The New Frontier, The Great Society and all the progressive legislation that was passed and signed. Hubert Humphrey proposed the Peace Corps. John Kennedy sent in Federal Marshals to integrate the University of Alabama, and Lyndon Johnson pushed through the Civil Rights Act of 1964 and the Voting Rights Act of 1965. But there were sad moments also, when John Kennedy, Robert Kennedy and Martin Luther King, Jr., were gunned down, yet there was still a reservoir of compassion as the country actually tried to fulfill its promise. Those were the years when I first marched for civil rights, and for an end of the war in Vietnam. It was a grand time for a liberal to be alive.

Yet the challenges nearly tore us apart. We knew we were off track during the terrible years of the Vietnam War, and the decade neared an end in the convulsions of the 1968 racial riots, the violence at the Democratic Convention in Chicago, and the election of Richard Nixon. Since then, many liberals (including myself) felt the country had lost its way. The years of Reagan and the two Bushes were a time when the country no longer seemed to care about those left behind; the focus was on tax cuts, defense spending, and slashing government programs. There was a modest attempt to renew our purpose during the Carter and Clinton years, but we were no longer committed to care about everyone. It was different and we all knew it.

The ideals of liberals were mocked on cable news channels as we fell off the path of using government for the collective good of all. The new heroes were rugged individualists who prided themselves on avoiding taxes and breaking labor unions. Political leaders turned their backs on helping those who couldn't help themselves. It was like the nation had forgotten The New Deal, The Fair Deal, The New Frontier, and The Great Society. We had lost our way.

Poor and middle-class people lost their homes, their jobs and their faith that someone cared about them. Before 2016, few recognized the widespread sense of betrayal felt by many voters who were looking for someone (anybody) who wasn't tainted by politics. Angry voters turned in desperation to a political amateur, a carnival barker who bellowed out the slogan, "Make America Great Again." Trump was a boisterous candidate, without much content, but he spoke the language of those who resented the establishment.

The inspiring message of progressive politics had been traded in for a message of fear and an eagerness to blame everyone else for our problems. It hardly seemed possible that the rhetoric of Hubert Humphrey had given way (in my lifetime) to the crude, threatening white nationalism of Donald Trump. Where did the good times go? Who let us fall into this reactive pattern? Have we forgotten the message of the "Happy Warrior?"

Liberals of today are in retreat to the extent that they no longer even call themselves "liberals." It's not stylish any longer to idealize the purpose of helping those left behind. Trump calls liberalism "a disease." He has espoused a new ethic: "It's a dangerous world out there and everyone has to watch their own back." Trump is in the process of disassembling all the agencies and programs that gave people a second chance. The government that inspired people to help each other is being refashioned and privatized so it will yield a profit for the wealthy above the heat of the struggle. We are now in the era of the "morning after" when people are waking up to the changes that are taking place.

Is liberalism dead or have we just entered a prolonged time when we no longer feel obligated to educate everyone, clean up the air and water, and deal with the reality of climate change? Have we forgotten history, or are we just resigned to go back into a boom and bust economy? Do we really want to discredit the free press in exchange for a regime that wants to undo all the good things done by Barack Obama? Will we feel comfortable in a world where a politicized clergy can hide behind a tax-free status while endorsing and funding political campaigns? How does it feel to be the only nation in the world that denies climate change? What will be the result when we cut public funding for schools and early childhood education? Is it a good idea to arm the teachers to defend the children from a mass shooting? Do we really need a $20 billion wall on the Mexican border? Is it OK to separate young children from their parents on the border? How about destroying our alliances with other democratic nations while crawling in bed with the Russians? What will be the result when we ban specific religious groups from entering this country? How can we respect a president who abuses women and makes fun of the handicapped?

We have lost our political soul since the days when we were inspired to "give to our country" rather than just "taking as much as we can get." According to Fox News, liberals of today are seen as "foolish" and "unrealistic" when they advocate helping the powerless. It's become naive to talk about sacrificing individual advantages for the sake of the nation. The Donald Trump crowd is laughing at us.

I heard a television commentator make fun of a *New York Times* front-page story noting that the temperature of the earth had risen again (for the third straight year) and there was concern that we might have reached the tipping point on climate change. I couldn't help but wonder if the liberal sense of obligation for the planet has been completely lost? Will a collective concern for humanity ever return?

It's so much easier to tear down than build up. Programs passed by liberals were high risk to begin with because they were aimed at persistent problems like poverty, environmental pollution, and wholesale discrimination against minorities. It wasn't an easy fix and a lot of things could go wrong. It was comparatively easy to find something wrong with programs designed to help everyone. Now all these programs are being systematically disassembled.

"Every man for himself" has become a part of the American creed. The goal, out on the marquee, is to deregulate the country and "Make America Great Again." The sign out front says it's to increase freedom, bring back jobs, to silence "fake news," and to get rid of troublesome groups like labor unions. But in the back room there is another set of goals that are more sinister—it's to increase corporate profits, destroy the credibility of the mainstream media, privatize government services, promote the gun culture, and undercut workers who need a living wage.

When I was 16 years old, I had a brief, part-time job working on a carnival that came to my hometown. I was hired because it was my hometown, and most people in the community knew and trusted me. It was the old scam of throwing a baseball at five metallic-colored plastic milk bottles (3 on a bottom row and 2 stacked on top). First, I was shown how to draw in a potential customer (usually a man) by showing them how easy it was to knock down the whole pile. All the bottles looked the same but one of them was filled with lead. If I put the heavy bottle on the top row (and if the ball hit any part of the pyramid) all the bottles went down, and the man won a prize. It was so simple. If the heavy bottle was on the bottom row it was nearly impossible to win.

They taught me how to catch the eye of a rube (a customer) who was wandering down the midway that looked like an easy mark. I would throw the ball myself showing him how easy it was to knock down all the bottles, and how they could win any one of these prizes for just one dollar. My take was 25 cents. It was a surefire way to con a customer. But I quit after one hour because I couldn't bear to cheat people in a rigged game. It was dishonest and I couldn't abide by the hoax to take people's money, especially from individuals I knew.

The milk-bottle swindle came to mind as I watched the 2016 election campaign. It was the old trick of hoodwinking the public by making them believe it was easy to win at a game that was based on a lie. It was based on deceiving the voter.

Donald Trump drew people in through mass deception. He distracted the public by making brash, outrageous promises he couldn't keep, and insulting all those who questioned him. It was the old milk bottle trick, fashioned at a mass rally shown on national television. But there was one important difference: the carnival could leave town before the people caught on. Now, however, the voters are becoming aware that something that "seemed too good to be true, was not true to begin with."

In a televised interview during a moment of candor, Donald Trump said he would like to be remembered and compared with P.T Barnum of the Barnum and Bailey Circus. It was the world-famous showman Barnum who said, "There's a sucker born every minute."

An Autobiography of a Conservative

Two friends of the author on opposite ends of the political spectrum volunteered to write companion pieces on their political beliefs. The following autobiography offers a nonfiction account of the origin and development of this person's conservative perspective.

I was raised to be independent. I was taught self-reliance as a child and have tried to practice it all my life. I believe that it is incumbent upon each of us to make a contribution to our families, our communities and our nation. Relying on others to do things that I should be able to do for myself is not on my radar.

I went to school, joined the Navy, worked my way through college, became a law enforcement officer and launched a successful business career. Along the way I had the privilege of raising a great family. While I did attend public schools I neither asked for nor received any assistance from the government. I accepted responsibility for my own life and believe that it is necessary for each of us to do that to the best of our ability. There are those, who through physical or mental disability or lack of education cannot assume responsibility for themselves. Only then should government step in to help. Dwight Eisenhower said, "Democracy is an opportunity for self-discipline." I am a conservative and that sums up the foundation of my personal philosophy.

I experienced poverty as a child. My father was poorly educated and he had to quit school to help support his family. As soon as he became of age, he joined the Navy and sent his pay home to help feed and clothe his five siblings. His dad made a meager living, first as a sharecropper in east Texas and then as a low-level railroad employee in Utah. His family lived in a small house with no plumbing or electricity. No one gave them anything. By contrast, my mother came from a wealthy family in Chicago that had lost it all in the market crash of 1929. My parents came from very different backgrounds but both contributed immensely to my current attitude. From my father I learned the value of hard work and from my mother I gained an appreciation for education.

I was born in Los Angeles just prior to World War II. Though I was very young I still recall how united we all were in the "war effort." Everyone participated in their own way and this country was truly one nation. We may never again see this near total unity. How sad.

My family, including my grandmother, lived in a tiny one bedroom house in south-central Los Angeles. When the war ended my uncle and his wife moved in with us. We were all piled in there but I recall it was a happy time. Jobs were scarce in Los Angeles so we moved to Utah where an unfinished basement was to be our home. My dad found work as a plumber. The winters were brutal and my dad suffered severely from working outside in the cold. Our circumstances would have been dire except for the loving kindness of our church, family and friends. The Federal government had not entered the welfare business at that time so we were on our own.

To get dad out of the cold we moved back to California where he went to work in a union shop which provided a reasonable income and, eventually, the opportunity to retire with some degree of comfort. I began to appreciate unions when their demands were reasonable. But I soon discovered that union demands were not always "reasonable." I can remember when the United States could boast of the greatest steel industry and the best railroads in the world. We had unmatched manufacturing facilities and our automobiles were the envy of everyone. The stamp "Made in the U.S.A" meant high quality at a fair price.

We reached a point, however, when unions were so powerful that they became the tail that wagged the dog. Union demands for wages and benefits far exceeded the value of the product. Manufacturers were forced to raise prices or lower quality. To compete in a global market, it became necessary for many to leave the country for a better labor market. I have only to look at Pittsburgh or Detroit to see the effect of all-too-powerful unions.

I joined the Navy at age seventeen. My ship visited many ports and this allowed me to witness abject poverty. I saw large families living in filthy huts. They had no clean water. No underground pipes to carry sewage away. No refrigeration. None of the things we might consider essential. Forget about cars, vacations, fine dining, washers or dryers, air conditioning or new clothing. Reality was a handful of rice and maybe a little meat.

One might think this would make me more of a liberal, but the opposite occurred. I came to believe that poverty was not caused by a lack of resources, but by large overbearing government. Those at every level in government accumulated all wealth with little actually going to those who produced it. Governments have a voracious appetite and, if unchecked, can consume everything and everyone. The people were driven down to a level in which poverty was the norm. The worst part was that people also suffered a poverty of aspirations—they no longer believed they could help themselves.

I was an enlisted man in the Navy and, upon entering, saw that officers were treated royally and the rest of us not so much. I observed that some of these officers were knuckleheads but they had a college degree and thus were able to be commissioned. I was determined, then and there, that come hell or high water, I would graduate from college.

While I was in college, the State of California passed the Rumford Fair Housing Act that banned discrimination on the sale of homes. This was a time of growing strife and the racial integration of neighborhoods was a hot subject. "Block busting" was rampant in California as black families moved into white neighborhoods, much to the displeasure of other homeowners. In response, the white homeowners would scramble to sell, and the housing market became chaotic. The Rumford Act was very controversial. A successful repeal campaign was launched by the real estate association but the California Supreme Court finally ruled that the repeal efforts were unconstitutional. The Rumford Act was upheld.

At the beginning of the controversy I argued that homeowners should have the right to sell a home to the persons of their choosing. They paid for it and it should be up to them to dispose of it as they saw fit. A very liberal professor managed to make me realize that I was wrong. He countered that the Bill of Rights was a two-edged sword. On one hand the majority should rule, but on the other, the rights of minorities had to be protected from the tyranny of the majority. No individual or group should ever be denied a right that is available to all others. I've never forgotten that situation because it taught me there were two sides to every question.

I worked my way through college while providing for a wife and two children. I received no government assistance. After college I applied for, and was accepted by the Federal Bureau of Investigation. The FBI academy was tough as most of the members of my class were lawyers and accountants. I knew little about federal law so it was difficult to keep up. I managed to graduate and was commissioned as a special agent. Looking back, I was impressed with the quality of the people I worked with. With few exceptions they worked hard and maintained very high ethical and moral standards.

But after fifteen years with the FBI I decided to resign. My career in law enforcement exposed me to some of the least worthy citizens of our country. I discovered that my constant exposure to the worst among us was giving me a jaded view of humanity. I was constantly exposed to people who had fallen through the cracks. I saw what government was doing to help the least fortunate, and how that effort was failing on a daily basis.

For example, I came in contact with very young mothers with multiple children fathered by multiple males. These young women were practically kids themselves. Some were totally illiterate and could hardly take care of themselves, much less their children. They got by with help from their mothers and from government assistance. But it wasn't working. Each generation repeated the same mistakes and the government actually participated by ignoring the chance to act in a positive manner.

Rather than simply supplying more cash each time another baby is brought into this world, we must tie welfare payments to literacy and learning job skills. Even little ones need to be educated in infancy to learn that there is a good life to be had outside of the circle of poverty. I learned this from my own family situation and know it's true. Our government cannot spend people out of poverty. As a conservative I believe in the old saying, "give a man a fish and you feed him for a day. Teach him to fish and you feed him for a lifetime."

I have seen billions of dollars spent to eradicate poverty, but it has, instead, institutionalized it as a way of life for some people. They say that the definition of insanity is doing the same thing over and over again while expecting a different result. We've done the same thing for nearly fifty years. Are we insane?

Several years ago, we were introduced to the Affordable Care Act, or "Obamacare." We were told, "if we like our doctor, we could keep our doctor. If we liked our health insurance, we could keep our health insurance." Neither was true. The promise was made that families would save twenty-five hundred dollars per year. Also not true. Obamacare was enacted through trickery, lies and fraud. Some members of Congress were completely ignorant of the details, because were told that they would have to pass the act before they could read it. Apparently, Nancy Pelosi knew that this monstrosity would never pass if her fellow Democrats knew that it belied all of the assurances that she and President Obama had promised. Several Democrats were reluctant to sign on. Several billions of dollars went to the renegade Democrats states in the form of government projects to buy their vote. In the end all of the lying and conniving worked and the law narrowly passed. No Republican voted for it.

The act is now in death throes as premiums and deductibles have gone through the roof. The Republicans are perplexed as to how to replace it. As a conservative, I believe the government should get out of the health care business and provide block grant money to the states which are much more capable of determining how to take care of their own sick. Liberals, on the other hand, are pushing for a total takeover of healthcare with a "single payer" system.

If you want a single payer system you have only to look at the way the government runs the Veterans Administration health care. It is a shambles and a government takeover of all healthcare would be like the Veterans Administration system on steroids. Liberals point out that we are the only industrialized nation without universal health benefits. My neighbors are Canadians who reside here during the winter months. They compare their system to the Veterans Administration program in that it is not unusual to wait for months or even years for non-emergency services. They usually wind up paying for those services themselves.

Another unintended consequence of Obamacare is the loss of full-time workers in small businesses. The cost to employers to provide health care has become so unmanageable that many have resorted offering only part-time work. Employers do not have to provide health care to part-timers. Many workers have to get two of these jobs just to make ends meet. Obamacare mandates these people must buy individual coverage or pay large fines so they struggle even further to meet this cost. In the end we have formed a very large group of people who are dependent on the government. For the liberals this means "mission accomplished."

Liberals always seem to want create divisions. They use "identity politics" to split us up into racial, gender, age, and sexual groups and then pit each against the other. They espouse the use of hateful names, charging that some people are racist, sexist, homophobic, misogynistic, xenophobic, or Islamaphobic. It is rare to hear a conservative use these terms but they are frequently found in the vocabulary of liberals. A very small percentage of Americans deserve to wear these labels, but if we do not agree with the liberal viewpoint we get so named.

Trump was criticized for saying things in the campaign that were controversial, but Hillary made a few comments that really defined who she was, and what she thought about regular people. She said Trump supporters were "a basket of deplorables." Trump responded by saying this showed her "true contempt for everyday Americans," and it did. Without fully realizing it, Hillary Clinton showed her true self, and voters remembered it. I know I did.

Liberals have got to recognize that some people have different points of view in regard to LGBT practices. It is not a matter of hate rather it is following their conscience. Some churches preach against it from the pulpit. In doing so they are exercising their right to freedom of religion, to assembly and free speech as guaranteed by the First Amendment to the Constitution. These groups are regularly castigated by liberals. Why are liberals so intolerant?

I am upset by other ways liberals trash the First Amendment. Conservatives are not allowed to speak on many college campuses. Some have even feared for their personal safety. Colleges used to be bastions of free speech. Once again, conservatism is not engaging in hate speech as it is labeled by liberals. It is just another political point of view. The free exchange of ideas fosters progress and unity. There is nothing to fear from other ideas. One of the first steps toward totalitarianism has been the suppression of free speech. Fox News has been under constant attack. Will conservative publications be next? This repression could cause the very foundations of our democracy to crumble.

It was difficult to get excited about any of the presidential candidates. In November of 2016 it came down to just two choices: Trump or Hillary. It was a choice between a bombastic businessman or a woman under investigation for destroying subpoenaed documents. He promised a new approach and she was more of the same. Not much of a choice.

We are a divided nation. From the halls of Congress to the chaos in our streets we have met the enemy and it is us. Republicans cannot agree on anything and the Democrat's new watchword is "resist." There is no effort on either side to find common ground. It was the same under the Obama administration. He accepted little input from Republicans and now, likewise, the Republicans have all but shut out the Democrats. What ever happened to statesmanship?

* * *

To what extent did the beliefs of the two men in this section reflect the three eternal questions of Chapter 3? What is the nature of humanity? How should the institutions of society be constructed? And which political strategies should be employed in society?

Advantages and Disadvantages

When comparing the left and the right it is tempting to see them as the *yin* and *yang* of politics—the Chinese symbols that interact equally in life. But it turns out that they are not equal—they are not a counterbalance to each other. If we look at them more carefully, we discover that each has built-in advantages and disadvantages that can be exploited by those who understand the qualities of each.

In most affairs of life, conservatives have the advantage of playing to a hometown audience. There is a natural inclination for human beings to conserve what is familiar in their lives, and right-wing groups are good at defending home-spun values. Most people are born as conservatives—they favor the current interpretation of their own religious, political, social, racial, and economic institutions. There is a real human built-in affection for what is familiar. When folks think of the "good old days," they remember that everything was simpler and easier to understand, even if it wasn't. Keeping things the way they were seems more sensible. Nostalgia is a good friend of conservatism.

It not only feels good to show reverence for the past, it's also smart if one wants to get ahead in politics, business or religious life. Taking a conservative position is inherently safer than proposing a grand new idea. There's no need to go out on a limb to justify what people already believe. In most circles, it just sort of makes everyone feel better if we revere the past. Most leaders learn not to rock the boat with their peer group if they want to succeed in life. It's the prudent thing to do, and it also feels good to have other people agree with you.

One could make a strong argument that the idea of God is a conservative concept because the underlying beliefs of religion are built around an established, righteous society that sets up a pattern for a traditional, virtuous life. Moreover, conventional religious morality is an enduring, permanent idea that is thought to be everlasting. Over the centuries, organized religion and conservatism have gone hand-in-hand. They are usually the twin building blocks of society.

Conservatives usually see themselves as being responsible for promoting and maintaining order on this earth; they are the self-appointed guardians of the righteous life. To them an orderly society is harmonious, even when it covers up inequality. Right-wing groups are usually champions of custom and continuity. They see their task as preserving society, despite the destructive nature of humanity. People on the right are fond of saying, "individuals are foolish, but the species is wise," consequently they generally respect custom. Conservatives often feel like they are the only adults in the room; they believe whole-heartedly that humans are frail creatures and it is necessary therefore to have a God-fearing society to keep them in line.

The view from the left is very different. Liberals seek a secular-based society where regular, orderly reforms and services are provided because it is the right thing to do, regardless of whether individuals believe in God. People on the left are fond of saying that human beings can be good without a fear in God—that they are rational and perfectly capable of thinking for themselves and criticizing the institutions of society, including the age-old churches. When leftists speak of liberty, they often are thinking about the right to dissent against the old, moralistic codes of conduct that hinders a new way of viewing the future.

There is a constant hope among liberals that society can be improved when leaders show a good example; they reject the idea that fear of enteral punishment is the only thing that keeps people in line. Progressives around the world dream of the day when conservatives will no longer see God as the great enforcer, but conservatives are content that that day will never come. In the meantime, left-wing groups are forever promoting changes with the belief that government can improve the lives of people on this earth rather than waiting for a reward in heaven.

Yet it often feels like a lonely task for conservatives who are fighting a continuous rear-guard action to repeal these changes brought about by liberals. Since the 1930s, there has been a steady upheaval in nearly every aspect of American life, ranging from New Deal legislation to the Civil Rights Movement. In some years, the left seemed to be almost unstoppable. Conservatives today have their backs up against the wall in nearly every area from the effects of climate change to challenging women's issues, race, and LBGT rights.

Yet the defensive posture of conservatives has made them stronger and more resourceful; they always seem able to regroup to reclaim their position on the field of battle. In the late 1970s, right-wing groups launched a series of think-tanks and foundations that helped them develop issues. There is always a ready-made group of conservative spokespersons prepared to go on television talk shows. The message from the right has never been stronger, more generously funded, or better organized. Progressives now seem to be in a defensive position.

One of the problems for the left is that they think their ideas are so well-supported by research and so self-evident that they should stand alone without a public relations campaign. For example, liberals are surprised and dismayed that everyone is not convinced that climate change is threating the earth. They report that scientists are annoyed that persons without any specialized training will call into question conclusions documented by decades of careful study. Yet a near unanimous scientific community can be held back by persons with no particular scientific background who simply say they don't believe the studies. A favored comment on the right is to say, "I'm no scientist, but I don't think we really know if humans have caused climate change." Then they add, "The government is wrong about a lot of things."

Conservatives have come to understand that all they need to do is sow the seeds of doubt about climate change, and that alone will halt any meaningful efforts to control greenhouse gas emissions. Doubt has become the new conservative strategy for blocking proposed carbon control legislation. The right has discovered that it is not necessary to disprove the effectiveness of environment programs of the Environmental Protection Agency (EPA)— just introduce the nagging notion that these kinds of programs are very expensive and usually don't work. Often it is only necessary to remind the public that government itself doesn't work. That's enough.

Progressives suffer from being overburdened with complex talking points when dealing with diverse issues ranging from the causes of poverty, how to stimulate the economy, or whether to use a land army to continue fighting terrorism in the Middle East. Conservatives have the relatively easy task of casting doubt by simply saying that leftist concepts have no provable merit. *It's easier to just keep doing the same thing.* Ordinary people are quick to stand by simple solutions. It's easy to see why the left can be caught off guard by claims that we don't need all those new theories about what to do next.

Another problem for liberals is that they usually talk about what is wrong in society –racism, poorly educated youth, or children who are abused by their parents. Ordinary people get sick of hearing about all the things that are wrong, and they are relieved when conservatives focus on positive stories like tax cuts and getting rid of government regulation. Worse yet, the message from liberals is often taken personally by voters who think they are being accused of being racist, not maintaining their schools, or beating their children.

Conservatives often gloss over the problems in society because they don't want to start expensive programs to solve them. Right-wing groups are usually more popular because they talk about patriotism and stories of individual success. All of this gives conservatives a real advantage at election time.

On a day-to-day basis, traditional conservatism warms the heart of American Main-Street culture. Prevailing values are seen as a set of sensible principles that made the United States great. There is a feeling here that is exemplified in Norman Rockwell paintings. People in the pictures of Americana are wholesome, a bit rough around the edges, their clothes don't fit all that well, but they do the right things for the right reason. Conservatives will look you in the eye and say clearly, "Our people are different than any other." Implied is the unspoken belief that "We have a special insight that others may not have." Traditional, conservative values have an authenticity of hometown wisdom that is not found on the left. Somehow crusading liberals don't seem to fit well into a Norman Rockwell painting.

An added factor that favors the right is that patriotism and nationalism have always come easy to them. There is no limit here on loving the country or waving the flag. The general public is quick to accept the idea that certain kinds of cherished beliefs are worth fighting and dying for. Even when there's evidence the war was fought in error, it is still regarded as a noble venture that brought out the best in the nation. Even if a veteran lost a leg or arm in the war, no one wants to hear him talk about fighting for a "lost cause."

During times of war, conservatives have an ideal position—the nation rallies around the old-fashioned values that have always been defended. The symbols of heroes and battles past are steeped in stories passed down from earlier generations. Standing up for one's country just naturally appeals to a wide slice of the public who are more likely to call themselves conservatives. People on the right side of the spectrum seem to have more flags and patriotic reminders around their houses. They are not shy about loving the "American Way of Life" and it shows.

In an almost natural way, the right often provides the warriors that defend society when we are threatened by an outside force, while the left often takes up the mantel of being the caregivers when the warriors are disabled. To a great extent, each promotes their role as being critical to building a good social order, and each minimizes the role of the other. For example, when is the last time you heard liberals talk about the need to enlarge the military, or conservatives propose providing a safety net for the homeless?

On the issue of immigration, liberals generally side with the new arrivals. They empathize with those that are looking for a better life. This is especially true in urban areas where there are many established neighborhoods of immigrants. Several large cities and states have declared themselves to be sanctuary areas, declaring that local law enforcement officials will not go out looking for persons who don't have documentation of their status. Left-wing groups usually take a strong position favoring diversity in language, culture and race. They support clearly written immigration laws, but they line up in defending persons already in the U.S. that are not guilty of any crimes. Nearly all progressives in Congress voted to relax immigration laws to allow the *Dreamers* to stay in the U.S. (These were the young people who were brought into the country as children by their parents, but do not have a legal right to stay.) In recent times this issue divided the left and right more than any other.

Conservatives are more inclined to restrict new immigration. Conservatives say their only concern is obeying the immigration laws, but many are especially sensitive to people of another color who don't speak English. Some are worried that American culture will be diluted by alien customs and practices. Still others fear that the new arrivals will someday outnumber them and vote in leaders with foreign-sounding names. Call-in shows on radio and television feature conservatives who say that immigrants are "taking our jobs, crowding our schools, and filling our prisons," but the most important reason may be cultural and emotional because there is a fear that new arrivals will undermine American values. It is not uncommon for conservatives to say they want to stop the flow of immigrants by almost any means, "before it's too late."

The Trump policy of separating children from their parents at the southern border divided the country into opposing camps, but it was grudgingly accepted by many conservatives who saw it as a deterrent to more Hispanics coming into the United States. Cable news outlets on the left focused on small children in cages crying for their mothers, while right-wing television commentators spoke of keeping drug dealers and gang members out of the country.

Donald Trump chose to come down hard on the immigration issue in the 2018 midterm elections. He ordered 15,000 troops to the border to combat a "caravan of bad people" who were threatening to "invade" the United States. There was no proof, but Trump speculated that the caravan might contain folks with leprosy and small pox. He warned that Democrats were financing the caravan because they "hated America," and believed in an "open border."

There has always been a strain of nativism in American politics as insecure segments of the population reacted to the most recent arrival of new immigrants. Looking back at the 19th and 20th centuries, new groups like the Irish, Italians and Greeks were not welcomed by many Americans. But after a period of integration, descendants from those same groups were opposed to newer groups coming in from south of the border. Turning against newcomers is as American as cherry pie. It is an interesting factor in life that folks who were recently at the bottom of the social structure are the first to demonize new immigrants.

But regardless of how long one has been here, virtually every American has a sense of loyalty to the country, yet conservatives have a sneaking suspicion that they are more loyal than liberals. After all, those on the left are forever talking about mistakes the U.S. has made in foreign policies. Critics of American foreign policy are accused of being un–American. It's a bit more complicated for people on the left to say they support our troops abroad because liberals often criticize U.S. military involvement in the world. In international affairs, progressives usually have explanations that end up suggesting that America has done something wrong. It's seldom very popular to remind others of the glaring mistakes that have been made in our foreign policy. To avoid a charge of being unpatriotic, many on the left have learned to tone down their criticisms unless they are willing to have their loyalty called into question.

As a group, conservatives become strangely silent when the topic comes up of whether the United States should have intervened in some foreign hotspots around the world such as Vietnam or Iraq. Large numbers of people on the right still have trouble admitting that these wars were a mistake. Pride is a powerful factor, and criticism of the national policies doesn't fit well in the conservative temperament. It is more satisfying ideologically for persons on the right to focus on what "we've done right," rather than what "we've done wrong." Standing by the country is much more comfortable for conservatives in both foreign and domestic affairs.

To add to this situation, leading members of the power structures in most communities support a conservative point of view. Existing institutions such as churches, banks, and corporations have a lot of time and money invested in maintaining the status quo. There are deep financial pockets on the right, and many powerful and affluent people are willing to spend large sums to keep things the way they are. Corporations are eager to fund projects that tell how well the present system works. They spend an inordinate amount of time and resources convincing people that it's a good idea to stay in line on right-wing issues and resist major changes. These organizations make the point that everything works better when there is continuity in everyday life. Through this perspective, major changes should come slowly, if at all, in the realm of politics, culture, religion, and economics.

Along these same lines, there is a strong belief among conservatives that enterprising people deserve the most rewards. It seems self-evident that those who have already attained wealth must have worked the hardest and therefore should be admired and compensated at the highest level. It goes without saying that those on the bottom have probably not applied themselves completely, and therefore don't deserve the most important privileges of life. The public generally accepts these conclusions. There is a deep admiration in most localities for those who succeed in business and other walks of life. Among low income people there is the hope that someday they may "strike it rich," so they don't want to undermine the position of the rich because, in their fantasies, they imagine themselves to be there some day.

Liberals have a suspicion that conservatives think they are more deserving and better than anyone else. It shows up in legislation when the wealthy get more of the rewards and the poor are conveniently forgotten. The left is forever saying "everyone is equal," while the right has a stoic silence suggesting that they have no interest in that particular topic. Inequality is something that is accepted on the right—it's even defended on an economic and religious level. Liberals secretly suspect that conservatives think they are closer to heaven and better than anyone else. What do you think?

In recent years, some Christian ministers have expanded the gospel by preaching that God wants us to be rich, that financial and spiritual rewards go together when individuals work hard. The old idea that Jesus identified with the poor is not heard as often with this segment of the population. Many of the seminars on "how to be rich" have a religious type of following. They attract disenchanted folks who dream of succeeding on both fronts.

There is also a continuity of opinion as it relates to crime and punishment. The right has the general view that negative, antisocial behavior will be curbed if there are severe penalties for law-breakers: "If you do the crime, you do the time." The death penalty is favored by many conservatives because they believe it will serve as an example of what will happen to folks if they commit a capital crime. The implication is that fear of punishment keeps people in line. Liberals strongly disagree. What do you think?

People on the left are less inclined to view punishment as a deterrent to crime. Liberals are quick to say that minorities are often treated unfairly by the justice system, and that society should focus on early childhood education as a means to reach young people before they turn to antisocial behavior. Leaders on the left are fond of pointing out that even if we ignore the human costs, it is far cheaper to educate someone and make them into a taxpayer, than it is to lock them up for life in prison. Conservatives don't seem to have a good answer to that point.

Right-wing groups are not inspired by the idea that society needs to provide special early childhood education to aid children who grow up in crime-infested neighborhoods. In this area, conservatives see everyone as free agents who choose their own path—to be a law-abiding citizen or a law-breaker. They are more concerned with the morality of right and wrong than social engineering, and are seldom attracted to the proposition that education should be the top priority in society for both social as well as economic reasons. The bottom line of this issue is the belief that those who break the rules should pay the penalty. The left-wing has real difficulty arguing against this moralistic point of view, especially if it involves punishment for a horrendous crime. Progressive candidates are often accused of being "soft on crime," and are often trying to explain why they can't bring crime rates down.

Along similar lines of morality, right-wing organizations support personal gun ownership as a defense against crime. There's a belief that less-worthy people behave only when the citizenry is armed. "The only way to stop a bad guy with a gun is with a good guy with a gun." Conservatives are firm believers in the constitutional "right to bear arms," and they often are vocal backers of the National Rifle Association. There is a lot of talk on the right about buying and owning guns, and there's also a built-in expectation that conservatives are more likely to use firearms as a means of self-defense.

After every mass shooting, progressives propose tighter controls on buying guns. Within hours after the killings, liberals bring out plans to control the sale of particular kinds of weapons. The conservative response is this is time for mourning the dead, not a time for politics. Liberals come back with the point, "but when is the proper time for a debate on this subject?" The response from the right side of the spectrum is a loud silence.

On gun issues and many other topics, conservatives seem to be more confident than liberals—they often appear as the most "sensible citizens." The right doesn't have to mince words. There is no need to lower one's voice when defending the current ways of thinking. The tone of voice is strong when defending the respected principles of the past. There's a feeling of being on the right side of history because the majority generally agrees.

Critics of the status quo almost always labor under the displeasure of the ruling elites. It's risky to argue for change. Ask anyone who has started a new religion, proposed a different economic system, advocated social reforms, or sought more rights for minority citizens.

Liberals are often the most unpopular people in the room. Much of "respectable society" sees the left as being soft-headed and out of touch with reality. The present way of doing things always seems more sensible, even if it's disastrous. It's almost always safe to say, "I think liberals have lofty motives, but they really don't seem to have a firm grasp on reality."

But the left often waits in the wings as the need for reform builds out on the street. The public only turns to liberals when society is in drastic need of reform. The economic collapse of the late 1920s brought about the New Deal of the 1930s. One hundred years of Jim Crow segregation made the Civil Rights Movement inevitable. Women lived in a form of gender slavery for hundreds of years until feminist rebels fought for and won some measure of equality. The LGBT community was treated as outcasts until very recently. Progressive change of this type is often an insidious idea until "respectable society" feels the time for reform has come.

But even if the present system fails, new ideas are still criticized for being ill-conceived, unnecessary, too expensive, or out of step with our traditions. The programs and policies that came out of the New Deal in the 1930s are often credited with saving American capitalism, yet it is still acceptable in some circles to say they were unnecessary or ill-conceived.

New programs like Social Security and Medicare are still being scrutinized decades later. Public attention is focused on some particular problem areas; credit is almost never given to the main portion of the program that is succeeding as planned. The result is that even when new ideas are successful, they are deemed a failure because negative news is always remembered more by the public. Liberals seldom get credit for positive changes. It's a lonely position to advocate novel ways of thinking, even if they work.

To add to this situation, unfounded criticisms of new ideas can be made without the critic being held accountable. Somehow opponents from the right get a free pass to make unproven charges because the public generally likes to hear that newfangled ideas will probably crash and burn. Predictions of doom are repeated over and over even though a new concept is progressing well. But the negative charges are remembered by the public.

Most social and economic programs that expand government services can be traced back to liberals with a vision for taking on new tasks. Later the program is developed to encompass more functions that were not in the original design. Progressives often get their foot in the door with a pilot program that later grows into something more substantial. Obamacare was a case in point; it was first enacted in 2010 as a government-sponsored insurance program with the expectation that it would later become a fully funded universal health care program. Conservatives knew this and it was picked as a prime target for repeal when Donald Trump became President in 2017.

Programs like Obamacare are often designed to take care of society, to ward off some widespread problem that involves nearly everyone. It may be climate change, gun violence, poor schools, injustice, voting rights, air quality standards or other nationwide challenges. A built-in problem for liberals is that the function of *providing for everyone's welfare* is too general in tone and it may even sound naive or impractical. Somehow it is more difficult to sell the idea that we should all give up something for the sake of the common good. It is much more acceptable to hear about alleged losses of individual freedom in religious, economic or social affairs. The negative response to over-regulation of the economy or alleged government fraud stimulates a crowd much quicker than a warning about air quality.

A basic tenet on the left is the belief that everyone in society should sacrifice for the sake of the rank-and-file of the majority. This is especially true when addressing the needs of those without personal power. There is a long-standing position among liberals that everyone should care about the less fortunate, but somehow this kind of thinking sounds too much like socialism or a do-gooder idea that is out of touch with reality. It does not blend well into Americans values.

On the economic front, liberals are motivated by promoting a shared prosperity that rescues those at the bottom of society. There is a belief on the left that a rising tide lifts all boats—that public economic investment benefits everyone. There is an argument here that a broadly based economy is more stable because everyone has a stake in maintaining the system. Conservatives wouldn't necessarily disagree with this point, but they seldom advocate policies that provide immediate opportunities for those at the bottom of the structure. Liberals are fond of voicing the philosophy that we are all in this together, and therefore the first thought should be promoting policies that aid us all. On the conservative side there is the underlying thought that each of us is here pretty much on our own, so don't worry too much about the other guy. These two ways of looking at politics are major factors in how we shape public policy.

The conservative side of individualism is much more popular. The basic belief is that society can be benefited most by encouraging everyone to seek their own goals through personal initiative rather than government programs. As a matter of principle, the right does not feel much enthusiasm for a collective responsibility to aid to those who do not (or cannot) help themselves. What do you think?

The two sides actually think differently when it comes to delivering assistance to those in need. The right generally favors private agencies where voluntary contributions can be targeted to a specific cause. The word "voluntary" is the key. Conservatives see public giving as a virtue, but they draw the line when government gets into the picture. There is reluctance for using tax monies for disaster relief, especially if it occurs in a different part of the country such as a hurricane that hits only a small portion of the country. There's a nagging feeling on the right that those folks should have known better than to settle in areas that are often hit by storms. This point of view, of course, is not expressed by conservatives who live in the battered areas.

The left has a very different approach in providing public assistance in times of emergencies. Generally, liberals are of the opinion that if there is a legitimate need the government has an obligation to step in. Progressives don't disapprove of private charities such as churches or the Red Cross, but they oppose the transference of public obligation to private groups because the funding may be cut off if public interest wanes.

There is an assumption on the right that business experience qualifies one to administer government agencies. When conservatives win the presidency, they regularly put corporate executives or retired military leaders in the cabinet, thinking that managing business and commanding the military is the same as managing government, but that's really not true. Business executives and retired generals are often annoyed when they need to negotiate and compromise with members of the bureaucracy and Congress. There is no command structure in politics as there is in private business and the army; that kind of experience is a poor training ground for political leaders because political executives cannot give orders to members of legislative bodies. Running a political organization calls on special skills that involve convincing and bargaining with others to follow the leader; these are leadership traits that are not necessarily found in business or the military.

In a related strand of conservative thinking, services offered by private industry are considered to be superior to those performed by the government. There is an assumption that non-governmental activities are more efficient, better formulated, and less expensive. The expectation is that the profit motive streamlines operations, cuts red tape, reduces waste, and makes everything work better. Privatization of public service is expected to provide better services while reducing taxes. They say, "It's just a matter of common sense."

These are the arguments made by conservatives to privatize a major part of the services presently performed by federal, state, or local governments. They include law enforcement—garbage collection—retirement pensions—toll roads—lotteries—government buildings—schools—air traffic control—prisons—fire protection—highway and street construction and maintenance—public assistance—postal services—commando operations in war zones—voting services—parole officers—waste water treatment—administration of public lands—Army Corps of Engineers—public transportation—libraries—food safety—water services—snow removal—border patrol—parking meters—airport and seaport management. And recently there has been a very prominent effort to privatize several government departments including Homeland Security, Veterans affairs, plus a longtime effort to privatize Medicare, Medicaid, and Social Security.

Progressives have fought privatization on the primary point that governmental services are not meant to be run as businesses where cutting cost and avoiding waste are the main goal. They believe that schools, police departments, and libraries were established to provide services regardless of profit/loss, and that they should not be run as a business. There is a fear that the whole idea of governmental accountability for services will be lost in a business-model program. Liberals maintain that privatization of services ignores human needs that cannot always be measured on a purely statistical basis. This topic has been debated vigorously since the Trump administration launched an effort to privatize several governmental functions.

The debate to privatize services highlights the basic values of the right and the left. Liberals idealize the teacher who teaches a child to read, the social worker who personally helps a former prisoner get a job, or the public health employee who works overtime to maintain the purity of the city's water supply. Progressives are troubled when the free-market approach is applied to the public services. They stress that government is for people, not for profit. Conservatives, on the other hand, speak of government waste, inefficiency, and old-style administrative practices. Right-wing proposals focus on cutting costs, streamlining services and avoiding bureaucratic rules. The emphasis is on a non-partisan approach with the motto, "there's no Republican or Democratic way to pave a street." What do you think?

Morality

Why do liberals want to help folks who can't help themselves? Why do they see themselves as the self-appointed guardians of the least fortunate? Why are many progressives willing to raise their own taxes for the benefit of people they don't even know?

A simulation game highlighted these questions in a setting that featured a self-described liberal newspaper editor and a wealthy, conservative businessman who was the mayor of a medium-sized city. It turned out that a sense of empathy for victimized people drove the editor while the mayor was more pragmatic in following his own personal self-interest.

Simulation games can teach us a lot about politics and ourselves. Not long ago I organized a simulation game to be played with a group of men who were community leaders in an American city. I had no idea that the game would reveal the basic differences that separate liberals and conservatives in meeting real-life problems.

The game was designed to illustrate the problems of poor people who wanted to improve their ghetto-like neighborhood by pooling their resources, getting involved in community action projects, and generally providing hope, despite the depressing circumstances of hardcore poverty. Each player drew cards that decided their individual fate. The different cards had an immediate impact on their life chances—they lost their jobs, had their welfare payments cut, got evicted from their apartments, or flunked out of school. Included in the game was the enticing chance to engage in crime that might solve some of their personal problems, but would cause the neighborhood to be infested with illegal drugs, an increase in street crime, and more of the players would be arrested and sent to jail. It stimulated bare-knuckled politics where everyone was on their own in a dangerous environment.

As the game progressed, players began to see that the odds were stacked against improving the neighborhood, and individuals turned to anti-social behavior as a means of survival. The simulated society became more dangerous as crime rates rose and individual players lost control of their future. Frustration turned to anger as players were pitted against each other for the scarce resources. Community action projects were abandoned because it simply made no sense to work together for long-term community improvement. Folks felt increasingly isolated as the simulation degenerated into a crime-ridden situation that went steadily downhill.

There were eight people playing the game, but two of them stood out. First was the mayor (a Republican) who owned a successful local timber products company. He was a solid conservative political leader who was the first to catch on to how to succeed while living in extreme poverty. It wasn't long before the mayor rose to become a crime boss by threatening low level criminals. At the end of the simulation he was skimming ten percent off of all the illegal drug sales. He bought off the police and generally adjusted very well to the severe circumstances. The second person of interest was the editor of the local newspaper (a Democrat) known as a "crusading liberal." In real life he supported local schools, defended civil liberties, community health clinics, and campaigned for measures to increase cooperation between the city and the county. But the editor had a problem: he couldn't bring himself to engage in criminal behavior in the simulation. He continued to sponsor community projects that failed miserably because other players would not support programs that didn't help them in the short run. Everyone else in the simulation (the other seven players) adjusted to a life of crime in the game despite the fact that all of them (in real life) were law-abiding, upstanding members of their real community. There was one physician, an attorney, and four business leaders. In real life, none of them had ever engaged in crime.

After the simulation ended, we had a debriefing session to discuss the dynamics of the game. Seven of the eight players (excluding the editor) spoke of how they had to change and adapt to new circumstances as their lives were impacted by "terrible conditions" in the ghetto. The mayor was quite proud of himself as he spoke of how the "situation out on the street" evolved and he applied "pragmatic strategies" to survive. The seven of them agreed that they learned something about how frustration could cause a person to break the law. But the editor of the newspaper was very quiet. He sat over in a corner, chain-smoking, and he was obviously frustrated by the simulation. Finally, the editor spoke up and said he had taken a "moral stand" in the simulation to help everyone else even though no one would work with him. He said he couldn't do the "wrong thing" even if it were only a game. It soon became clear that he personally couldn't let go of his "crusading spirit" because, he said, it would have been "immoral."

The most intriguing part of the debriefing session was an unplanned, lengthy discussion on morality in politics, and how sometimes liberals wanted to lead the community to a "better place" even when some in the community didn't want to go. The editor confessed to being frustrated in his real life when individuals in his city voted against school levies and refused various reforms because it would raise taxes. He confessed that liberals were probably doomed to frustration because "doing the right thing" is often unpopular. In his words, people on the left have a "special burden" because they feel responsible for "everyone's welfare." The editor said he never really understood people who didn't "feel responsible" for the entire community.

The mayor interrupted by saying, "I hope you don't mean to suggest that conservatives don't care. We do feel a clear obligation to help people, but we believe that they should be responsible for their own lives." He went on to say that he didn't really see a great moral problem in the simulation because people need to be free to react to situations with pragmatic responses. The mayor added that—in real life—he never felt personally "devoted" to projects that involved everyone, and he couldn't understand why some people (like the editor) got so "hung up" on issues like improving city/country cooperation. The mayor laughed when he talked about the simulation. He added,

"I could see that being a do-gooder wasn't going to work so I did what I had to do."

Since that day, I've thought a lot about how the conservative mayor and the liberal editor acted, and how an allegory of the simulation could delve deeper into explaining how liberals and conservatives might see the morality of supporting programs that might be good for society, but unpopular with most of the voters. Perhaps the Affordable Care Act (Obamacare) is a prime example. Liberals enthusiastically put together a program that enabled about 20 million Americans to gain health insurance through a program that conservatives strongly opposed. So what drove President Obama and the Democratic Party to launch a program that was to be so unpopular in the short run? Liberals were not set to profit from the program economically or even politically. They lost their congressional majority in 2010 and never recovered during Obama's term of office (2009–2017). Leaders on the left knew they were taking a huge political gamble by pushing through a program that proved to be a huge political problem. So why did they do it? What do you think?

And perhaps just as importantly, what motivated the Freedom Caucus of the Republican Party to fight Obamacare? They were also driven by doing the right thing for the right reason—also with a sense of morality. As a matter of principle, these conservative Republicans could not vote for a government program that took away the freedom of individuals to provide for their own health care. They objected strongly to the idea that "health care was a right." GOP leaders contended that just because health care was important, didn't mean the government should make health insurance mandatory. They stood firm on a moral political principle.

Liberals were motivated by a sense of political morality in providing a program that they thought people needed. Progressives at all levels told stories about how people couldn't afford medical care, and how many ordinary, responsible folks filed bankruptcies because they couldn't pay their medical bills. The liberal sense of empathy went into overdrive. You may remember the dedicated look in Obama's eyes as he defended Obamacare. He seemed to be motivated by something that he believed in, but something that brought him many sleepless nights. Obama, like the newspaper editor, was thinking about those lower income folks who would benefit, but both Obama and the editor faced the public reaction from ordinary people who were saying: "I'd rather do it myself."

But health care is just the tip of the iceberg. The morality issue comes up in nearly every social welfare/civil rights issue on the books. Think outlawing racial discrimination, funding inner-city schools, voter suppression, women's rights, gerrymandering, community welfare centers, Medicare, Medicaid, Social Security, Head Start, food stamps, abortion, affirmative action, same-sex marriage, and most anti-poverty programs. The issue of left-wing morality comes into play on every program.

Liberals (like the newspaper editor) are committed to these kinds of programs even while they are criticized for waste, mismanagement, and questionable goals. People on the left often appear to be inflexible when they are not willing to abandon their original purpose. Conservatives, on the other hand, are more flexible (like the mayor) and are more pragmatic as they adjust to the reality of a situation. The left is caught in the role of advancing humanistic goals, while the right enjoys the role of appearing to be more sensible and practical. Both stand by their moral principles. Maybe the editor was right—*maybe empathy is a burden*. What do you think?

Morality is not something that can be proven; it's an abstract concept in the individual's conscience that motivates them to do the right thing for the right reason. The liberal sense of empathy is difficult to explain, but it comes up every time people on the left talk about the folks that are having trouble making ends meet. Morality for progressives is all about putting themselves in the shoes of those who have the least. Programs like these have only limited success, but liberals are willing to risk it all and accept that situation because they have a different moral mission.

But conservatives have morals too. From their perspective, it is immoral to undermine the human spirit by turning people into wards of the state. They argue that everyone has challenges in life like getting sick, losing their jobs, or not saving enough to retire, and that individuals will learn a more important lesson in life if they have to take personal responsibility for their own welfare. There is an implication that the lessons of life should leave a scar that hurts a little—that the best way to learn is through the school of hard knocks. The traditional point of view is that government does not make people better by giving them things they do not deserve. Conservatives focus on the waste of a poorly designed, expensive program that never should have been enacted.

People on the right usually save the word "morality" for discussing religious or ethical concepts—of serving as an example to children, or behaving in an honest way that strengthens the family and the country. Conservatives contend that they are not just cutting the funding of programs for their own self-interest. They believe that people have the potential to take care of themselves, and government should not stand in their way of becoming more independent.

Neither the left nor right is inherently wrong, but they certainly have a different vision of morality. Most conservatives and liberals don't understand each other. Folks on the right tend to get angry when they see a program as unnecessary or ill-conceived, while people on the left are dismayed when they hear critics say that everyone is on their own. Both are like ships in the night that pass each other in the dark without appreciating how and why other side applies a different set of moral standards to govern the nation.

Questions for You

1. Apply the three functions of an ideology to the political party of your choice. How well does it do in deciding: what's wrong with society— how to fix it—and the individual's role in the process?

2. How do the stories of getting indoor plumbing and providing for national defense illustrate the positive role for government? Do you have any personal stories that illustrate how you acquired any particular political value? Did your family generally have a positive or negative view of government as an institution?

3. The stories of Scott and Susan are similar in the beginnings but dramatically different in later years. What do you think were the key events in each life that changed the outcome of the socialization process? Can you point to any particular event in your life that changed you politically?

4. Read and analyze "An Autobiography of a Liberal," and "An Autobiography of a Conservative." What do think were the earliest events in each case that shaped their personal ideology? Could you personally identify with either one of them? Consider for a moment how you would write An Autobiography of yourself. What would be the major events that shaped your political points of view?

5. After reading the section, "Advantages and Disadvantages," which of the two major ideologies do you think has the greatest number of built-in advantages? How about built-in disadvantages? Why do you think public opinion generally favors one group over the other?

6. Why is immigration such a sensitive issue for conservatives? Do you share some of those concerns that were stated in this section? Why or why not?

7. Compare and contrast the typical positions of the left and right on national defense and supporting recent wars. Why are liberals thought to be disloyal in some conservative circles? How do you feel about this topic?

8. What are the consistent positions of the left and right on income equality, crime and punishment, early childhood education, and gun ownership? Why, according to the author, are conservatives more confident when discussing these kinds of topics?

9. According to the author, what is the common public response to proposals that are designed to benefit everyone? Why is it usually easier politically to block a legislative program than to support it? Can you cite any examples of this in American politics?

10. Google "privatization of government services." What is the logic that supports more privatization? What is the opposing position? How do you feel about the issue?

11. What did you think of the comment in the "Morality" section that liberals want to take people to a "better place" even when they don't want to go? How about the statement that liberals have a "special burden" for taking care of everyone's welfare? Is Obamacare an example of this? Why or why not?

How Did You Learn Your Political Values?

Where did your political values come from? Which life experiences have made you who you are? On a separate piece of paper, check off the following possible sources and arrange them in rank order with the five most important factors at the top.

Here is the list: family—church—school—length of residence in country—age—social class—life partner—media exposure—work mates—race—political party—gender—nationality—music—your neighborhood—friends—the Internet—income level—sports—military experience—geographic residence—occupation—ethnic background—or finally an inspiration leader you followed in your life.

Are there other sources of your political socialization that should be noted here?

5

Expectations and Deprivations

Democracy is based on the assumption that there are multiple ideas of value in the political arena and that everyone has a right to be heard. In the past, both the left and right had a pride in defending democratic values. But in recent years it has become increasingly difficult for some to listen to other opinions. Some of us wonder whether the practice of democracy itself is under assault. What do you think?

On the local level there's been a rash of incidents on college campuses in which students have protested the appearance of speakers that hold an opposing point of view—both left-wing and right-wing speakers have been barred. Opposing talk radio and cable TV news have had a field day, leaving the impression that only one side was "afraid to hear the other side." There is a real fear that colleges are being infected by the same political virus that has contaminated the rest of society. What used to be the haven for new ideas has become a place to shout down speakers with opposing points of view. Have you seen this happen through your own experiences?

Today there's a growing notion (in some quarters) that all the truth is on *one* side. In our lifetimes, we have never seen such one-sided thinking on the political, social, religious, racial, and economic issues of the day. These positions blot out any thought of objectivity and appreciation for the other side. Minority rights have become a thing of the past. Some folks are willing to close down the government—and undermine the rule of law—rather than compromise with the opposition. More and more it is becoming apparent that we are living in an era of the *true believer*, a time when some think they have an exclusive insight into the truth and that they have no obligation to let anyone else speak. In an unbelievable show of arrogance and anger, some political leaders are willing to short-circuit the democratic process to achieve narrow partisan goals. There are new examples of this sorry state of affairs nearly every day.

The above allegations about American politics and society in general would have been considered completely unfounded a few years ago. When I reread the above paragraphs, I recognize that no one would have believed me if I would have written these comments as predictions 10 or 15 years ago. Then, most of us thought we had outgrown the kind of blind partisanship that surrounds us today. Perhaps even more disturbing is the thought that this kind of thinking has become the new normal. Is it possible that the belief in pluralism and tolerance is dying? There is a real fear that this is the way it's going to be in the United States unless we can find some way to bring civility and tolerance back into our national life.

Role of the Central Government

It may sound farfetched, but the most contentious issue of all is deciding the proper role for the national government. The most persistent and divisive political question between the left and right is deciding what the federal government should or should not do on a wide range of subjects. Virtually every hot-button issue is a sub-topic under that general heading.

Opinion leaders on the left argue that we need a strong national government to maintain an accountable consistency across the country. Liberals believe that a strong central government should be responsive to all, regardless of gender, race, wealth, or power. The right is alarmed at the growing scope and expense of supporting a federal government that they believe undermines individual initiative and impedes the forces of the marketplace. Conservatives warn that unnecessary government rules and regulations are sapping the energies of entrepreneurs who have made this country great. Liberals strongly disagree, arguing that only the national government has the authority to step in to promote everyone's interest in a modern society.

The first priority of the right is to roll back regulations they say intrude on everyone's lives. They see big government (and the taxes to fund it) as public enemy number one. Increasingly, conservatives see government regulations mushrooming out of control at every level. Liberals see government as the prime vehicle for promoting fairness and equality.

The issue that comes up the most frequently in Washington, D.C., is deciding the role of the federal government (or any government) in a multitude of critical areas. Favoring or opposing governmental action is predictable on nearly all issues. The left and right are lined up on opposing sides on topics as diverse as same-sex marriage—head start programs—teaching evolution—Planned Parenthood—Social Security—women's rights—Middle East refugees—student debts—banking regulations—gun control—climate change—income inequality—immigration—drug laws—LGBT rights—the minimum wage—legislative redistricting—immigration—affirmative action—aid to education—prison reform—environmental standards—abortion—military spending—capital punishment—privatization of public services—race relations—voter rights—Wall Street regulations—militarization of police—Medicare—Medicaid—food stamps—Obamacare—campaign spending limitations—arming classroom teachers—clean energy—tax policies—right to work laws—carrying concealed weapons—prayer in school—consumer protection—college costs—budget deficits—Iranian nuclear non-proliferation treaty—Paris Climate Change Accords, and a host of other topics.

Every one of these issues has further polarized ideological groups on the left and right. If one side prevails in setting policies in a particular area, it leaves scars that are not healed until the policy is reversed. Everyone has long memories. There is endless talk about annulling what was done, and amending the constitution so something else can no longer be done. Distasteful political wrestling matches are common as the same old group tries some new tactic to win a propaganda battle. Even those who support a particular issue usually know (deep down) that the arguments are made up just to counter what is being said on the other side. No one ever seems to question why there is such uniformity on both sides, and why people assume they always have legality and rationality on their side. It is tribal politics, pure and simple.

Constitutionalism

In this day in age, when the claim is made loudly that some particular policy is "constitutional," it means the speaker is for it, and the reverse is true as well. Clearly the Constitution has been (and is now) interpreted for political reasons and the meaning of the document has changed dramatically. It was used to legalize slavery, and later to outlaw racial segregation. In the late 19th century, the Supreme Court ruled that labor unions were a violation of anti-trust laws, but in the 20th century the right of unions to organize was upheld. The list of dramatic reversals continues into the present as the left and right reduces or expands the specific powers of the Constitution for their own political purposes.

Legal scholars often quote Supreme Court Justice Charles Evans Hughes who said, "The Constitution is what judges say it is." In a real sense, the Constitution has no binding meaning until the Supreme Court interrupts it, and that meaning has changed in important ways since it was written. Some professors of constitutional law have jokingly forbidden their students to read the Constitution itself because it would mislead them as to what it really means today. In truth, it has always been a political document that changed with the times and the political temperament of the country, as it should. Changing its meaning is the real power of the Supreme Court.

It is popular on both the left and right to charge that Supreme Court judges are acting in an improper manner by making "political decisions." Both sides have contended that judges should only interpret the law, not make the law. In fact, judges have always been politicians in robes who have acted in a subjective manner. The Court has repeatedly chosen a new path in key areas whenever it was considered necessary. Each time it happens, however, the critics of the decision act as though the justices are expected be non-partisan. That has never been true.

Everyone knows the President and Congress are driven by partisanship but the Supreme Court is driven in the same manner. This point is readily apparent in surveying key decisions made since the 1930s because—for long periods since then—all three branches of government have had a strong preference for liberal policies. This was especially painful for American conservatives. Consider the number and scope of new social programs and government regulations that were created in the past century. In most cases, liberals have been pleased by the changes, and conservatives have vowed to reverse the outcomes as soon as possible. Much of the political conflict today is based on conservatives trying to regain the ground they lost in the past.

Setting the Scenario

There has been a massive increase in the size and scope of the federal government since the early 20th century. With very few exceptions, there has been a rhythm to the process: the left moved to increase the scope of government while the right opposed that action. This may sound like an oversimplification, but it has actually reoccurred in a distinctive pattern.

The scenario took on a definite form when Franklin Roosevelt became President in 1933. The great depression of the 1930s jeopardized nearly every aspect of American life. The bottom dropped out of the economy. There was a run on the banks as depositors drew out their money. Jobs, investments, and consumer confidence disappeared overnight. Few anticipated the sudden financial collapse, and when it happened, no one had any idea of what to do. The immediate result was to turn against the policies that many believed were responsible for the dramatic downturn. Old, familiar economic principles and policies were set aside as Franklin Roosevelt experimented with a variety of New Deal measures. No one knew for certain where the country was going, including the president.

It was an upsetting time for conservatives, who sensed that their policies were being rejected. From Wall Street to Main Street, liberals were taking control and passing new laws that were to change the way politics and business were conducted. Roosevelt called for a "New Deal" as public works projects were organized to provide jobs—new business regulations were approved—the social security system was set in place—labor unions were promoted—the minimum wage was endorsed—stock market regulations were established—and the U.S. was taken off the gold standard. It was a time right-wing Americans will never forget or forgive. The changes enacted by liberals in the 1930s were fiercely resisted by many on the right. Decades later, conservatives are still trying to undo much of the New Deal.

In addition to the economic problems of the 1930s, it was also a time of fluctuating weather patterns as drought, extremely high temperatures, and severe dust storms hit the plains states. The Dust Bowl added to the economic problems faced by farmers. Some of the most productive land in the nation turned to dust and blew across the middle of the country. Thousands abandoned their farms and moved west as popularized by John Steinbeck's book, *The Grapes of Wrath*. This natural calamity stimulated the Roosevelt administration to expand federal agricultural subsidy programs in an effort to stabilize farm income and foster better land-conservation practices. The result was more New Deal policies favored by liberals and opposed by conservatives.

On the international front, World War II (1941–45) began before the Great Depression ended. Industries that had been shut down by hard times reopened their doors making materials necessary to fight the war. The economy went into high gear in all sectors on the home front. The military drafted able-bodied men so the path was open for many who wanted jobs. Almost overnight, the U.S. moved from high unemployment to a labor shortage. New jobs were plentiful along with new government regulations. Under the pressure of rising prices in an expanding economy, the federal government expanded economic controls on prices, wages, rents, and other critical parts of economic life. Again, conservatives opposed many of the changes.

World War II may have been the only so-called "good war" in our history. The war effort had nearly unanimous public support because the stakes were so high. I recall my father telling me, "We had to win because our whole civilization was on the line." He and nearly everyone else saw the aggression of Nazi Germany and Imperial Japan as a direct threat that had to be overcome. People were willing to accept sacrifices in their personal lives. Food and scarce resources such as sugar, rubber and gasoline were rationed. The American people became accustomed to yet another set of government regulations. After the war, some of the regulations were repealed, but in the post-war period, the federal government took on increased responsibilities for maintaining national security, economic growth, and fiscal stability. Conservatives were troubled again by a long list of new laws and regulations.

The war also brought social changes that were greater than anyone could have imagined. Women had new opportunities during the 1940s working in war plants, earning wages of their own, away from the role of housewife.

These women became the heads of households because men were away in the armed forces. "Rosie the Riveter" was an image of the new woman with her sleeves rolled up, working in the war plant with a sense of independence as she learned to deal with life on her own. This newfound status for women would lay the foundation for the women's movement that would be popularized by many liberals, much to the opposition of rank-and-file conservatives. The winds of change not only altered gender roles, they were about to transform American education as well.

The GI Bill opened the door for returning veterans to get a college education, enabling them to enter the middle class. University campuses mushroomed in size and importance as new ideas were tested and welcomed. Liberal intellectuals gained a foothold in college classrooms across the nation. The newly educated post-war generation was about to change the way we thought about nearly every aspect of American life. Social, economic, and racial movements gained supporters among the young who were exposed to new (some would say radical) ways of thinking. The "free speech movement" was centered on college campuses as students questioned the prevailing attitudes of middle-America. Conservatives soon discovered that college campuses would become a hotbed for leftist ideas and protest movements.

After the war, formerly stable urban neighborhoods changed dramatically as emerging, low-income groups moved into big cities and middle-class people fled to the suburbs. The core around the center of cities became more blighted as ghettos grew in size and intensity. More money was spent on freeways and mass transit systems so commuters could flood into the cities every morning and leave every evening. New tensions arose between conservatives and liberals on the question of how to fund the needs of the cities, especially dealing with poverty and rising crime rates that resulted from the huge population growth in urban areas across the nation.

Until the mid–1960s, conservatives still had a secure hold on the American electoral process. Cities were grossly underrepresented by gerrymandered districts that maintained rural control over entire regions. Most states had not reapportioned legislative districts for decades, so the population movement into the cities had been largely ignored in terms of elected representation. Many of the upper houses in the state legislatures represented each county equally so at the time, Los Angeles County, with approximately 6,500,000 people, had only one state senator, as did Kings County in central California with fewer than 60,000 people. In the mid–1960s, one out of every three people in California lived in Los Angeles County, but they were represented by only one of the 40 state senators.

Congressional district boundaries were also drawn in a manner to clearly underrepresent urban voters. To compound the situation, nearly all congressional committees were chaired by conservatives from the Democratic solid south. The result was that most of the growing problems were in the cities, but the legislative power to solve these problems was still in the hands of rural, small-town America. In an unexpected series of cases, the U.S. Supreme Court dramatically changed how people were to be represented at the state and national level, much to the disapproval of rural conservatives.

There was yet another trend that was equally important. America was becoming more secular. The war had brought new stresses on many traditional institutions. There were discussions on college campuses on whether "God was dead." Churches faced new competition from non-religious organizations as weekly church attendance decreased. Prayer in public places such as schools and city council meetings was being challenged by secular groups. Families were undergoing increasing strains as divorces were becoming more common. Young people were moving from rural areas into the cities. Small-town values were being contested by social norms that were popular with the younger generation. The pace of social change was accelerating in most areas of life. Many on the right were upset by all these dramatic changes.

Another byproduct of World War II was the movement of African-Americans away from the South into the armed forces and wartime jobs up North. Blacks moved into every major city from coast to coast. Like "Rosie the Riveter," black men and women also gained a new sense of economic and social independence. This new feeling of independence laid the foundation for the Civil Rights Movement that was to intensify later. Those who moved out and up were never going back to their old submissive role at the bottom of the economic, social, and political pile. During the war, there were race riots in cities where African-Americans were pushing up against the racial, political, and economic ceilings that had been in place since before the founding of the nation. But despite those warning events, there was a sense of growing euphoria as the war ended in a victory.

There was a song written during World War II that captured the popular public imagination and expectations. The title, *When the Lights Go On Again All Over the World*, implied that everything would return to normal again when World War II ended. There was a kind of innocence as Americans celebrated the end of the war. Few had any idea that the war had unleashed forces that would disrupt society on countless fronts for many decades to come.

Yet there was a sense of optimism spreading across the land that a new dream was in the making. The old principles of small-town America were being replaced by rising aspirations that were economic, religious, political, sexual, social, and racial. There seemed to be no limit on the controversial subjects that were explored in movies and magazines. The media spread the upbeat message that nearly everything was possible. Everything that was for sale could be put on a credit card. There were countless breakthroughs in medicine and technology. Television encouraged everyone to accept new ideas and lifestyles. Many thought the new world shouldn't have any restrictions. Gay and transgender people were getting ready to come out of the closet. Boundaries were being pushed back in science, social mores, racial attitudes, and income projections. It was a stimulating combination—a great time to be alive. There was an atmosphere of optimism coast to coast. It was an exciting time to live.

But there were also dark clouds on the horizon. The Cold War was developing with the Soviet Union. The threat of Communism was not only abroad, it loomed within the United States as well. Congressional investigations focused on alleged Communist Party members in nearly every walk of life; suspects were barred from labor unions, Hollywood studios and university classrooms. People across the country became fearful that schools, churches, and the U.S. government itself had been infiltrated by a new kind of subversive, international thinking that would weaken America from within. Even moderates were suspected of being disloyal. My high school history teacher was condemned for saying he thought the best hope for world peace was in the United Nations. Local critics in my hometown reminded everyone there were "a lot of foreigners in the UN."

Consequences

Increased uncertainties and conflict were just around the corner in many areas of life in the United States, but the issue of race would bring the most sweeping, fundamental changes of all. No one could have imagined how violent the struggle would become, and how long it would continue, nor could anyone have predicted how a few judicial decisions could activate people on both sides of the issue. What followed was the most dramatic example of how perceived deprivation could collide with rising expectations.

When May 17, 1954, dawned, no one had any idea what was in store. That was the day the U.S. Supreme Court decided *Brown vs. Board of Education of Topeka*. Chief Justice Earl Warren read the decision for a unanimous court declaring that segregation of public schools was unconstitutional. The Court was careful not to set a deadline, but it was an obvious threat to the prevailing system of racial segregation. On the following day there were editorials in some newspapers announcing resistance, not only to the integration of schools, but to any other form of "race mixing." Soon after the decision, the *Impeach Earl Warren* bumper sticker began to appear. It was the beginning of an era that would increase racial, political, and economic tensions across the land. Even many liberals felt the court had moved too far, too fast.

Segregation had been a way of life for many whites who dug in their heels to oppose the court. On the other side, black people saw this as the first ray of hope that might change their lives. The clash of "expectations versus deprivations" on both sides set the stage for decades of conflict. Southern conservatives lined up on the side of continuing segregation policies while many, but not all, liberals favored integration of the races. There was a kind of unspoken racism beneath the surface across the land that was becoming more evident as events unfolded.

I was just eighteen years old when I first visited the South; it happened to be just months after the *Brown* decision. I was told by everyone I met that nothing had changed, and nothing would ever change as a result of the case. White folks I talked to had nothing but contempt for the Supreme Court decision. I didn't meet any black people. There were two separate worlds. In public, and in private, the color line was drawn sharply. Everyone knew their place, and no one was expected to challenge the separation of the races.

All the signs of segregation were there: two sets of waiting rooms in bus stations, white and colored drinking fountains, "Whites Only" signs in restaurants, and of course, the segregated schools. I had heard about all these examples of separating the races, but the one that sticks in my mind was one I saw at a South Carolina service station. I went around back to use the restroom and found there were three of them—men, women, and colored. (The hinges on the colored restroom were broken and the door was ajar.) It illustrated to me that black people were not worthy of gender privacy. Somehow, those signs said it all. They weren't regarded as being real people entitled to rights. My southern friend said, "That's the way it's always been."

During this time in the 1950s, the Ku Klux Klan became active again. As unrest grew among whites, the Klan expanded and vowed to defend against "race-mixing" and preserve the white way of life. Underneath the Klan, discontent was a strong feeling of white deprivation (not just in the South but across the nation) who felt that African-Americans were somehow getting preferential treatment. The promise from the Klan raised expectations among some whites that blacks would be kept in their place and white rule would continue. The white governor of Alabama, George Wallace, said it all in 1963: "Segregation now, segregation tomorrow, segregation forever."

On the other side of the divide, rising expectations brought out another brand of dissatisfaction. African-Americans had carried strong resentments to segregation for a long time as they had faced public humiliation for hundreds of years. The scar of inequality had been etched deeply into black culture against their will. But until the *Brown* decision, they didn't see any legal route for their cause. But in the 1950s, they sensed things were about to change. Black churches and ministers organized around the court ruling. Expectations were rising sharply. There was tension in the air as the Civil

Rights Movement moved into high gear. For decades, the question of racial prejudice had been swept under the rug. Now it was discussed everywhere, and not always in a civil manner. The issue was picked up by the media and debated on college campuses in every part of the nation. White America was slowly becoming aware of the heritage of segregation and racism. It was becoming clear to everyone that racial equality was a fiction throughout the country. Black America was beginning to feel empowered as they confronted the old ways and White America was fighting back. The country would never be the same again.

The political/racial temperature went up on both sides. All kinds of marches increased in size and number. Weapons were brandished in public. There was a split in the Civil Rights Movement as some became more militant. High-powered rifles were used to assassinate black leaders. Many civil rights protesters (white and black) were injured and some were killed. Lunch counter sit-ins and freedom rides spread across the country. In response, there were cross burnings at Klan meetings that attracted white people who never would have attended such a gathering in the past. Local police used attack dogs and high-pressure fire hoses against black civil-rights protesters. The Arkansas National Guard was ordered into operation by President Eisenhower in 1957 to integrate Central High School in Little Rock, Arkansas. America watched the conflict unfold on the televised evening news. The nation was becoming more alarmed as all the dark corners of America were being exposed. Few if any could have predicted that all of this would happen as a result of several Supreme Court decisions. There was a spin-off that affected attitudes across the country. Some people became more tolerant, others less so. It still hasn't ended. (See Chapter 7 for interviews with Ku Klux Klan members.)

Post-World War II (1945 to the Present)

Since the end of World War II, there have been a string of Supreme Court decisions, acts of Congress, presidential actions, investigations, key elections, and special events that have increased tensions and angered people on both sides of the political spectrum. It has been a time that illustrates how disruptive situations can develop when feelings of deprivation collide with rising expectations. Just a partial listing of events is a sufficient reminder of how actions have triggered the right and left to focus on the classical controversial issues of our time. Most of the current conflicts of today arose during this post–World War II period, especially in the 1960s.

The following is a short list of actions that divided the country after 1945:

- To offset the expected economic decline after World War II, the Employment Act of 1946 declared that the federal government would use all practical means to promote maximum employment, production, and purchasing power. The legislation established the Council of Economic Advisors to make annual recommendations to the president on economic policy and required the president to submit an economic report to the Congress.

- Congress passed the Taft-Hartley Act of 1947 over the veto of President Truman. The law limited labor unions ability to strike, and required union leaders to sign a loyalty oath declaring they were not supporters of the Communist Party. The legislation prohibited the closed shop (where one had to be a union member before they went to work) and permitted states to pass right-to-work-laws (making paying union dues voluntary) which, of course, would weaken unions.

- In 1948, President Harry Truman ordered the desegregation of the armed forces. Many military leaders openly resisted the order to integrate. In reality, military personnel continued to be segregated for several years by individual commanders who assigned blacks to special units that were engaged in support operations.

- Congress passed the Internal Security Act of 1950 over the veto of President Truman. The law set up the Subversive Control Board to investigate alleged subversive activities and enforce the requirement that American Communist Party members register as "agents of a foreign power." None of the party members ever registered.

- Starting in 1950, Senator Joseph McCarthy (R) of Wisconsin held a series of hearings in which he charged there were 205 members of the American Communist Party employed in the State Department. He later held congressional hearings to investigate alleged communist influence in the US Army and other sectors of American society.

- *Dennis v. the United States* (1951): The Supreme Court upheld the conviction of 11 top American Communist leaders on the grounds that the United States should not have to wait until the Communists attempted to overthrow the US government. The public strongly supported the decision.

- Julius and Ethel Rosenberg, a married couple from New York, were convicted of passing top secret information to the Soviet Union and were executed in 1953.

- *Brown v. Board of Education of Topeka* (1954): The Supreme Court declared that racial segregation in the public schools was unconstitutional. The Court waited until 1955 to order states to begin desegregating "with all deliberate speed."

- *Yates v. the United States* (1957): The Supreme Court decided that the "mere belief" by Communists in overthrowing the US government did not warrant conviction of treason.

- *Engle v. Vatale* (1962): The Supreme Court held that government written prayers recited in schools were unconstitutional. It has become known as the "prayer case." Since then, several states have challenged this decision unsuccessfully.

- *Baker v. Carr* (1962): The Supreme Court declared that the federal courts could intervene and require redistricting in cases involving malapportionment of legislative districts. The case increased representation for people in cities across the country.

- The Clean Air Act of 1963 was designed to control air pollution and set environmental standards on a national level. It authorized creation of the Pollution Control Administration to set standards for factories where toxic chemicals were being used or emitted.

- The Office of Economic Opportunity was established in 1964 to administer the War on Poverty that included the Job Corps and VISTA.

- The Civil Rights Act of 1964 outlawed discrimination based on race, color, religion, sex, or national origin in the workplace and in public facilities. This law caused most southern whites to shift their political allegiances from the Democratic Party to the Republican Party.

- *Reynolds v. Sims* (1964): The Supreme Court laid down the "One Man, One Vote" rule that congressional districts within a state must be nearly equal in population, and that all state legislative districts within a state must be based on population.

- The Water Quality Control Act of 1965 was enacted to restore and maintain the integrity of the nation's water resources. It authorized the newly created Water Pollution Control Administration to set standards when states failed to do so.

- The Housing and Urban Development Act of 1965 provided for rent subsidies for low-income families and rehabilitation grants for low-income homeowners. The legislation established a cabinet-level department to coordinate federal housing programs.

- The Social Security Act of 1965 authorized Medicare for those 65 and older and created Medicaid, providing medical care for low-income people.

- The Elementary and Secondary Education Act of 1965 provided federal aid to public education, especially programs for early childhood education in low-income areas.

- The Voting Rights Act of 1965 provided nationwide protection for voting rights and prohibited state and local governments from enacting laws that discriminated against minorities. The law provided nationwide protection of voting rights and outlawed literacy tests and other devices that disenfranchised racial minorities. In 2013, the Supreme Court struck down a key provision of this law making it possible again for states to pass laws that made it more difficult to vote.

- *Loving v. Virginia* (1967): The Supreme Court ruled that state laws banning interracial marriages were unconstitutional. The Court struck down all state laws banning interracial marriage.

- The Fair Housing Act of 1968 prohibited discrimination concerning the sale, renting, and financing of housing based on race, religion, gender, or national origin.

- The Environmental Protection Agency (EPA) was established in 1970 upon recommendation by President Nixon. Since then, the federal government has taken an active role in enforcing environmental protection rules across the nation.

- *Roe v. Wade* (1973): The Supreme Court decided that a women's right to an abortion was protected by the Constitution. Since then, several states have attempted to circumvent the ruling by restricting medical clinics performing abortions.

- Richard Nixon resigned the presidency (1974) A congressional investigation concluded that President Nixon had obstructed justice when he was involved in the cover-up of the burglary of the Democratic National Committee at the Watergate complex in Washington, D.C.

- *Regents of the University of California v. Bakke* (1977): The Supreme Court upheld affirmative action rules permitting race to be one of the criteria for admitting students to the University of California medical school. The case banned "racial quotas," but permitted race to be used as a criterion for admission to the university.

- President Ronald Reagan in 1981 fired 11,345 members of the Professional Air Traffic Controllers Organization (PATCO) that were on strike. The union had refused a presidential order to return to work. Reagan's mass firing slowed air traffic, but did not cripple the system.

- *Communication Workers of America v. Beck* (1988): The Court found that unions could not compel the collection of fees for political purposes that workers might oppose.

- Impeachment of President Bill Clinton (1999): The president was impeached by the US House of Representatives on one count of perjury and one count of obstruction of justice, but he was acquitted by the US Senate.

- *Bush v. Gore* (2000): By a 5 to 4 margin, the Supreme Court ordered a halt to the 2000 presidential vote counting in Florida and declared George W. Bush to have won the presidential election over Al Gore. The court declared this case could not serve as a precedent for the future.

- *District of Columbia v. Heller* (2008): In a 5 to 4 verdict, the Supreme Court struck down provisions of the Firearms Control Regulation Act of 1975 as unconstitutional, declaring that individual firearm rights were protected by the Second Amendment to the Constitution.

- Barack Obama was elected as the first African-American President of the United States in 2008.

- The federal government appropriated $700 billion in 2008 as a bailout to stabilize Wall Street firms in a massive financial emergency. No major executives on Wall Street were ever prosecuted for involvement in illegal actions that brought on the most serious recession since the Great Depression of the 1930s.

- President Barack Obama signed the Affordable Care Act into law in 2010. Obamacare was challenged and was upheld twice by the Supreme Court.

- *Citizens United v. the Federal Election Commission* (2010): The Supreme Court held by a 5 to 4 vote that the freedom of speech clause in the First Amendment prohibited the government from regulating political campaign spending by organizations such as corporations and labor unions.

- *National Federation of Independent Business v. Sebelius* (2012): In a 5 to 4 decision, the Supreme Court upheld congressional authority to enact the Affordable Care Act (Obamacare).

- *Shelby County, Alabama v. Holder* (2013): By a 5 to 4 margin, the Supreme Court declared that several southern states would no longer be required to undergo special scrutiny before changing their voting laws. This repealed a key section of the Voting Rights Act of 1965. As a result, several states established voter suppression laws that have had the effect of reducing voter turnout for elderly voters without picture ID, first-time voters, and racial minorities.

- *Burwell v. Hobby Lobby Stores* (2014): In a 5 to 4 decision, the Supreme Court struck down a provision in the Affordable Care Act (ACA) that required employers to provide health insurance for women that included contraceptive care.

- President Barack Obama's Executive Order of 2014 provided temporary legal status to nearly 11 million unauthorized immigrants in the United States.

- *King v. Burwell* (2015): The Supreme Court upheld the constitutionality of Obamacare for a second time by a 5 to 4 margin.

- *Obergefell v. Hodges* (2015): In a 5 to 4 decision, the Supreme Court required states to grant marriage licenses to same-sex couples and required the recognition of those marriages throughout the nation.

- *Whole Woman's Health v. Hellersdedt* (2016): The Supreme Court struck down a Texas law designed to shut down abortion clinics thereby making it easier for women to get an abortion. Some states continued to limit the number of women's clinics in their jurisdiction.

- Donald Trump was elected President of the United States in 2016.

- Investigation of Russian influence in the 2016 election (2017): Robert Mueller III was appointed as a special counsel to investigate Russian meddling in the 2016 election.

- *Epic Systems v. Lewis* (2018): By a 5 to 4 decision, the Supreme Court ruled that workers can be prohibited from banding together in disputes over pay and working conditions.

- *Husted v. A. Philip Randolph Institute* (2018): The Supreme Court upheld an Ohio law by a 5 to 4 majority that permitted a state to remove voters from the rolls who have missed voting in a single election.

- *Gill v. Whitford* (2018): In a 5 to 4 verdict, the Supreme Court refused to consider a case involving alleged partisan gerrymandering from Wisconsin for procedural reasons.

- *Abbott v. Perez* (2018): The Supreme Court, by a 5 to 4 margin, upheld the design of Texas legislative districts on the grounds that they were not drawn in a manner to discriminate against Hispanic voters.

- *Janus v. American Federation of State, County, and Municipal Employees* (AFSCME) (2018): In a 5 to 4 decision, the Supreme Court ruled that government workers cannot be required to pay a "fair share" of union expenses if they do not approve of the sum being taken out of their pay.

Unfinished Business

Put simply, the most important political struggles in modern American politics have been the effort on the right to repeal many of the political and judicial actions taken since the 1930s, while on the left there's been a rearguard action to hold onto these policy decisions. The long list of issues above has brought about an ongoing conflict that has resulted in a political gridlock between the two sides—not since the Civil War have emotions been so raw. It has been a see-saw battle as one side scores some success while the other group loses ground.

Despite the string of battles won by the left, the trend has not always gone in one direction. For example, the right has been more successful in reversing policies as it relates to labor unions, controls over campaign financing, voter's rights, and gun control. The election of Donald Trump in 2016 began a series of actions that reversed several legislative, judicial and executive policies. Several legislative acts have been weakened by amendments. Steve Bannon, the reclusive mastermind of the Trump administration, said the goal was "the deconstruction of the administrative state." That means the wholesale repeal of major governmental actions since the 1930s.

Now it was time for the left to be on defense. Since the 1930s, there has been a mindset among liberals that once an issue has been decided, there was no need to organize a defensive action. They'd been wrong. People on the left side of the spectrum often think no one would dare reverse policies that were so obviously a sign of forward-thinking. They were wrong again. Many progressives view American politics as a one-way street in which major changes were considered permanent and wouldn't be undone later by the opposition.

Conservatives, on the other hand, have never viewed politics that way. A major task for the right wing has always been to reverse what they find objectionable policies from the past. Generally, the right has been better organized for this kind of politics because they have tested specific models and methods to reverse public policies. Conservatives are very adept in framing issues with words designed to win public favor. For example, when discussing anti-union measures, they speak of "right-to-work-laws," which seems completely acceptable. When arguing against the estate tax it is called the "death tax," which sounds completely unacceptable. In justifying the use of guns, they use the phrase "stand your ground laws," which seems to be a sensible matter of self-defense. And finally, when trying to stop family members joining other family members already in the country, they use the term "chain migration." Once phrases like these have been launched into public debate, they are very effective in shaping public reaction. After time, well-framed issues like these build up a public image that become a part of American culture, especially among people whose views are reinforced by the right-wing media.

Liberals have never been good at framing issues to defend existing programs. This is especially true on matters concerning public assistance programs. It's always been difficult to answer the charge that welfare recipients were lazy and undeserving. It seems the left has never really had wide public acceptance for these programs, in part because there is negative public perception on this issue. The right has been quick to capitalize on any shortcomings.

Perhaps the greatest advantage enjoyed by the right in repealing certain measures is the built-in tactic of finding fault with a particular program. As noted earlier, every public policy has at least one glaring problem that can be used as a reason to revise it or even repeal it. It's easy to focus on a negative. It is easy to find waste and fraud that would seem to justify shutting down a particular program. Claims have been made that eliminating a particular public program will bring great improvements, such as better health care if Obamacare is abolished, or better planning for individual retirement if Social Security were made voluntary. There is also the tactic of focusing on the loss of constitutional choices. For example, by prohibiting prayers in public schools, individual children are said to be "denied their right to pray." On gun control laws, citizens are being "denied the right to defend themselves."

The overall point is that those who wish to repeal a practice need only to find one fault, while those who wish to retain it must defend all features of the program. Liberals have the disadvantage of being on the defense while conservatives have much greater latitude to pick the battles they can wage at a time they wish to take up an issue.

The election of Donald Trump in 2016 provided conservatives with a ready-made opportunity to even up the score on a multitude of issues. All three branches of government could be activated in turning back the clock in many areas. The Trump Administration has commenced the task of dismantling federal agencies by undermining their purpose and pushing career civil servants into early retirement. There has been a focus within the Trump Administration to appoint conservative judges to the federal judiciary so conservative viewpoints will continue far into the future.

Attacking the System

When surveying the last century, it is easy to see why conservatives have taken a position of opposing big government. From their point of view, nearly all the undesirable things that have happened have been at the hands of a large central government. Every decade has brought more governmental regulations and changes. For those on the right, it is as though some unseen hand has intentionally upset the established patterns and stirred up movements to launch left-wing policies at all levels of society.

When frustrated people are faced by events they cannot accept or control, they typically invent false narratives to account for the unwanted developments. It is little wonder that there has been a host of conspiracy theories that have arisen on the right to explain offending actions taken by the Supreme Court, the President, and the Congress. It has been absolutely necessary for the right to hatch out these unique explanations, because if they did not, they would have to accept these changes as natural, evolutionary changes. That would be even more unacceptable.

While there is conspiratorial thinking on both the extreme left and right, there is no question that right-wing groups have depended more on voicing unlikely schemes to explain unbearable changes. Groups such as the Ku Klux Klan and the American Nazi Party believe there is a malicious agenda to weaken the white race. For example, they often focus on federal programs that (they say) have intentionally debased the purity of the white race, and promoted "race-mixing." It is easy to see why programs that promote integration of the races are not just seen as evolutionary developments—they are seen instead as something evil that has been intentionally done to deteriorate our national character and promote "inferior people" into places of leadership. When presented in this context, it is an epic struggle that cannot be lost.

Along with the hostility toward racial integration, there is a sharpened opposition to the idea of government itself. It's now fashionable to blame government for all that has gone wrong. There is a growing conviction that society would be better off without a government. Grover Norquist, president of the *Americans for Tax Reform* said, "I'm not afraid of abolishing government. I just want to shrink it down to the size where we can drown it in a bathtub."

Liberals are shocked by the likes of Grover Norquist and the unexpected suggestion that modern society could exist with no government. While the left may not admit it publicly, big government has been their best friend—it has been used as the main vehicle for the liberal agenda. Federal legislation, presidential actions and court decisions have aided liberals in transforming American economic, political, religious, and social life. Conservatives are well aware of this trend, and they are now fighting back and see "government" as their main enemy. The idea of reducing the size and scope of government is a principle on which nearly all conservatives agree. It is often touted as the single move that would increase prosperity and freedom in society.

For the first time in recent American politics, a significant number of elected officials are voicing a strong opposition to the concept of government itself. Rank-and-file conservatives are talking openly about "destroying" the ability of government to take actions they think are "unconstitutional," and American public opinion is slowly coming around to the position that "a smaller government is (almost automatically) a better government." Conservative candidates are nearly unanimous in their goal of reducing the role of government. But sometimes their over-zealousness destroys the public trust in the institution of government which, of course, runs counter to long-term conservative values.

Perhaps the most well-known example of this approach developed in the first years of the Trump era. In their effort to defend Donald Trump's involvement in clandestine Russian affairs, members of his party openly attacked the Department of Justice and the FBI. Trump supporters were willing to undermine public trust in the government justice system for very partisan purposes; they seemingly did not care that they were destroying faith and confidence in government itself. Their only goal was to undermine the justice system as a means of disproving Trump's association with the Russian government.

There had always been an old norm in politics for congressional leaders to defend the integrity of the political system because it was more important than narrow issues of the day. But now that former ethic has been replaced by a slash and burn tactic that justifies destroying public institutions as a means of gaining a political advantage. This change in political thinking may be the most serious danger in the new divisive political thinking patterns.

There is a real danger that American politics has become dysfunctional to the point where lies and deception have become the new normal, and citizens no longer believe any agency of the government. It is difficult to overemphasize the catastrophic consequences of living in a society where there is no trust, where political leaders are not held accountable for dividing the public to the point that governing is no longer possible. What do you think about this situation?

Success and Anger

Every controversial change cited in the previous sections of this chapter has created a list of winners and losers. Understandably those that lost were upset, but even those that won had a sense of frustration because there was always a feeling of "why did it take this long?" In politics, change never comes fast enough and never goes far enough to suit those who have been waiting for a long time.

An even stronger sense of deprivation, of course, is felt by those on the other side who lost out because of changing polices. The first response of those who lose is always an effort to try to reverse the events—to put the genie back in the bottle. This is especially apparent when considering matters involving racial, religious, social, or sexual issues, and there is often a move to blame the government for either doing too much or not enough.

During the 1960s, individual leaders of both the extreme left and right shared an intense anger against the federal government. Separately, they both concluded it was necessary to resort to violence. In response to new gun control regulations, an armed leader of the *Posse Comitatus* told me he had proof that the U.S. Justice Department was "under the direct control of the devil." He carried around a picture of an FBI show badge with the number "666," which is regarded in biblical circles as the mark of the beast. This particular leader indicated this was proof that the devil had taken over the entire federal system of government. He declared that all Christians had a "duty" to take up arms against any and all federal agents.

During the same period, a left-wing faction, calling itself the *Weather Underground* in Berkeley, California, indicated that they planned to increase their bombing campaign to "smash the capitalist system" across the country. It is interesting that they, too, had conspiratorial stories that "proved" that the federal government was controlled by unseen hands. Surprisingly, it is not uncommon for groups on both extremes to agree, but for very different ideological reasons.

The rapid changes of the 1960s upset both the left and the right. It is a classic truism of politics that a democratic society is in the greatest danger of upheaval when it tries to reform itself. Making an effort to remedy social, political, racial, and economic inequities awakens feelings of deprivation and expectation on both sides. It brings about an intense competition between contending groups. Because of this dynamic, reformers unwittingly create unsettling conditions that contribute to angry confrontations from both camps. Once the conflict begins, it is difficult, if not impossible, to go back to peaceful times again.

The lesson is that rising expectations can turn into bitterness very quickly. I watched this develop at a personal level during the 1960s with a young former student who received a federal grant to help prostitutes in San Francisco. The strategy was to contact these women and offer them federal scholarships to go to school so they could start different careers. According to my student, the prostitutes were very skeptical at first and reluctant to trust her, but slowly small groups of women enrolled in the program. My former student was very enthusiastic because she said, "Finally I am doing something that will change these women's lives." The problem arose when the program was cancelled because the government was running short on money to fund the Vietnam War. The next time I saw my former student, she was outraged. She had the task of telling each of the young women that they would no longer receive scholarship funds. I'll never forget her quoting one of the women who said, "It would have been better that you never raised my hopes—because for a few months—I thought someone really cared about me. Now I know that was never true."

That same situation is present every time a popular social program fails. It is so tempting for government leaders to promise a great improvement for society without thinking through the need for resources to support that pledge. Both liberals and conservatives are rather casual about raising the hopes of those who are frustrated by the present situations. When people are disappointed and abandoned again and again, they become cynical about believing anyone or anything in politics. Today, both the left and right are making promises they cannot keep, and many folks have simply stopped believing either of them. It has become fashionable in some circles to assume the government is lying about all kinds of issues. In some media outlets, telling lies about political events has become their signature approach to politics. There is a sort of wild west journalism out there where anything goes. The lead story is often based on allegations that are simply not true. We no longer bat an eye when we hear a political reporter or candidate make a statement that is clearly designed to mislead the public. Political paranoia is more prevalent than ever. Peddling anger and fear are powerful ways to get noticed. It increases the number of TV viewers and the amount the network can charge for running commercial spots.

There has always been an effort to twist the political facts, but today it so saturates the airwaves that many people are totally buying into conspiratorial explanations of events. According to *Fact Checker*, President Donald Trump made 4,120 false or misleading statements in his first year in office. The result is that an increasing number of voters were confused, afraid, and unsure of who to believe. The mainstream press has concluded that Trump is responsible for much of the current political division across the country. What do you think?

There is a festering anger out there because of all the competing stories and unsettling changes that have occurred in this country since the end of World War II in 1945. (See the earlier list in this chapter of judicial cases, presidential/congressional actions and key elections that have continued to the present.) Then add in the threat of mass shootings, domestic and international terrorism, and the declining sense of governmental legitimacy. The result is a real threat to a democratic society. This whole situation may be more serious than we think.

Our minds go back to the memorable circumstances in the 1976 movie *Network*. A deranged TV newscaster, Howard Beal, was so upset by recent events that he threatened to kill himself on air and later he persuaded viewers to hang out their windows and shout, "I'm mad as hell and I'm not going to take it anymore."

The movie was meant to be a comedy but the unethical character of the TV network executives is similar to some in the media leaders today. The underlying message in the movie was that the television network was willing to exploit Howard Beal's madness just to boost audience ratings. The TV executives took no responsibility for stirring up the entire nation. Like many broadcast executives today, they are interested only in the bottom line of how much profit can be made. Not many years ago, journalism had standards of truthfulness that are certainly not being observed today. The time of Walter Cronkite on the evening news is gone. There is no longer a voice that everyone can believe.

Voters are brought together by what they oppose, not by what they favor, and they turn out to vote in large numbers. Recently one middle-aged white women protester on television said, "What unites us is the fact that the government no longer pays attention to us." She may well have been speaking for millions of people.

To compound the situation, there are some in the media who are willing to intentionally raise the feelings of public anxiety, fan the flames of public indignation, and put anything on the air to increase the public outrage and thereby raise their TV ratings. Real *fake news* may be here to stay. The result is that fear and anger have come to dominate political campaigns, especially at the national level. Added to this situation of enflaming the public is the fact that the Russian government has learned how to manipulate American public opinion—that may be the most ominous development of all. Real and imagined campaign issues may be formulated by persons who never enter the United States. There are folks in office who benefit from this state of affairs.

There is a growing group of militants in this country who hold professional politicians in utter contempt. Anyone with experience in public office is believed to be partially responsible for all that they think has gone wrong. It's a time when a political outsider—with a reassuringly strong voice—can rise in the polls while making statements that can be proven false. This situation is remindful of Bill Clinton's statement: "When people feel uncertain, they'd rather have somebody that's strong and wrong than somebody who's weak and right." What do you think?

Questions for You

1. What is the present position of the left and right on the question of having a strong central government? Why has the role of the central goverment become such an emotional issue?

2. What does the author mean on the point that deciding on the proper role of government has "become automatic thinking for both sides?" Do you see any inconsistencies on either the left or right in accepting government controls in one area, but opposing it in others?

3. Explain the meaning of the statement, "what the left proposes, the right opposes." Cite examples of this pattern that emerged after 1933. Are there examples of this today? If so, name them.

4. What do think were the most important changes in political, economic, social, cultural, sexual, and racial policies after World War II? In your judgment, how have these changes affected American institutions? Do you anticipate this trend of rapid change will continue? Why or why not?

5. Explain why the *Brown vs. Board of Education of Topeka* case of 1954 set into motion a conflict based on perceived deprivation and rising expectations. How did this decision change political party loyalties in the United States?

6. Read through the list of court decisions, congressional acts, and presidential actions from 1946 to the present. From your point of view, which area of change do you think has divided the country most of all? Why?

7. Why haven't liberals been very good at framing issues? What are the apparent advantages held by conservatives in this area? Why does the right wing find it comparatively easy to use negative issues in politics? Why do you think liberals are constantly on the defensive?

8. Why have conspiracy theories become a necessary strategy for the right-wing in politics? Why is the government viewed as "the enemy" in right-wing conspiratorial thinking?

9. To what extent has rapid change since World War II been the cause of much of the conflict in current politics? Which changes have made the greatest impact on you and your family? Do you see a resolution of this particular problem in the near future? Why or why not?

10. Describe your response to the Bill Clinton quotation in the last sentence in this chapter: "When people feel uncertain, they'd rather have somebody that's strong and wrong than somebody who's weak and right." What does that warning say about the future of democracies in times of rapid change?

11. Have you felt a sense of political deprivation? Cite an example of how you or a member of your family has felt a sense of disappointment or deprivation about a government action that changed public policies. Have you ever felt angry or disillusioned about a decision made by the government? Did it change the way you might act politically?

6

Left-Wing Values

No one is a pure example of a liberal or a conservative. We all have unique experiences and shades of opinion reflecting our associations with the many political, religious, economic, racial, social, ethnic, or cultural groups that we may be a part of. And because of our complex backgrounds and experiences, we may even hold contradictory attitudes within ourselves. For example, some on the left may consider themselves to be racially tolerant, but they still voice racial stereotypes or harbor ethnically insensitive attitudes. Some may feel embarrassed because they are prejudiced on the topics of race or gender roles. It is possible to have inconsistent ideals without feeling like a hypocrite. It's just part of being human.

While the Democratic Party has the largest cluster of leftists, there is much diversity within its ranks. Many party members are from different racial or ethnic groups. Income levels range from the very rich to the very poor. Some favor the status quo in public affairs while others are actively involved in reform movements. Watch the Democratic Party in their national conventions, and you'll see floor fights that threaten to split the organization. But despite all these contrasting factors, there are some consistent themes that most members support.

The three major beliefs that seem to motivate the political left are that:

1. Human beings are inherently cooperative and their lives can be improved when living in an affirmative, free, and open society.

2. Government can play a positive role in improving the lives of humanity by taking collective action that benefits the majority.

3. The major institutions of society should encourage more policies and practices that benefit the least fortunate.

What They Believe

The key perspective on the left is a sense of empathy and equality combined with a belief that ordinary people and nations can work together successfully in a positive environment. They are optimistic about the fate of humanity. Virtually everything liberals believe springs from their affirmative views on improving the prospects for those on the middle and lower rungs of society at home and abroad. Whether it is funding for public schools in the ghetto, taking care of the handicapped, or public health needs in the Third World, liberals are focused on those in need.

They have a firm belief that people are at their best when they are being of service to others. There is a belief that everyone is connected—that we are all in the same boat—and therefore everyone should cooperate in seeking goals that promote the public welfare; this is especially true on the issue involving those without political power. Heroes on the left are those who reach out to the powerless minorities that need to be accepted. Martyrs in the Civil Rights Movement will always be remembered on the left. Liberals have always been driven to roll back all kinds of discrimination wherever they find it.

Since the French Revolution, the left has aspired to greater economic, racial, social, and political opportunities for the working classes. It has been involved in a quest for human equality, especially for the poor and downtrodden. Progressives have pressed hard for equal justice, elected representation, and the development of all persons through education, regardless of social class. They have generally felt a strong empathy for the plight of racial, social, ethnic, and sexual minorities. Generally, the left has been a strong supporter of women's rights, same-sex marriage, abortion rights, and LGBT issues across society and in the workplace.

Liberals are fond of saying they are for the "little guy," and those whose opportunities have been narrowed. On the issue of crime, they believe that many people in prison are often the product of poverty, and that former lawbreakers can be reformed if given a second chance. Left-wing leaders generally favor shorter prison sentences and the decriminalization of drug offenses.

People supporting feminist causes generally feel most comfortable on the left. Folks on this side of the spectrum also stand up for dissenters and those involved in various civil rights movements. Progressives strongly support the right to protest out on the streets.

Throughout history, the left has favored policies making it easier for immigrants to enter the country, gain citizenship and integrate into society. First generation immigrants are frequently attracted to left-wing candidates.

It has been a guiding principle for the left to oppose systems that perpetuate privilege, wealth, and power in the hands of a few. Leftists have favored taxation based on the ability to pay, and funding of programs that redistribute the wealth to lower income groups. They are staunch defenders of guaranteed retirement systems and programs that aid low-income seniors. Most on the left believe society should be mobilized so the less fortunate can gain a greater share of the benefits in life. They have campaigned for expanding the right to vote for racial minorities and also for the young and the poor. Liberals support greater participation in elections and they are strong opponents of voter suppression laws. They favor stricter controls on the use of large, unaccountable campaign funds that subvert the election process.

There has been a persistent belief on the left that most people are rational in their decision-making and that they should vote for candidates that will improve conditions of their own lives. They believe government should aid lower and middle-class consumers in society, especially as it relates to government-sponsored health programs, retirement plans, consumer protection, and the rights of organized labor in the workplace. There is a focus on regulating big business and major banks so they are more accountable to society. In addition, there is an effort to monitor air and water pollution so environmental standards are maintained. The left is convinced that climate change is real, and that international programs should be established to reduce greenhouse emissions to preserve the livability of the planet.

Reform on the left has been associated with the introduction of concepts that benefit those with the least amount of influence. There is a great faith that government can be used as a positive instrument to improve society. Those on the left have been impatient with slow-moving, incremental change. In politics they often initiate major new social/economic programs that are idealistic in tone. A sense of altruism prevails among liberals; there is seldom much thought given to policies or ideas that might benefit just themselves or their economic class.

In foreign affairs, the left has a long history of supporting anti-colonial movements and developing nations from the third world. They are noticeably less nationalistic and more inclined to favor international cooperation with bodies such as the United Nations and foreign aid packages aimed at improving living conditions around the world. On occasion, leaders on the left have been critical of their own government in cases involving human rights abuses.

Here are 20 examples of policy objectives on the left and far left:

- Enforce racial, ethnic, and gender equality throughout society.
- Close tax loopholes for corporations and the wealthy.
- Launch publicly funded health care programs.
- Expand coverage of unemployment insurance.
- Repeal voter ID laws and other practices that suppress the vote.

- Reduce tuition costs and interest rates for students in higher education.
- Remove discrimination in wages based on race and gender.
- Raise the minimum wage for unskilled workers.
- Stimulate the economy with more infrastructure investment.
- Protect labor's right to organize, collect dues, and strike.
- Enact stronger consumer protection laws and workplace safety regulations.
- Encourage people to join VISTA, the Peace Corps and other voluntary groups.
- Increase funding for Head Start and early childhood education.
- Preserve public assistance and food stamp programs.
- Prohibit unlimited financial campaign contribution.
- Provide women's health care and abortion services.
- Permit same-sex marriage and preserve LGBT rights.
- Strengthen laws protecting the quality of air and water.
- Favor international cooperation to control climate change.
- Require background checks before purchasing firearms.

In Their Own Words

What follows is a representative sample of left-wing thought that spans many topics. Persons quoted here were chosen not because of their political labels, but because of their beliefs on specific subjects. Statements are from political philosophers, writers, politicians, people in the labor movement, prominent writers, and also from little-known persons who were on the frontline of public affairs. Some of the pronouncements are ancient while others reflect current thinking. In total, these clearly worded declarations represent the underpinnings of leftist philosophy as it has developed through the ages. Some of the phrases may sound extreme because they reflect an emotion that is at the edge of left-wing politics—a few uncensored words can sometimes go to the heart of what people really believe. These comments are a series of "this I believe" statements. People on the left side of the spectrum won't agree completely with every quotation, but they likely won't completely disagree either. Like other things in life, political opinions are a matter of degree, and it is helpful to note the shades that make up the whole. In most cases, people on the left will at least appreciate how and why these statements were made. This section is meant to be read slowly with the reader reflecting on the full meaning of each statement. These quotations are from the "Brainy Quotes" website.

It is the greatest good to the greatest number of people which is the measure of right and wrong. **Jeremy Bentham**

We hold these truths to be self-evident: that all men are created equal; that they are endowed by their Creator with certain inalienable rights; that among these are life, liberty, and the pursuit of happiness. **Thomas Jefferson**

The planter, the farmer, the mechanic, and the laborer ... form the great body of the people of the United States, they are the bone and sinew of the countrymen who love liberty and desire nothing but equal rights and equal laws. **Andrew Jackson**

I distrust those people who know so well what God wants them to do, because I notice it always coincides with their own desires. **Susan B. Anthony**

No woman can call herself free who does not own and control her own body. No woman can call herself free until she can choose conscientiously whether she will or will not become a mother. **Margaret Sanger**

Every creature is better alive than dead, men and moose and pine trees. **Henry David Thoreau**

Patriotism is the willingness to kill and be killed for trivial reasons. **Bertrand Russell**

What has destroyed every previous civilization has been the unequal distribution of wealth and power. **Henry George**

We do not want churches because they will teach us to quarrel about God. We do not want to learn that. We may quarrel with men sometimes about things on this earth, but we never quarrel about the Great Spirit. We do not want to learn about that. **Chief Joseph**

Religion is the impotence of the human mind to deal with occurrences it cannot understand. **Karl Marx**

Show me the country that has no strikes and I'll show you the country in which there is no liberty. **Samuel Gompers**

We shall overcome. **Charles Albert Tindley**

If the workers want to win, all they have to do is recognize their own solidarity. They have nothing to do but fold their arms and the world will stop. The workers are more powerful with their hands in their pockets than all the property of the capitalists. **Joseph Ettor**

All day long I have listened to heartrending stories of women evicted from their homes by the coal companies. I heard pitiful pleas of little children crying for bread. **Burton Wheeler**

I am an agnostic; I do not pretend to know what many ignorant men are sure of. **Clarence Darrow**

True individual freedom cannot exist without economic security and independence. People who are hungry and out of a job are the stuff of which dictatorships are made. **Franklin Roosevelt**

The United Nations is designed to make possible lasting freedom and independence for all its members. **Harry Truman**

A hungry man is not a free man. **Adlai Stevenson**

None of us got where we are solely by pulling ourselves up by our bootstraps. We got here because somebody—a parent, a teacher, an Ivy League crony or a few nuns—bent down and helped us pick up our boots. **Thurgood Marshall**

A child born to a black mother in a state like Mississippi has exactly the same rights as a white baby born to the wealthiest person in the United States. It's not true, but I challenge anyone to say it is not a goal worth working for. **Thurgood Marshall**

The environment is everything that isn't me. **Albert Einstein**

We won't have a society if we destroy the environment. **Margaret Mead**

When we try to pick out anything by itself, we find it hitched to everything else in the universe. **John Muir**

Every gun that is made, every warship launched, every rocket fired, signifies in the final sense a theft from those who hunger and are not fed, those who are cold and are not clothed. **Dwight Eisenhower**

Those who make peaceful revolution impossible will make violent revolution inevitable. **John F. Kennedy**

There is no greater calling than to serve your fellow men. There is no greater contribution than to help the weak. There is no greater satisfaction than to have done it well. **Walter Reuther**

If there is technological advance without social advance, there is, almost automatically, an increase in human misery. **Michael Harrington**

A community is democratic only when the humblest and weakest person can enjoy the highest civil, economic, and social rights that the biggest and most powerful possess. **A. Philip Randolph**

It was once said that the moral test of government is how that government treats those who are in the dawn of life, the children; those who are in the twilight of life, the elderly; and those who are in the shadows of life, the sick, the needy and the handicapped. **Hubert Humphrey**

The biggest lesson I learned from Vietnam is not to trust our own government statements. I had no idea until then that you could not rely on them. **J. William Fulbright**

I'm fed up to the ears with old men dreaming up wars for young men to die in. **George McGovern**

Until justice is blind to color, until education is unaware of race, until opportunity is unconcerned with the color of men's skins, emancipation will be a proclamation but not a fact. **Lyndon Johnson**

There are those who look at things the way they are, and ask why … I dream of things that never were, and ask why not? **Robert Kennedy**

I grew up in the South under segregation. So, I know what terrorism feels like— when your father could be taken out in the middle of the night and lynched just because he didn't look like he was in an obeying frame of mind, when a white person said something he must do. I mean, that's terrorism, too. **Alice Walker**

The civil rights movement was based on faith. Many of us who were participants in this movement saw our involvement as an extension of our faith. We saw ourselves doing the work of the Almighty. **John Lewis**

When you grow up in a totally segregated society, where everybody around you believes that segregation is proper, you have a hard time. You can't believe how much it's a part of your thinking. **Shelby Foote**

Segregation was wrong when it was forced by white people, and I believe it is still wrong when it is requested by black people. **Coretta Scott King**

We must learn to live together as brothers or perish together as fools. **Martin Luther King, Jr.**

The organizers and perpetuators of segregation are as much the enemy of America as any foreign invader. **Bayard Rustin**

My personal feeling is that understanding evolution led me to atheism. **Richard Dawkins**

When people really understand the Big Bang and the whole sweep of the evolution of the universe, it will be clear that humans are fairly insignificant. **George Smoot**

I know of no wars started by anyone to impose lack of religion on someone else. We have lethal Sunni v Shia, Catholic against Protestant, but no agnostic suicide bombers attack crowded atheist pubs. **Simon Hoggart**

The greatest single cause of atheism in the world today is Christians who acknowledge Jesus with their lips and walk out the door and deny Him by their lifestyle. **Brennan Manning**

In some cases non-violence requires more militancy than violence. **Cesar Chavez**

Free speech has been used by the Supreme Court to give immense power to the wealthiest members of our society. **Noam Chomsky**

We did not make the laws in this country. We are neither morally nor legally confined to them.

We did not make the laws in this county. We are neither morally nor legally confined to those laws. Those laws that keep them up keep us down. **H. Rap Brown**

I think people are entitled to march without a permit. When you have a few hundred thousand people on the street you have permission. **Tom Hayden**

Now then, in order to understand white supremacy we must dismiss the fallacious notion that white people can give anybody their freedom. **Stokely Carmichael**

America preaches integration and practices segregation. **Malcolm X**

Human rights are the soul of our foreign policy, because human rights are the very soul of our sense of nationhood. **Jimmy Carter**

We have a tendency to condemn people who are different from us, to define their sins as paramount and our own sinfulness as being insignificant. **Jimmy Carter**

Prisons don't rehabilitate, they don't punish, they don't protect, so what the hell do they do? **Jerry Brown**

Global warming is real. It is happening today. It is being charted by our satellites. It is being charted by our scientists. It is being charted by those of us in this body, and I think the real key is if we are ready to admit that fact and take the action to make the necessary conversion. **Dianne Feinstein**

The only way to be true to our American tradition is to maintain absolute governmental neutrality regarding religious beliefs and practices. **Bill Bradley**

The corporate lobby in Washington is basically designed to stifle all legislative activity on behalf of consumers. **Ralph Nader**

By the time a man gets to be presidential material, he's been bought ten times over. **Gore Vidal**

Education is the most powerful weapon you can use to change the world. **Nelson Mandela**

The cry of the poor is not always just, but if you don't listen to it, you will never know what justice is. **Howard Zinn**

There is no flag large enough to cover the shame of killing innocent people. **Howard Zinn**

We cannot build our own future without helping others to build their future. **Bill Clinton**

The rich are always going to say that, you know, just give us more money and we'll go out and spend more and then it will all trickle down to the rest of you. But that has not worked the last 10 years, and I hope the American public is catching on. **Warren Buffett**

The entire North Polar ice cap is disappearing before our very eyes. It's been the size of the continental United States for the last 3 million years and now 40 percent is gone and the rest of it is going. **Al Gore**

I saw courage both in the Vietnam War and in the struggle to stop it. I learned that patriotism includes protest, not just military service. **John Kerry**

Every one of my positions cuts out half the country. I'm pro-choice, I'm pro-gay rights, I'm pro-immigration, I'm against guns, I believe in Darwin. **Michael Bloomberg**

Reproductive choice has to be straightened out. There will never be a woman of means without choice anymore. That just seems to me so obvious. The states that changed their abortion laws before *Roe* are not going to change back. So we have a policy that only affects poor women, and it can never be otherwise. **Ruth Bader Ginsburg**

If the Founding Fathers could have looked into a crystal ball and seen AK-47s and Glock semi-automatic pistols, I think they would say, you know, "That's not really what we mean when we say bear arms." **Michael Moore**

Capitalism works better from every perspective when the economic decision-makers are forced to share power with those who will be affected by those decisions. **Barney Frank**

I think the environment should be put in the category of our national security. Defense of our resources is just as important as defense abroad. Otherwise what is there to defend? **Robert Redford**

No fundamental social change occurs merely because government acts. It's because civil society, the conscience of a country, begins to rise up and demand change. **Joe Biden**

Service to others is the rent you pay for your room here on earth. **Muhammad Ali**

More people have been slaughtered in the name of religion than for any other reason. **Harvey Milk**

We are all socialists who support public education, state-funded universities, government-run hospitals, Medicare and Social Security. **Lawrence O'Donnell**

Human rights are not only violated by terrorism, repression or assassinations, but also by unfair economic structures that creates huge inequality. **Pope Francis**

Do all the good you can, for all the people you can, in all the ways you can, for as long as you can. **Barack Obama**

I found that at Princeton, no matter how liberal and open-minded some of my white Professors and classmates were toward me, I sometimes felt like a visitor on campus,as if I really didn't belong. **Michelle Obama**

Without liberals we wouldn't have unions. We wouldn't have environmental protections. We wouldn't have seat belts or birth control or the ACLU! Any of those things! **Janeane Garofalo**

Electoral politics was always an objective of the Black Panther party, so Barack Obama is a part of what we dreamed and struggled and died for. **Bobby Seale**

Liberals were liberators—they fought slavery, fought for women to have the right to vote, fought against Hitler, fought to end segregation, fought to end apartheid. Liberals put an end to child labor and they gave us the five day work week! **Barbra Streisand**

And Jesus, the heart of the Christian faith is the wildest, most radical guy you'd ever come across. **Bear Grylls**

The anarchy gang is quick to malign government, but when was the last time anyone called for regulators to go easier on companies that put lead in children's toys, or for food inspectors to stop checking whether the meat in our grocery store is crawling with deadly bacteria, or for the FDA to ignore whether morning sickness drugs will cause horrible deformities in little babies? We never hear that. **Elizabeth Warren**

It is unacceptable that someone can work full-time—and work hard—and not be able to lift themselves out of poverty. **Sherrod Brown**

The modern conservative is engaged in one of man's oldest exercises in moral philosophy; that is, the search for a superior moral justification for selfishness. **John Kenneth Galbraith**

We do not want to live in a theocracy. We should maintain that barrier and government has no business telling someone what they ought to believe or how they should conduct their private lives. **Robert Reich**

I have yet to hear a man ask for advice on how to combine marriage and a career. **Gloria Steinem**

In a democracy there are only two types of power: there's organized people and organized money, and organized money only wins when people aren't organized. **Ben Jealous**

For too long in this society, we have celebrated unrestrained individualism over common community. **Hillary Clinton**

We must stop thinking of the individual and start thinking about what is best for society. **Bernie Sanders**

You know, I think many people have the mistaken impression that Congress regulates Wall Street. In truth that's not the case. The real truth is that Wall Street regulates the Congress. **Bernie Sanders**

Basic Problems for the Left

Liberals think differently than the rest of the world. They focus on what could be rather than on what is. Their strong humanistic optimism inspires them to want to help those at the bottom of society, but they usually fall short. There's almost always a gap between what they set out to do and what they actually achieve, so it's comparatively easy to criticize them for not finishing the job. Typically, this discrepancy is due to the fact that they take on the great problems of the era: human rights, poverty, universal health care, world peace, and climate change. They have an uncompromising incentive to take on the great challenges of their generation even when they know that success is probably not going to happen in their lifetimes.

That means the left always has two problems. The first is they never get it all done—next year there's always more to do. And secondly, they have a reputation for frustrating themselves and their followers because progress today is a watered-down version of what they really wanted. Yet the left is not deterred. They continue to take on the tough problems of the world that many think are impossible to resolve.

Liberals see politics as a human responsibility. They believe that we can't sweep serious problems under the rug. They argue that someone has to take on the big issues that are holding humanity back. Leftists pride themselves in doing the right things for the right reasons. They also assume that other people will agree with them and support a cause that benefits the general welfare. Unfortunately, many human beings have a different focus—not everyone is altruistic and willing to put their time and energy into the big issues that involve everyone's interest.

Progressive-minded leaders are often astonished when the electorate rejects self-sacrificing programs that are meant to benefit minorities who need it the most. There's always been an expectation on the left that the average person can be enriched by a society that educates and nurtures, but there is sometimes a negative reaction from the very people who are being helped. American culture idealizes those who make it on their own. It is the classic example of the parent who helps too much and is resented by the child. One can almost hear the child saying, "Mother, I'd rather do it myself."

Progressives are driven to do good things for people even when people don't ask for it, and in some cases, when they don't want it. Leftist agendas are full of policies designed to help those who can't help themselves, and they frequently are surprised when the help is criticized as coming from "do-good-ers" or "bureaucrats" who really don't understand our problems. It is a truism in American life that the populace often resents the aid they receive from others, especially when it comes from those in positions of power.

Liberals have more than their share of PhDs who quote statistics and write studies. These academicians mean well, but they sometimes come off as looking down on the group they want to help. Most of the new federal programs originated with White House "brain-trusts" who worked closely with supportive congressional staff members. The New Deal, the Fair Deal, the New Frontier, and the Great Society were all hatched by people with advanced university degrees. Former governor of Alabama, George Wallace, called them "pointy headed intellectuals," and "eggheads." Ordinary people outside of Washington, D.C., have always been suspicious of ivy-league reformers who grew up with silver spoons in their mouths.

Conservatives campaign on the promise of repealing most of the programs that liberals set in place. Traditionally right-wing leaders have a different approach to these issues that is more consistent with American mythology; they promise those in need that they can raise themselves up (without government help) through greater economic freedom, tax cuts, and making wise financial investments. But left-wing leaders know that those promises don't work for people that have no job, no skills, and have lost their homes. Self-help policies from conservatives appeal to the sense of being self-sufficient. It feels better—even if it doesn't work.

The result is that the left is seen as out-of-touch elitists who mean well, but who are usually out of touch with enduring American values. Programs like federal aid to education, affirmative action, defending voter rights, Social Security, Medicare, Medicaid, and Obamacare are designed to aid everyone, but these programs don't fit well into the American dream. The liberal argument of aiding the public welfare is often resisted by those who don't think the programs are necessary and don't trust the people who are proposing them.

It is a strange fact of politics that lower income people often look up to the wealthy and fantasize that they might be there someday if they got a few breaks in life. American novelist John Steinbeck wrote that the poor don't see themselves as "an exploited proletariat but as temporarily-embarrassed millionaires." Low-income Americans are more interested in books on how to get rich rather than government programs that actually share the wealth. Many working-class Americans think they may be rich someday. There's always been a "rags to riches" dream among folks at the bottom.

The mythology of the American dream has caused some unexpected reactions. As stated earlier, the left has assumed that the populace would always cherish social welfare programs. But an increasing number of people no longer have a sense of gratitude. Looking for someone to blame for a failing program supersedes any sense of gratitude.

The left keeps bringing up the same issues every year, and after a while, liberal reformers are blamed for the problem. The War on Poverty of the 1960s and the Civil Rights Movement are examples; both are still remembered by some in Middle America as liberal failures because poverty and racism continue to be a problem. Conservatives are fond of saying that both problems would have gotten better if left alone.

In a strange twist, many hold government responsible for the ills of the world. Working-class Americans love to tell stories about how government programs were put together by do-gooders who didn't understand what's like to "work for a living." Conservatives silently applaud this belief and focus instead on reinforcing the values of self-made people who work hard and become wealthy despite their race and station in life. Every school child has heard the story of the boy who started out as a mail-room clerk and went on to become chairman of the board. This story is much more in tune with American mythology.

On a related topic, progressives are amazed that blue-collar workers and the elderly are less willing to vote for their own economic self-interest. Democrats still don't comprehend why many voters are more concerned about why a particular government program doesn't work, and less concerned about the benefits they may receive personally from that same program.

President Ronald Reagan always got a hearty laugh when he said, "The most terrifying words in the English language are: I'm from the government and I'm here to help." It surprises liberals to find out that government itself is seen as the enemy by an increasing segment of the voting public.

In real life, the government may be quite efficient in building roads, fielding an army, and providing clean water, but that success is never very newsworthy. The compelling story that gets coverage is failure—everyone is interested when roads and bridges crumble, the army is in retreat, and there are high amounts of lead in the water.

Bad news is easy to understand and remember. For example, pretty much everyone knows about the rising national debt. There is also an increasing fear about the shortcomings of retirement funds and health care programs. The prevailing view out on the street is that the government is going broke because it can't afford all those so-called "entitlement" programs. Warnings are issued every day that young people will never be able to retire on a pension. The left is doing a poor job of defending the measures they felt were their major accomplishments, and the right is profiting politically from the situation.

Both liberals and conservatives are selective in how they speak of the mounting national debt. Liberals bring it up when huge tax cuts are passed for the rich; they worry that the decreased revenue that will increase the deficit. Conservatives are generally silent in that case, but they voice concern about the debt when there is increased spending on social programs. But the two situations are not equal in the public's mind. When compared, the public is more likely to accept the idea that tax cuts for the rich is more defensible than increased social spending. Again, it goes back to the negative view Americans have about social welfare programs.

A growing number of people are dependent on government benefits, but they oppose receiving help from the government. Many of these people need medical help, some are disabled, and others are simply unable to find a job. Recipients of government aid often feel guilty and frustrated because they shouldn't need help. It is not uncommon for people to deny their own self-interest and instead support candidates who promise to cut the very programs they depend on for survival. Americans want to live out the image of being financially independent even if it doesn't work for them individually. The mythology is more important than the reality.

The bottom line is that the Democratic Party is on the defensive when it comes to extending government benefits to those who need it the most. Republicans have targeted welfare cheating, government red tape, ineffective job retraining, and Obamacare. Fox News delights in running stories that illustrate how government is failing the people. Special attention is given on right-wing television to the failing of left-wing governments in Venezuela or Cuba, focusing on the point that socialism doesn't work anywhere in the world.

Again, the point is made: bad news crowds out good news. Saying that government works is not really news at all. But liberals have been slow to recognize that they are victims of a very effective political public relations campaign. They don't seem able to defend themselves in the face of the many charges against major programs and leftist governments around the world.

Liberal activists have the unexpected situation of making progress only to have their followers turn against those achievements later. Each generation seems to forget the hard-fought battles won by their parents. New ideas and reforms have always been a bit unwieldly. No program works the way it was intended and there are always unforeseen consequences that no one expected. Because of this, progressives have had to resell concepts they once thought were firmly established. The problem is that there is frequently a political memory loss among those who were helped the most by these programs.

Liberal reformers will tell you they are constantly battling the tendency of humanity to become complacent and lose their appreciation of what government can do in real life. Those who sponsored the reforms become disillusioned when they see their life's work being undone by time and inaction. They wonder whether it was worth the effort in the first place. The following is a case in point.

Saul Alinsky

Several years ago, I invited an old college friend to speak at a university symposium on the subject of political change. At the conclusion of his prepared comments, he took questions from the floor and got sidetracked on the issue of the futility of politics. His sense of optimism faded as he said:

> Most of the progress we make is lost by new leaders who turn out to be just as set in their ways as the old leadership. As years go by, reform organizations lose momentum and drift back into the old pattern. The new commitment to help the poor, minorities, and the powerless is undermined by people who are more concerned about getting and keeping power for themselves.

He went on to say:

> Over the years all organizations lose sight of their original purpose. They all betray their founders, so why should we throw our hearts and souls into a cause that ultimately will be lost?

My friend's logic was enough to dampen everyone's enthusiasm. Students who heard him seemed to withdraw from the dialogue and showed less interest in the topic of political change. "What would be the use "to engage in politics?" they thought, "In the long run, what good would it do? It all gets undone later."

At the symposium lunch break, my friend went on with his remarks in a smaller group and concluded, "in the end we will all be dead, and what good is political reform then? We'll all be just as dead, and it won't make any difference to anyone."

At this point, another guest speaker at the symposium interrupted sharply by saying, "Shut up, I've heard enough of this crap!" The other person was Saul Alinsky, considered at that time to be the foremost radical community organizer in the United States. He had earned his reputation as an irreverent, street-wise organizer who had taken on the old political leadership of Chicago, Oakland, Philadelphia, and other large American cities; he prided himself on using political power to organize the least fortunate segment of society. Alinsky was clearly bothered by the negative direction of this conversation, which seemed to undermine the motivation of politics itself. In a loud, dominant voice he said:

Now don't interrupt me until I'm finished. I want to tell you about a time I went to Albert Einstein's home for dinner. I was there with a member of the Princeton University faculty. The three of us, Einstein, the professor and I talked over dinner about the immense size of the known universe, the role of God, and the relationship between God and humanity in the universe. Einstein did most of the talking. After dinner we went into another room for brandy, and Einstein asked the two of us a question he said school children often ask each other. "The question is simple," Einstein said, "but great minds have pondered it for centuries. The question is this: If you could have anything, what would you ask for?" Einstein added, "Don't respond until you know you have the correct answer."

According to Alinsky, the professor and he sat silently for a full 45 minutes as Einstein sat between them sipping brandy. Then, according to Alinsky, the silence was broken. Alinsky said:

Mr. Einstein, I have the answer: *I would want to know what to ask for.* As a human being, we don't know enough about the universe to know what is the most important question to ask. But this is not a weakness on my part. It is rather an awareness of my role on earth.

Alinsky went on, speaking to the students with building anger in his voice:

You see, we don't always know everything about the results of our labors. Some of what we do may be lost or undone. But that is not an excuse for doing nothing. Each of us must have a zest for life in all we do. We must do things that need to be done and hope for the best.

Alinsky looked deeply at everyone in the group and concluded:

Now I don't want to hear any more crap about in the end we'll all be dead. Hell, that's not profound. It's just a copout for doing nothing!

In truth, Alinsky had a realistic view of leftist politics. There is no certainty in political affairs. Everything may be undone tomorrow. But, of course, that is true about everything else as well, and that does not stop us in other areas of life, does it? Nothing is ever settled permanently in politics. The ink doesn't dry on laws and rules before a group is organizing to change the new decrees. People sometimes become selfish and lose their crusading spirit to help others. The pulse of politics is a steady beat of conflict, choice, change, and sometimes reversal. Sometimes it's necessary to do it all over again.

If they live long enough, liberals get to see many of their great achievements repealed. It's just a matter of time before the clock runs out on the process of progressive reform. This is the reason why leftists were universally depressed after the election of Donald Trump in 2016. Everything in the field of health care, environmental protection, education, progressive taxation, and social issues was jeopardized when President Obama left office. In foreign affairs the United States became the only nation in the world to leave the

Paris Climate Change Accord, and the US also dropped out of the international nuclear agreement with Iran. Trump found it comparatively easy to undo much that had been done during the past 75 years. For liberals, it was the same old story of having to start all over again.

Revolutionaries on the Left

But there is a world of difference between non-violent leftists like Saul Alinsky and those who advocate a revolution they believe will remake the world. Revolutionaries on the left are not satisfied with reforming the system and making it better, they are prepared to use violent means to smash all the rules of society and begin anew.

In following a Marxian model, radical revolutionaries hold the conviction that all governments exploit the poor around the world, and that a violent revolution and class struggle against these governments will occur as a result of the exploitation of the working class. Human beings will be united through their misery and rise up against the right-wing capitalist class. Society will be remade through a dictatorship representing the working class so that the full potential of humanity can be realized.

Their faith in human nature is so great that they believe that, after the revolution, when the dust settles, everyone will live at peace in a classless society without the need of government. Proponents of these ideas often come from small groups of intellectuals who dream of eliminating the present institutions of society and setting up a whole new order based on an all-encompassing confidence that humanity can be trusted to live in a society without repressive rules. But in building that order, they will use any and all means to eliminate their foes. Their underlying belief is that someday society can be purged of all its bourgeois values because agents of the revolutionary regime will expose them one by one, and finally re-educate everyone through a class struggle that will bring out the true, non-exploitive nature of humanity.

It is interesting that leftist revolutionary leaders seldom come directly from the working class they profess to represent. Those who instigate rebellion are usually well-educated, middle-class intellectuals who have the time and opportunity to study, write and converse with other idealists about why a revolution is justified. Many of them led a privileged life. Examples include Lenin in Russia, Mao in China, and Castro in Cuba. Poor people in these countries were too busy scratching out a living to plan a revolution. As a group, the poor and downtrodden were reluctant to confront the power structure because they were afraid they would lose the little they have. It is the middle-class idealists who have stirred up workers and peasants and convinced them to revolt.

But for every revolutionary radical who leads people to the barricades, there are scores who never leave the coffee house where they plot the coming rebellion. Because they are so out of step with the rest of society, they often become a closed group with little contact with anyone who disagrees with them. I knew self-declared Marxist, revolutionaries in Berkeley, California, holed up in small, dark apartments, living inside their own world, writing long position papers about liberating the working class with whom they had no contact. I interviewed an old leader of the Communist Party in San Francisco who wanted to lead young radicals, but was "turned off," as he put it, by young men with long hair. In southern Oregon there were radical revolutionaries up in the mountains, many miles away from the revolution they hoped to lead. As far as I know, they are still up in the mountains waiting for the right conditions before they come down to the valley floor to start the revolution.

Yet there are celebrated left-wing revolutionary leaders around the world that have moved from the theory to the practice of instigating popular revolutions. Perhaps the examples in Russia, China, and Cuba are classic cases of fomenting a successful revolution. In organizing the revolt, they created mass movements inspiring those considered to be the "the powerless people" to rise up and take power through use of force.

The issues of revolutionaries on the left are not identical around the world, but there are some elements that come up often, both at home and abroad. What follows are 10 typical goals for revolutionary radicals in the United States today:

- Abolish corporations that oppress people around the globe.
- Free political prisoners held in imperialist jails.
- Supply weapons to revolutions against right-wing dictators.
- Destroy the capitalist banking system that enslaves the world.
- Attack companies that destroy the environment.
- Join liberation terrorist groups on other continents.
- Organize direct action against law enforcement bodies.
- Encourage armed resistance for ethnic, racial, and minority groups.
- Advocate disobedience to objectionable laws.
- Detonate bombs in public buildings to publicize their cause.

Problems for Revolutionary Radicals

The authority and ability of an industrialized 2st century capitalist state to put down a revolution is impressive. Even repressive regimes have the built-in advantage of an official respectability that intimidates most potential revolutionaries. Those who consider an armed rebellion are dealing with very long odds. The whole apparatus of the state looms large with a professional army, the police and governmental officials. On the other side, it's difficult to attract a band of supporters worried about their own personal welfare. Most people are fearful of losing the little they have and are reluctant to join in such a chancy adventure. The success records for revolutions is not encouraging, especially in a modern Western country.

The United States is one of the least revolutionary nations in the world. When riots have occurred, the U.S. approach has been to view it as a police problem (or if it is serious) the government calls in the Army or the National Guard. The general posture has been one of using overwhelming force to suppress the unrest. U.S. officials do not negotiate with leaders of a protest movement even if they have legitimate issues.

Perhaps the clearest example of this was in 1932 when the U.S. Army burned down the encampment of World War I military veterans (known as the Bonus Army) in Washington, D.C. World War I army veterans were lobbying Congress for financial benefits that had been promised. There were 43,000 marchers in all, and approximately 17,000 of them were veterans with certificates they thought entitled them to a cash bonus. The great majority of the marchers were loyal Americans who felt they had a just cause.

One of the noteworthy reactions to the Bonus Army was that there was no negotiation with the veterans. Despite the fact that they had all served their country, President Hoover and the Congress made no attempt to grant them even a small stipend so they could return home. Under the command of General Douglas MacArthur, the encampment was knocked down, and tents and other enclosures were burned as the veterans and their families fled for their lives. Two people were killed in the melee.

There's a lesson here for groups that assemble illegally to seek redress of their grievances. If this is how the United States treated certified veterans who had risked their lives in combat and been promised a bonus, imagine the response to full-fledged revolutionaries who want to overthrow the government. The United States does not bargain with revolutionaries.

The chance of a leftist revolution getting off the ground in the U.S. is almost zero, and there is no legacy of how to integrate revolutionary groups into the American system. Once a group goes out on the street, they face the awesome power of law enforcement officials who will hunt them down. It is an article of faith that the government leaders will smash any and all uprisings. Anyone who understands American politics and culture would realize immediately that they will be treated harshly if they attempt to use violence against the government.

In addition to the political problems of confronting the regime, there is an important organizational problem within radical revolutionary movements. On the one hand, their ultimate goal is to build a non-exploitive society where everyone can live peacefully in complete harmony. However, the willingness to use violence against the regime in power creates an environment where brute force is often used to settle disputes within the movement. It is very difficult to promote an idealized environment while fighting a violent revolution.

In an effort to consolidate their own power, leaders often purge dissenters. The use of repression against opposing points of view is especially disruptive when used against faithful members of the revolution. It is not uncommon for leaders who rise to positions of power to become more motivated in getting and keeping power for themselves rather than building a classless society. Quite often there is a reign of revolutionary terror resulting in the purging of all dissenters, even those who were devoted followers. As a consequence, the original goals of the revolution are often betrayed by those who are driven to consolidate their power. It is a sad and violent story that is played out over and over around the world.

Sometimes thoughtful radical revolutionaries reflect on their lives by concluding that they made society worse instead of better. Their problem began when they expected the "inherent goodness" of humanity to emerge after the negative features of society had been cast out. As we shall see in reviewing recent history, real revolutions usually turn out different than planned.

The Communist Party

A few years ago, I knew a woman who was involved in leftist revolutionary politics. Evelyn was a Russian Jew who had been born in New York City. Her parents raised her to believe that average, working-class people could make this a better world. At the age of 16, Evelyn joined the Young Communist League, which was the youth arm of the party. She grew up with personal friends that were to become the leadership of the American Communist Party. Among her friends were party leaders Eugene Dennis (later general secretary of the party), longtime member Harry Bridges (San Francisco longshoremen), and Gus Hall (chairman of the national party committee). One of her best friends was Peggy Dennis, wife of Eugene Dennis, General Secretary of the Communist Party. Evelyn married another party member, Steve, who was editor of the *Daily Worker* newspaper in San Francisco.

Evelyn showed up at every left-wing protest demonstration in northern California and southern Oregon. She was a feminist, active in the "ban the bomb" movement; she opposed the Pentagon in general. (Think Barbra Streisand in *The Way We Were*.)

She didn't talk about it publicly out on the street, but privately Evelyn was a devoted member of the International Communist Party. She was on board when Stalin made a non-aggression pact with Hitler in 1939. Along with other loyal members, she "readjusted" her stance when the Soviets declared war on Germany in 1941. She personally knew and supported Julius and Ethel Rosenberg, party members who were executed in 1953 for being Soviet spies. She said she was always opposed to violence personally, but recognized it was absolutely necessary to spread the communist doctrine around the world. By her own admission, Evelyn followed the party line faithfully because she believed in Marxism and the Soviet cause.

Evelyn told me she had a "terrible personal crisis" in 1968 when the Soviets used tanks and guns against dissenting party members in Czechoslovakia. She watched filmed accounts of young, idealistic Communists being killed by Soviet troops. She couldn't get the images out of her mind. It violated her faith in the revolution because violence was being used against fellow party members who favored peaceful public participation. At first, she thought the press reports were just a part of "American anti–Soviet propaganda," but she decided later that what she saw on television was true. She said it "violated her soul" to see her Soviet comrades turn against other revolutionaries. It was a personal crisis that changed her life.

In a videotaped interview, Evelyn spoke to me about her faith in humanity, concern for the poor, and hopes for minority groups around the world. She believed firmly that the Communist Party workers' class struggle would ultimately bring forth a better world for everyone. I asked her how it felt to believe in all those things while watching the Soviet actions crush fellow revolutionaries in Czechoslovakia. She swallowed hard as she turned her head toward me and said, "How do you think it feels to find out your mother's a whore?"

Evelyn remained involved in radical causes for the rest of her life, but later she denounced the Communist Party activities as "counter-revolutionary." She spoke often about how the party suppressed dissent within its own ranks and refused to align with other radical groups that turned against the leadership. She and several other leading members of the party resigned after 50 years of membership.

When Evelyn was near death, she gave me a six-page, single-spaced letter written by her friend Peggy Dennis, wife of the late Eugene Dennis who had been General Secretary of the American Communist Party. The letter was written after Eugene Dennis died—it was Peggy's political resignation from the Communist Party. Peggy Dennis recounted how the "Party" had betrayed its followers by becoming "dogmatic" and how it used intimidation against its own members. She wrote, "there is only one side for a revolutionary in the class struggle," but—apparently feeling the Party had betrayed her—

she quoted the title of an old radical song by Pete Seeger by asking, "Which side are you on?"

The life of Evelyn, and her fellow Communist Party members, underlines a problem the revolutionary left has always had. Idealism in the revolution is followed by repression because the leadership justifies the use of force and intimidation against "enemies of the revolution." Often the first victims of the revolution are the idealists who supported the movement in its formative years. Like Evelyn, they were believers in the cause, but were not wired politically to personally engage in violence against their former commrades. It may be the great tragedy of the left that the idealism of a revolutionary movement is squandered by the brutality of leaders who use physical force to put down dissent after the revolution.

As we shall see in the next chapter, this has never been a problem of the right because their goal has never to create a classless society based on the inherent goodness of human nature. The right has always held a rather pessimistic view of humanity; they never "promised a rose garden" where people were expected to interact peacefully without conflict or disruption.

Questions for You

1. In your judgment, why is a sense of empathy so important for persons on the left? What evidence to you see that liberals are constantly putting themselves in the place of others? Do you admire this characteristic? Why or why not?

2. Read the 20 examples of policy objectives for the left and far left. Do you generally agree or disagree with those objectives? Which one do you agree with the most? Why? Which one do you disagree with the most? Why?

3. Read through the 80+ individual statements in the "In Their Own Words" section. Do you generally agree or disagree with those statements? Which statement do you agree with the most? Why? Which statement do you disagree with the most? Why?

4. What does the author mean in the statement, "Liberals think differently than the rest of the world?" Do you think they approach politics differently than conservatives? Why or why not?

5. Which aspects of American culture run counter to the way progressives conduct themselves in politics? Why does the author think the conservative approach is more in tune with American mythology?

6. Why are both liberals and conservatives very selective in how they speak about the national debt? In your judgment, why do many lower-income people support tax cuts for the wealthy while they oppose increased spending on social welfare?

7. What was your reaction to the story about Saul Alinsky having dinner with Albert Einstein? Do you think this story provides an accurate view of left-wing motivation in the face of setbacks? Why or why not?

8. What is the fundamental view of radical revolutionaries about government as an institution? In what way do their beliefs shape that view? What is your personal reaction to that ideological belief?

9. Why do radical revolutionaries usually come from the educated middle class? What is your reaction to the point that revolutionary radical intellectuals often come from a "privileged position" in society?

10. Read the 10 typical goals of revolutionary radicals. Do you generally agree or disagree with those goals? Why or why not?

11. What evidence does the author supply to support the statement that the "United States is one of the least revolutionary nations in the world?" If this is true, why do you think radical revolutionaries are still willing to risk their lives in an armed revolution?

12. Why did Evelyn, a dedicated Communist, turn against the leadership of the Communist Party? To what extent does this story demonstrate a built-in problem for thoughtful revolutionaries on the left? What would you do if you found that your ideological commitments were in conflict with your moral beliefs? Do you see any examples of this kind of behavior in current politics?

How Do You React to Left-Wing Values?

Select one statement from the "In Their Own Words" section and present a convincing argument as to why you believe that statement *is not true*. Provide examples to support your point of view.

Select one statement from the same section and present a convincing argument as to why you believe that statement *is true*. Provide examples to support your point of view.

Do you see an ideological connection between the middle-left and the revolutionary-left? On what points do they agree?

7

Right-Wing Values

The Republican Party has been the dominant force among conservatives for many years, but it has now been infiltrated by the Tea Party and the Freedom Caucus. Earlier, old-line conservatives worked well with liberals in legislative politics, but these new conservatives are very independent-minded and not willing to cooperate with outsiders. The situation became more complex with the rise of Donald Trump, who has no discernable ideology of his own; he also personally violated many of the basic principles of conservatism.

The new conservatives of today are frustrated with the old politics of making concessions and negotiating with the oppositions—they have lost interest in working with the other side. But they still stand firm against illegal immigration, opposing government regulations and any new taxes. Many have grabbed public attention with their high level of motivation which borders on religious fervor. But their movement is complicated by Donald Trump, who has overshadowed the Republican Party and muffled traditional right-wing values. Yet conservatism stands as one of the two major American ideologies—it will prevail long after Trump passes from the scene.

The three major sets of beliefs that have shaped political thinking on the right are:

1. Competition, individual initiative, free enterprise, patriotism, traditions, and faith in a supreme being bring out the best in human beings.

2. The main obstacles to prosperity, personal freedom and liberty are government controls and regulations of our personal lives.

3. Our country needs tough, respected, honest, and courageous leadership coupled with traditional values to maintain a well-ordered society.

What They Believe

The key perspective of the right is an independent spirit combined with a strong sense of nationalism and a belief in a higher power. Virtually everything conservatives believe in springs from their faith in their country, and their claim of rights against government controls—they stand up for the rights of the individual to be free in every sense of the word. Whether it is economic freedom or religious liberties, it always comes back to the enterprising individual being more important than the whole. This is especially true if a person succeeds against great odds. Heroes on the right include those who fight for their country—who win in sports, war, business, politics, or some other contest that requires great personal determination. It is the epic example of the highly motivated person who rises from humble beginnings to achieve greatness on their own strength of character. There is the compelling story of developing a sense of self-power through competition—of testing one's ability to succeed. Conservatives have always had a faith that freedom for the individual is the main pillar of society.

Throughout history, leaders on the right have believed there are natural differences among people and inequality is to be expected—it is a predictable part of a free society. Governmental policies that promote equality are seen as a misguided effort to punish those who create the most wealth and reward those who have done the least. There is a cardinal belief that those who work hard and smart should win out at the end. It logically follows that a completely free capitalist system is the best system ever devised by humanity because it enables free competition that naturally rewards individual genius and hard work. In this arrangement, sensible investors and entrepreneurs set the standard for excellence in the free market system. A great feature of capitalism is that successful enterprises at the top drive prosperity through the entire economy so all can benefit within the system. There is a belief here that successful people who have proven themselves to be superior and are entitled to their earned rewards. The most important citizens are those with the incentive to create wealth that is the life's blood of any successful society. Nothing should stand in their way.

There is a belief on the right that humanity is far from perfect and that the leaders in society should be ready to establish disciplinary rules for those who protest against the government. It is far better for individuals to work through the system than to show their disagreement in public.

Conservatives are of the opinion that undeserved benefits to less successful people will condition those folks to become less enterprising and more dependent on society. A much better approach to helping those in poverty is to show them how free enterprise can work for them. It is immoral to provide government handouts to protect individuals who lack initiative.

Right-wing groups oppose any relaxation of immigration standards because they believe everyone should follow the rules in entering the country and achieving citizenship. There is a special reluctance to let in persons who don't have the same language, religion or cultural values of the majority. A major concern is that new arrivals may not be personally motivated and will not participate in the free enterprise system that has made this country great.

For conservatives, the economic marketplace is a hallowed place, driven by supply and demand, plus individual self-interest and innovation. There is a self-correcting feature in most areas of human affairs; the government should stand back and permit prosperity to occur in its natural form. The government that governs best governs least.

The general posture on the right, therefore, has been to encourage pro-business policies, cut individual and corporate taxes, reduce government regulations, and defend free enterprise. A flat tax is fair with everyone paying the same percentage of their income. People deserve to keep what they have earned, and they should be able to pass it on to their descendants.

Conservatives are very individualistic in respect to employer/employee relations. They strongly oppose any effort of workers to organize in order to gain an unfair economic advantage by conspiring or striking against management. Employers are in charge and have every right to dismiss workers who try to organize a union.

Those who are very successful in life have an obligation to voluntarily give back to society in the form of philanthropy to worthy charities. Wise leaders should serve as mentors to inspire everyone to work hard in a wide-open, free-enterprise economy.

A consistent theme on the right has been the position that change should come at a measured pace, and never should there be a sharp break with past patterns, especially in matters relating to economics, social norms or public morality. Reform from the right often takes the form of merging the needs of the present into the enduring ways of the past.

Family values, established morality, and a faith in God are major principles on the right. These values are seen as the cornerstones of a well-ordered society. It naturally follows that there is a general opposition to secularism, abortion, and same-sex marriage.

The right believes that legally constituted force is an important factor in preserving our freedoms. Individuals have a constitutional right to own firearms and stand their ground against anyone who threatens them. In the international field, there is a duty to use military force to preserve national economic interests abroad. To this end, the right favors a vigorous national defense system so we can continue to be the strongest nation in the world.

Current examples of 20 policy objectives for the right and far right are to:

- Reduce regulation on business and ease environmental standards.
- Privatize more public services such as police, fire, schools, and prisons.
- Cut taxes on individual income, inheritance, private property and corporations.

- Restrict public welfare programs and unemployment insurance.
- Eliminate voter fraud by requiring a personal photo as proof of identity.
- Repeal and replace the Affordable Health Care act (Obamacare).
- Build security walls along the southern border to keep out all illegal aliens.
- Reduce public employment in unnecessary government programs.
- Protect a worker's right to not join a union or pay union dues.
- Continue the use of capital punishment for serious crimes such as murder.
- Maintain an economic system based on competition and free-market forces.
- Establish schools where curriculum matters are decided at the local level.
- Provide for daily prayers in all schools and public meetings.
- Require people to work rather than draw welfare or food stamps.
- Eliminate restrictions on owning and carrying legal firearms.
- Protect First Amendment rights for unlimited contributions to political campaigns.
- Retain employer's right to not provide abortion coverage in health care plans.
- Block federal and state funds used for abortions.
- Prohibit same-sex and interracial marriages.
- Display the national flag in private and public places.

In Their Own Words

What follows is a representative sample of right-wing thought that spans many topics. Persons quoted here were chosen not because of their political labels, but rather because of their beliefs on specific subjects. Statements are from political philosophers, religious leaders, politicians, military leaders, writers, persons in business, and from little-known persons who were on the front-lines of public affairs. Some of the pronouncements are ancient while others reflect current thinking. In total, these clearly worded declarations represent the underpinnings of right-wing philosophy as it has developed through the ages, and is still shaping our politics today. In some cases, the phrases may sound extreme because they reflect a sense of emotion that is at the edge of right-wing politics—but a few uncensored words can sometimes go to the heart of what people really believe. In some respects, these comments are a series of "this I believe" statements. People on the right side of the spectrum won't agree completely with every quotation, but they likely won't completely disagree either. Like other things in life, political opinions are a matter of degree, and it is helpful to note the shades that make up the whole. In most cases, those on the right will at least appreciate how and why these statements were made. This section is meant to be read slowly so the reader can reflect on the full meaning of each statement. These quotations are from the "Brainy Quotes" website.

The basis of a democratic state is liberty. **Aristotle**

The end of law is not to abolish or restrain, but to preserve freedom. **John Locke**

The real tragedy of the poor is the poverty of their aspirations. **Adam Smith**

Man is an animal that makes bargains: no other animal does this—no dog exchanges bones with another. **Adam Smith**

Good order is the foundation of all things. **Edmund Burke**

Those who will not be governed by God will be ruled by tyrants. **William Penn**

The great object is that every man be armed. Everyone who is able may have a gun. **Patrick Henry**

When government takes away the citizen's right to bear arms, it becomes the citizen's right to take away the government's right to govern. **George Washington**

When the people fear their government, there is tyranny; when the government fears the people, there is liberty. **Thomas Jefferson**

That government is best which governs the least, because its people discipline themselves. **Thomas Jefferson**

Democracy is two wolves and a lamb voting on what to have for lunch. Liberty is a well-armed lamb contesting the vote! **Benjamin Franklin**

Why has government been instituted at all? It is because the passions of man will not conform to the dictates of reason and justice without constraint. **Alexander Hamilton**

The power to tax is the power to destroy. **John Marshall**

The America Republic will endure until the day Congress discovers that it can bribe the public with the public's money. **Alexis de Tocqueville**

The proper role of government is to do for the people what they cannot do for themselves. Whatever they can do for themselves, government ought not to interfere. **Abraham Lincoln**

Compromise is usually a sign of weakness, or an admission of defeat. Strong men don't compromise. **Andrew Carnegie**

My idea is that if capital and labor are left alone they will mutually regulate each other. **Jay Gould**

Give tax breaks to large corporations, so that money can trickle down to the general public, in the form of extra jobs. **Andrew Mellon**

Patriotism is supporting your country all the time, and your government when it deserves it. **Mark Twain**

A man who is good enough to shed his blood for the country is good enough to be given a square deal afterwards. **Theodore Roosevelt**

Every immigrant who comes here should be required within five years to learn English or leave the country. **Theodore Roosevelt**

Socialism proposes no adequate substitute for the motive of enlightened self-ishness that today is at the basis of all human labor and effort, enterprise and new activity. **William Howard Taft**

It is impossible to mentally or socially enslave a Bible-reading people. The principles of the Bible are the groundwork of human freedom. **Horace Greely**

The parents have a right to say that no teacher paid by their money shall rob their children of faith in God and send them back to their homes skeptical, or infidels, or agnostics, or atheists. **William Jennings Bryan**

There is no more reason to believe that man descended from some inferior animal than there is to believe that a stately mansion has descended from a small cottage. **William Jennings Bryan**

I would rather see the United States respected than loved by other nations. **Henry Cabot Lodge**

There is no worse tyranny than to force a man to pay for what he does not want merely because you think it would be good for him. **Robert Heinlein**

Socialism is a philosophy of failure, the creed of ignorance, and the gospel of envy, its inherent virtue is the equal sharing of misery. **Winston Churchill**

Never do anything against your conscience even if the State demands it. **Albert Einstein**

I would like to electrocute everyone who uses the word 'fair' in connection with income tax policies. **William F. Buckley, Jr.**

Idealism is fine, but as it approaches reality, the costs become prohibitive. **William F. Buckley, Jr.**

Democracy is an opportunity for self-discipline. **Dwight Eisenhower**

Battle is the most magnificent competition in which a human being can indulge. **George Patton**

Duty—Honor—Country. **Douglas MacArthur**

Of all tyrannies, a tyranny sincerely exercised for the good of its victims may be the most oppressive. **C.S. Lewis**

I don't feel we did wrong in taking this great country away from them. There were great numbers of people who needed new land, and the Indians were selfishly trying to keep it for themselves. **John Wayne**

It is necessary for me to establish a winner image. Therefore, I have to beat somebody. **Richard Nixon**

The trouble is where scientists speculate about theology they don't know what they're talking about because they weren't there. They can't speculate about the origins of life because they weren't there either. **Pat Robertson**

It is the soldier, not the reporter, who has given us the freedom of the press. It is the soldier, not the poet, who has given us freedom of speech. It is the soldier, not the agitator, who has given us the freedom to protest. **Zell Miller**

The whole global warming thing is created to destroy America's free enterprise system and our economic stability. **Jerry Falwell**

There is no difference between communism and socialism, except in the means of achieving the same ultimate end: communism proposes to enslave men by force, socialism—by vote. It is merely the difference between murder and suicide. **Ayn Rand**

If you kill enough of them, they stop fighting. **Curtis MeMay**

A government that is big enough to give you something is big enough to take it all away. **Barry Goldwater**

My aim is not to pass laws, but to repeal them. It is not to inaugurate new programs, but to cancel old ones. **Barry Goldwater**

Politics, it seems to me, for years, or all too long, has been concerned with right or left instead of right or wrong. **Richard Armour**

Justice is merely incidental to law and order. **J. Edgar Hoover**

We who live in free market societies believe that growth, prosperity and ultimately human fulfillment, are created from the bottom up, not the government down. **Ronald Reagan**

Freedom prospers when religion is vibrant and the rule of law under God is acknowledged. **Ronald Reagan**

The First Amendment of the Constitution was not written to protect the people of this country from religious values; it was written to protect religious values from government tyranny. **Ronald Reagan**

No government ever voluntarily reduces itself in size. Government programs, once launched, never disappear. Actually, a government bureau is the nearest thing to eternal life we'll ever see on this earth! **Ronald Reagan**

I believe more people would be alive today if there were a death penalty. **Nancy Reagan**

The problem with socialism is that you eventually run out of other people's money to spend. **Margaret Thatcher**

What kind of society isn't structured on greed? The problem of social organization is how to set up an arrangement under which greed will do the least harm; capitalism is that kind of a system. **Milton Friedman**

Democrats are people who raise your taxes and spend your money on weird stuff. They steal your guns, and they spit on your faith. **Grover Norquist**

It's about time we all faced up to the truth. If we accept the radical homosexual agenda, be it in the military or in marriage or in other areas of our lives, we are utterly destroying the concept of family. **Alan Keyes**

If America shows weakness and uncertainty, the world will drift toward tragedy. That will not happen on my watch. **George W. Bush**

Literally, if we took away the minimum wage—if conceivably it was gone—we could potentially virtually wipe out unemployment completely because we would be able to offer jobs at whatever level. **Michele Bachmann**

There is only one kind of freedom and that's individual liberty. Our lives come from our creator and our liberty comes from our creator. It has nothing to do with government granting it. **Ron Paul**

Today the primary threat to the liberties of the American people comes not from communism, foreign tyrants or dictators. It comes from the tendency on our own shores to centralize power, to trust bureaucracies rather than people. **George H. Allen**

The invisible hand of the market always moves faster and better than the heavy hand of government. **Mitt Romney**

We believe in individual initiative, personal responsibility, opportunity, freedom, small government, and the Constitution. These principles, these American principles are key to getting our economy back to being successful and leading the world. **Mitt Romney**

To achieve world government, it is necessary to remove from the minds of men their individualism, loyalty to family traditions, national patriotism, and religious dogmas. **Brock Adams**

I believe my business and non-profit investments are much more beneficial to societal well-being than sending more money to Washington. **Charles Koch**

The fight we are in here, make no mistake about it, it is a fight of individualism versus collectivism. **Paul Ryan**

There's such cultural rot taking place, such disintegration throughout our culture. Values, morality, you name it. Standards have been relaxed, and people are not being held to them. **Rush Limbaugh**

The only thing that stops a bad guy with a gun is a good guy with a gun. **Wayne LaPierre**

The American people are screaming at the top of their lungs to Washington, 'Stop! Stop the spending; stop the job-killing policies.' And yet, Democrats in Washington refuse to listen to the American people. **John Boehner**

Halloween is a liberal holiday because we're teaching our children to beg for something for free. **Sean Hannity**

We should invade their countries, kill their leaders and convert them to Christianity. We weren't punctilious about locating and punishing only Hitler and his top officers. We carpet bombed German cities; we killed civilians. That's war. And this is war. **Ann Coulter**

I oppose the attempts of homosexual activists to treat homosexual activity as a civil right to be protected and promoted by the government. **Todd Akin**

If the Supreme Court says that you have the right to consensual [gay] sex within your home, then you have the right to bigamy, you have the right to polygamy, you have the right to incest, you have the right to adultery **Rick Santorum**

Armed and law-abiding citizens are a greater deterrent to violent crime than 1,000 laws passed by Congress. **Rick Perry**

The cities and states with the toughest gun laws have the most murder and mayhem. **Mike Royko**

We could also electrify this wire (on the border) with the kind of current that would not kill somebody, but it would simply be a discouragement for them to be fooling around with it. We do that with livestock all the time. **Steve King**

People need religion. It's a vehicle for a moral tradition. A crucial role; nothing can take its place. **Irving Kristol**

We will take the power of choice away from the unions and bureaucrats. **Jeb Bush**

One of the reasons more young women are giving birth out of wedlock and more young men are walking away from their paternal obligations is that there is no longer a stigma attached to this behavior, no reason to feel shame. **Jeb Bush**

The last 15 years, there has been no recorded warming. Contrary to all the theories that they are expounding, there should have been warming over the last 15 years. It hasn't happened. **Ted Cruz**

Obamacare is really, I think, the worst thing that has happened in this nation since slavery. **Ben Carson**

We ask why there is violence in our schools, but we have systematically removed God from our schools. **Mike Huckabee**

If the Democrats want to insult women by making them believe that they are helpless without Uncle Sugar coming in and providing for them a prescription each month for birth control because they cannot control their libido or their reproductive system without the help of the government, then so be it. **Mike Huckabee**

I do not support raising the minimum wage, and the reason is as follows. When the minimum wage is raised, workers are priced out of the market. That is the economic reality that seems, at least so far, to be missing from this discussion. **John Sununu**

The danger to a black child in America is not a white police officer. The danger is another black. **Rudy Giuliani**

When Mexico sends its people, they're not sending their best. They're sending people that have lots of problems, and they're bringing those problems with them. They're bringing drugs. They're bringing crime. They're rapists. And some, I assume, are good people. **Donald Trump**

My whole life is about winning. I don't lose often. I almost never lose. **Donald Trump**

I'm the president and you're not. **Donald Trump**

Where you have the most armed citizens in America, you have the lowest violent crime rate. Where you have gun control you have the highest crime rate. **Ted Nugent**

A conservative is a liberal who got mugged the night before. **Frank Rizzo**

Fear is a good thing. Fear is going to lead you to take action. **Stephen Bannon**

We have taken God out of our education system. We have taken Him out of government. You have lawyers that sue you every time you mention the name of Jesus Christ in any public forum. **Franklin Graham**

I'm a Christian, a conservative, and a Republican, in that order. **Mike Pence**

Basic Problems for the Right

There is a core value with conservatives that makes them appear to be insensitive to those outside their group. Many on the right identify with the inspirational story of the small business person who nurtured a start-up enterprise by making many personal sacrifices and finally achieved success. It is one of those stories of the small businessperson waking up at four in the morning, worrying about how to keep the doors open, how to meet the payroll, and whether some new idea will increase the cash flow. It is the familiar story of the entrepreneur who took the risk to launch a business they hoped would bear fruit, but with many bittersweet memories of working 14-hour days, 7-day weeks. The ultimate success gave them a feeling of personal triumph and also a strong conviction that may sound inflexible to those outside the business community. The following statement appeared in the letters to the editor in a local newspaper:

> No one else knows how much work I put into this business—no one else had the determination to follow through and put their heart and soul into this operation— and it follows that no one else has the right to tell me how to run my successful business. It's mine to do with as I wish.

This feeling of pride is appreciated by all those who made this kind of effort, but it is not understood in a positive light by those who didn't go through the experience. Successful entrepreneurs feel as though they did pull themselves up by their own bootstraps. There is often an overriding belief in this idea: "I made it on my own, and I don't need to share it with anyone else." The result can lead to the appearance of strong insensitivity to those who didn't go through that process. Self-made owners of a business may have a short temper with employees who demand higher wages, neighbors who want to control industrial emissions, or a government that wants to regulate workers' safety standards.

This point of view may explain the sharp negative reactions of conservatives at the 2012 Republican National Convention who responded to the following statement made by U.S. Senator Elizabeth Warren, and then repeated later by President Barack Obama:

> If you were successful, somebody along the line gave you some help. There was a great teacher somewhere in your life. Somebody helped to create this unbelievable American system that we have that allowed you to thrive. Somebody invested in roads and bridges. If you've got a business—you didn't build that. Somebody else made that happen.

For liberals, this statement made perfect sense, but to conservatives it was blasphemy. Obama's statement violated the central idea of capitalism:

A person owns what they create—it shouldn't be subject to outside control. Liberals, on the other hand, see success as a community-wide effort that includes the entire infrastructure that made it possible, plus the schools that educated the workers. This conflict goes to the very heart of the two ideological positions. For the "job creators," as they like to call themselves, comes the assertion, "I made it on my own—it is mine and no one should tell me how I should control it." Liberals, however, see a successful private business as a part of the total society, and therefore subject to public regulation.

One way of explaining this is to use the example of Amazon, created by Jeff Bezos to market on the Internet and distribute goods to consumers all over the world. Should Bezos have total control over the business? Or does the community have a vested interest in his success because Amazon uses the public Internet to display the products and an international distribution system to deliver the products to the public? Should Bezos have the right to create a monopoly because he created the business model? How about Mark Zuckerberg and Facebook? Does the government have any legitimate rights to regulate either of them? How do we separate public interest from private property?

There are many difficult questions on this subject, yet the view from the right on private property has been consistent. Conservatives have generally rejected the idea of government intrusion and focus instead on permitting the free market forces to operate without regulation. This belief has been the cornerstone of their thinking and practice for many generations. It is repeated by virtually every Republican candidate seeking public office. The implication is that there are automatic economic forces that promote public accountability, good quality products, and stability in the market place. There is also an expectation that poor quality goods, deceptive practices, and unsafe products will be driven out of the market by free competition.

A cardinal belief is that government regulation upsets these laws of economics by injecting rules that are poorly designed that may impede real competition. The right views the marketplace as the most efficient, cost effective, and freest system in the world. There is an underlying belief that it should not be restrained. "Let the market decide" is their favorite slogan. The idea of the self-correcting marketplace has also become an important public belief for the American people. It is the most effective argument to be used against government regulation because it is a popular, sensible idea that is part of American mythology.

But liberals charge that the free-market concept can have disastrous consequences. Monopolies can exist, price fixing can occur, and dangerous goods can be produced without controls, plus unsafe working conditions can result in injuries in the workplace.

In economic affairs, there's also been a long-standing belief of moderates on the right that a broad-based prosperity would benefit everyone. It is this *establishment group* that has accepted collective bargaining on the theory that a good working relationship between management and labor benefits both sides. There's always been a moderate segment among conservatives that believed in women's rights, a progressive income tax, and free education.

But that point of view is heard less often. There's now a competing group of economic conservatives that are more controversial. They have been more stringent in promoting economic deregulation, breaking unions, underfunding public schools, cutting social programs for the poor, slashing environmental regulations, and reducing taxes for high income groups. It is the so-called 1 percent segment of conservatives that believe in a more uncompromising form of capitalism that idealizes the job creators and shows little concern for those outside the top echelons.

In addition, there are also the social conservatives. Included here are major portions of the former Democratic Solid South that is now the Republican Solid South. This group is generally unsympathetic to racial minorities, new immigrants, and the poor. They generally oppose affirmative action programs to promote racial integration. In addition, they include the traditional values of fundamentalist religious voters that oppose LBGT groups and a woman's right to an abortion. There is also a strong opposition to controls on gun ownership and the rights to carry weapons in public. They are purists, and not willing to compromise with anyone.

The result is a unique brand of pro-business policies mixed in with down-home right-wing populism, anti-gun control attitudes, and religious fundamentalism. Then add in the positions taken by Donald Trump on a multitude of issues that don't fit any ideological framework such as trade wars and dropping out of international commitments. There is not a harmonious relationship between the moderate, old-line conservatives and this newer brand. There is an intense competition within the main body of conservatism today that threatens the entire movement. It is not uncommon for contending groups to turn on each other in primary election campaigns. The question in a nutshell is how do the various wings within the conservative movement manage to compromise and maintain a workable coalition? How can compromising moderates maintain a union with fundamentalists who distrust the practice of compromising?

There is a built-in problem for moderate conservatives to mount a national campaign and carry both sides into a coalition. Campaign statements that please one segment of the electronic may drive other voters away. What follows is a graphic example of a Republican candidate who found that his assets turned out to be his liabilities.

Mitt Romney

As a political person, Mitt Romney is an American success story. He is an extremely likable family-man who did well financially because he worked hard through the system. After amassing a sizable personal fortune, he turned to politics and became a pragmatic leader who could appeal to people in both political parties.

Early in his career Romney had a reputation as being a bipartisan. He registered as an independent and sometimes voted for Democrats. Later he became the Republican governor of Massachusetts, a very Democratic state. To the surprise of many, Romney proposed and implemented a health insurance system (similar to Obamacare) for the people of his state. He was a moderate Republican with a progressive record on social issues.

From a distance, Romney fit the ideal of a hard-working, sensible leader who proved he could make money, behave in a bipartisan manner, win an election in a Democratic state, and propose health care legislation that would benefit working-class people. In addition, he had an exemplary wife and family. He was also a Mormon who proved he could win votes among Catholics and mainstream Protestant voters.

But Romney is a prime example of the problem that successful business conservatives have when they run for public office. There is a chink in the armor of many wealthy Republicans when they face liberal Democrats in an election campaign. Even though Romney was strong in the polls, he was defeated in a 1994 bid for the U.S. Senate by Ted Kennedy in Massachusetts, and he also lost the 2012 his presidential bid to Barack Obama.

In both campaigns the Democratic candidates concentrated on the specific methods Romney used in building his wealth through Bain Capital, a private equity investment firm. According to the Democratic opposition research, Bain's typical approach was to engage in leveraged buyouts of companies, forcing them into debt, and then selling the companies at a profit after the firms had to lay off workers to avoid bankruptcy.

A Democratic 30-second TV ad featured workers who lost their jobs saying, Bain "came in and sucked the life out of us." The voice-over political message concluded, "You can tell by the way he acts, he doesn't care about working-class people."

Bain Capital and Mitt Romney acted entirely within the law, but the paid ads turned Romney's record of success into a liability. It made his business practices appear to be heartless and immoral. The average voter was suspicious of someone who they thought could amass a fortune by getting other people fired. His ideal qualifications in a successful business career didn't stand up to 30-second ads that told a very slanted side of the story.

In addition, it was revealed that Romney paid a tax rate of only 14.1 percent on an income of $13.7 million in 2011. According to Democrats, that tax rate was lower than a voter would pay who made only $50,000 a year. Also, it was charged that Romney had shifted some of his assets off-shore to avoid paying higher taxes. In both cases, Romney's actions were completely legal though these two issues were used against him.

And finally, Romney made a huge tactical blunder that probably cost him the election. He was recorded while speaking at a $50,000 per plate private fundraising dinner, saying that 47 percent of the people pay no income taxes and would vote for Obama because they saw themselves as "victims," dependent on the government for "health care, food, and housing." He was obviously addressing his remarks to the 1 percent faction in the room, and did not realize that he was really being heard by the whole world. A recorded video, made from a cell phone, was played again and again by the media and the Obama campaign. The 47 percent comment played directly into the stereotype of being the 1 percent rich guy that looked down on the average voter.

The crux of the problem for Romney and other conservatives is that their political/economic practices, pronouncements, and values are acceptable only at a distance in American politics. Everyone believes a citizen has every right to make a maximum profit within the law and legally to pay as little tax as possible, but the problem for wealthy Republicans is that very few voters can actually identify with being a millionaire. Average people don't have an income of $13.7 million a year, and only a tiny segment of the voters shift some of their assets off-shore for tax purposes. While most Americans admire success, they are suspicious of anyone who has that much wealth, and who can use the tax laws to pay such a low tax rate.

On paper, Mitt Romney was the perfect candidate in terms of his demeanor and temperament. But the very qualities of his millionaire personal success story became his major shortcoming. In the closing days of the campaign, the Obama television ads defined Romney as a man who didn't care about other people—not a good image for someone seeking the presidency.

Successful conservative Republicans look great in theory; they are venerated by nearly everyone who would love to have that much wealth. But liberal Democratic campaign advisors developed the message that anyone who has that much money must have exploited others on their way up. When rich Republicans run for office, there is a near automatic charge that they must have cut some ethical corners in their business practices. And, in a political campaign, the appearance of irregularities is more important than the reality of a situation.

The same problem exists for wealthy conservatives even if they are not running for office. The whole philosophy of free-market capitalism is criticized for being uncaring to lower-income groups. There is a general feeling that no one should have that much while others are scraping by just to put food on the table.

It is, of course, an important contradiction in this situation because the average person admires entrepreneurs as the engines of our economic system. It is assumed by the general public that the captains of industry and commerce deserve their wealth because they create new businesses and add jobs to the economy. But there is a fine line between success and excessive wealth—even if it's legal. Most conservative business-types are frustrated by this public relations problem because they usually follow the letter of the law so they shouldn't have to apologize for being successful. Moderates on the right get angry because they are proud of their success and therefore not very careful about showing their wealth in public. They seldom take care to avoid the role of the rich guy who doesn't care about the average person. It is a problem that leftist politicians will always exploit in a political campaign.

Revolutionaries on the Right

There is an enormous difference between regular conservatives (including Donald Trump and the Freedom Caucus) when compared to the extreme right-wing revolutionary brand, and it relates to the willingness to use violence. Real revolutionary reactionaries are ready to use guns and bombs to gain their objectives. They have no qualms about endangering human lives. Their goal is often to eliminate a particular race, religious or ethnic group from the general population.

Rank and file right-wing revolutionaries are generally drawn from the lower-economic class with backgrounds involving some level of personal struggles in their lives. They are frustrated by current events and want sweeping changes in society. They are staunch defenders of their region or nation despite the fact that they may be looked down upon by local upper-class people with power and prestige. It is ironic that revolutionaries from the lower reaches of society are more willing than anyone else to lay down their lives to restore their view of past greatness. It is a unique combination of intense patriotism and lower-class status.

I spent a few days with the Oakland chapter of Hells Angels in the early 1970s. I was interested to learn that most of the renegade motorcycle bikers supported the right-wing causes of the day. They told President Nixon they were "volunteering for combat" in Southeast Asia, and were ready to go to Vietnam (behind the lines) and "throw the fear of God into the Viet Cong." According to them, the White House never responded to their offer.

In an earlier era, Mark Twain had a very unfavorable view of self-appointed guardians of the nation. He wrote, "Patriotism is the refuge for scoundrels." Twain questioned the right of anyone to use violence to save the country from (what they consider) to be a shameful path. The idealism of the revolutionary on this side of the spectrum is framed by a strongly worded, highly nationalistic declaration to purge and cleanse society from unwanted elements. This group has been the core of fascism both at home and abroad.

Prime examples of the revolutionary reactionary group are the neo–Nazis, skinheads, and Ku Klux Klan members who are drawn together to fight a common enemy. They have high levels of anger and aggression against (what they consider to be) an inferior element that must be eradicated by force. More than anything, they want to eliminate inferior people who are responsible for all that has gone wrong. What starts out as segregating the "inferior people" in public can end up by pushing them into gas chambers. There is slippery slope for hard-core right-wing revolutionaries that can end in crimes against humanity.

A major focus for the right-wing revolutionary is to expose the decadence of the present and set out a specific doctrine that will reclaim a purity of purpose. They tell terrible stories about how society is rotten to the core and how it must be purified by a violent revolution. There is a revulsion towards all that has decayed morally, religiously and politically. Right-wing revolutionaries have a list of the traitors at the top who (they think) have deliberately sabotaged a once-superior culture by letting in inferior foreigners and/or non-believers. They are ready to name those people that have sold out the country.

These revolutionaries are also outraged by ordinary people who have lost their sense of loyalty to the original political and/or religious beliefs, and who no longer have strong moral values. Folks with a lot of personal problems can find a calling in life as patriots that will save their country. It can elevate a person overnight as they are dedicated to rooting out turncoats that have corrupted society. People with low self-esteem can gain a sense of pride and self-importance. It's a heady experience to be the self-appointed savior of your country.

Right-wing revolutionaries demand harsh penalties against their "enemies," and do not hesitate to kill those who stand in their way. The expectation is that only a violent revolution will reclaim the former path to greatness. To that end, these zealots amass weapons for a violent overthrow of the present government. They believe sincerely that assassination and armed insurrection are the only tactics that will purge society and restore a magnificent past. This is the mindset of fascists around the world.

The following 10 typical goals are supported by revolutionaries on the right:

- Remove all restrictions on owning and using firearms.
- Prohibit the use of any cultural practices that originate in foreign countries.
- Use force to stop illegal immigration and deport inferior aliens.
- Protect the preferred race by prohibiting interracial marriage.
- Block persons of other religions, cultures and races from entering the country.
- Require lessons of strict patriotism to be taught in all schools.
- Maintain national interests abroad by using overwhelming military force.
- Build and maintain a well-armed citizen army to seize power at home.
- Defeat all rival ideological groups around the world.
- Target state and federal agencies that threaten our patriotic groups.

Right-wing revolutionary groups are always in the wings when democracies begin to fail. Hitler's Germany may be the best example of a leader who established a fascist totalitarian regime by feeding on the frustrations of a desperate people looking for order in a democracy that was in chaos. There was also much turmoil in Mussolini's Italy and Franco's Spain. It was a time when a gang leader on the street could become a leader that could change the world. Everyone should remember that no democratic country is totally immune to fascism.

In the 1930s, American novelist Sinclair Lewis was disturbed by the rise of Hitler. He worried in his writings that an opportunistic politician could lead the United States down the same path without firing a shot. In his 1935 book, *It Can't Happen Here*, Lewis wrote, "When fascism comes to America it will be wrapped in the flag and carrying a cross." Lewis imagined a brash character with a mix of crude language and racist rhetoric combined with a dose of down-home Christianity. The main character was a spell-binding presidential candidate who was the master of mass rallies. Lewis warned readers that the United States was "so flabby that any gang daring enough and unscrupulous enough, and smart enough not to seem illegal, could grab hold of the entire government." Does that sound familiar?

The message of Sinclair Lewis is that right-wing fascism could be wrapped up in a popular package by an unprincipled demagogue. He emphasized that most people wouldn't think it could happen here until it was too late. What do you think?

Problems for Revolutionary Reactionaries

On the right end of the spectrum there's been a blurring between what some call hard-core activists and the more extreme variety of self-proclaimed revolutionaries. There's always the question of who is really a real revolutionary. Is it necessary to carry through with actual violence against people, or is threatening violence enough to put a person in that category? Sometimes violence can be on a sliding scale—beating up folks versus killing them in cold blood. How do we categorize individuals in a torch-light rally who advocate killing members of a particular ethnic group? How real does the threat have to be? What does society do with those who declare they are ready to kill others, but haven't done it yet?

Not long ago, a man in a rural area of Oregon warned a local sheriff that he was going to start a "bloodbath" by killing every law enforcement officer he could find. He bragged that he had a semi-automatic rifle and more than 1,000 rounds of ammunition. The sheriff locked him up, but the next question is what to do with armed people who have threatened to shoot other people, but haven't started shooting yet? A few days later, the sheriff had to let him go. As far as I know the man with the guns hasn't changed his mind.

There are some who say an armed citizenry is the most important characteristic of a democracy. There is the belief, in some quarters, that real liberty exists only when the government is afraid of the citizens. An ever-increasing number of right-wing groups are brandishing guns on the proposition that they are the only reason why some measure of liberty has been preserved. They go on to say that the government is trying to disarm them—they see themselves as the defenders of everyone else. From their vantage point, they are the only true patriots against a government that is coming after their guns. Charlton Heston, one-time president of the National Rifle Association, made this point to a cheering crowd at an NRA national convention: "I will give up my gun when they peel off my cold dead fingers around it."

The warning is also heard that the government is coming after your guns, but it is interesting to note that the only president who threated to take away guns was Donald Trump after the Parkland, Florida, school shootings in 2018. Strangely, after Trump made his threat, the NRA endorsed him again; the reason given was that Trump didn't "really mean what he said."

Does the First Amendment freedom of speech provision protect those who are plotting an overthrow of the government to save the Second Amendment? If so, how long does the government have to wait before it can defend itself against real revolutionaries? These are difficult questions that are being asked now by law enforcement officials.

Taking the law into your own hands is becoming more common in American society. Self-styled armed militia groups patrol the U.S. border with Mexico, ready to shoot those who would come into the U.S. illegally. Physicians who perform abortions have been assassinated by extremists. There have been armed stand-offs between federal officials and armed western ranchers against the Bureau of Land Management. The FBI and other agencies are watching a significant number of Americans who have vowed to take up arms against those they oppose.

Scores of armed, right-wing splinter groups such as the Ku Klux Klan and Nazi Party strongly identify with the symbolism of American culture. The American flag is displayed at their rallies. They voice a strong commitment to the U.S. Constitution, and a clear devotion to the Christian religion. Extreme right groups of this kind have a hometown advantage in many communities. Because of the emphasis on American symbols, there is usually some latent local support among many who conclude, "What's the harm in backing a group that's pro–American?" The result has been that a collection of homegrown right-wing groups have come to dominate state and local politics in many areas.

Virtually every time I have been with right-wing activists, I've noticed a tendency for them to imagine problems that aren't generally recognized by the rest of the population. Some quote President Trump in saying that left-wing folks vote several times by going to their cars to change their clothes. Many believe that foreigners can vote and change an election outcome, and that transgender people are lurking in restrooms just to watch little girls or women undress. The fact that these things aren't happening does not discourage the anger that can be generated. Often there is a tendency for ordinary folks to believe the worst. Some people seem to enjoy hearing stories about the awful things that are going on. It's the kind of story that is told by the guy sitting at the end of the bar in a local tavern. What starts out as an outrageous allegation goes mainstream in many localities.

The imagined problem can be enlarged to meet the needs of the moment. Make-believe stories are discussed as the storyteller talks about what should be done to those who threaten public morality. It is one of those situations where individuals (usually men) can boast about what they would do if an imaginary incident arose. It is especially satisfying for a man (with no particular personal achievements) to present himself as the defender of Christianity, white womanhood, the integrity of elections, and American culture. Being a savior of your country beats trying to explain personal failures. It makes a man feel important.

The Ku Klux Klan

My personal experience with the Klan grew out of a series of interviews I did several years ago with Klan members after mass rallies in Louisiana and Mississippi. I had some apprehension going to these rallies because of the violent reputation of the Klan, but I soon discovered that they were mostly ordinary, hometown people who were the product of their own communities.

At the time, I was working as a freelance journalist, which was perceived by Klansmen as a great opportunity for press coverage. My approach was strictly objective, asking open-ended questions so they could tell their story. I worked by myself with nothing but my press credentials, a ballpoint pen, and a reporter's notebook. I was a northerner with Oregon auto license plates so there was always some suspicion of why I was there. I introduced myself as "Bill," and I was surprised that they usually remembered my name throughout our conversations.

Klan members were understandably cautious because there had been many attempts by law enforcement agents to infiltrate their ranks. For this reason, I never asked for names and they, in turn, were careful not to give me any details about themselves. My questions were always general in nature. I always made it a practice to present myself honestly because I had nothing to hide. I learned early on in life, when doing interviews with folks on the extreme right and left, always tell the truth. If they catch you in a lie there could be a real problem.

These Klan get-togethers were clearly a chance for the whole family to come out and talk about issues that concerned them all. There were an unusually large number of young men present. Some Klansmen had on the full regalia of gowns and hoods, but nearly all the people were just in street clothes. I didn't stand out as an outsider in the crowd, and contrary to my earlier feelings, I felt completely safe.

The four Klan rallies I attended were very similar, featuring a speaker from out of town who would excite the crowd with condemnations of the civil rights leaders, the so-called Jewish conspiracy, and the intrusive actions of the federal government. These mass meetings were held during the early summer; all them were outside in open fields at the edge of small towns. There were homemade signs posted as to the time and place of each gathering. I was always on the lookout for these signs along the road that directed me into small towns off the major highways.

My tactic was to ask questions to men standing near me about who was speaking and what was going on locally. Typically, I would say something like, "Boy this is quite a turnout," before asking anything about the rally itself. The northern accent of an outsider always made heads turn. My introduction to them was, I am writing for a newspaper in Oregon, which was true. I had press credentials, but no one ever asked to see them.

Sometimes I asked about the local high school football team, which always got a quick response. When a person is alone, it's amazing how fast one can strike up a conversation with total strangers. People love to talk, especially about what makes them proud or angry. The pride was in being white and anger was about national political leaders. These two themes were woven into all the speeches at the Klan rallies. From their point of view, their local way of life was being threatened, and coming to the rally was one way they could express their fears about the present. The Klan also "passed the hat" to support their activities

As each event was winding down, I would continue to talk to men in small groups at the meeting site, in parking lots, on park benches, and in one case at a local tavern. There was always a thin line on when to stop asking questions; instinctively I knew when I was pushing them too far. I was alone in their town and it was important to not attract unwanted attention.

Those who attended the rallies always turned the topic to race relations and the federal government trying to shove integration "down their throats." The conversation focused on their hatred of black civil rights leaders and their delight in the assassination of Martin Luther King.

When asked, I told them that I was writing for several newspapers in Oregon. My role was to ask questions and never argue. I was the uninformed northerner who obviously didn't know much about the South; the questions were all soft-ball inquires under the general heading of, "how do you feel about that?" All my contacts were with young men in street clothes who took this an opportunity to tell their story. Generally, the longer we talked the more comfortable was the conversation.

Only on one occasion did I speak briefly to a Klansman who was dressed in robes. That was a very different experience. I soon discovered how intimidating it was to make eye contact with a person wearing a hood with eye holes cut out. Seeing the dim outline of the eyes and hearing a deep voice coming from inside made me wonder if I was safe speaking to someone who advocated violence, or perhaps had engaged in some actions against victims. I had no specific reason to feel threatened, but the whole regalia made my blood pressure go up a few points. The man in his robes spoke with a little more authority than the others. He especially wanted to know more about me and why I was there.

It was that this point that I realized that the Klan had a certain mystique designed to terrify an outsider like me. There was something about the hood that sent shivers down my spine. Afterwards I imagined what it must be like to be an African-American or a Jewish person to face this figure on a back street in a small town, and to remember that local law enforcement officials weren't known for protecting a stranger with a northern accent.

All the Klan members brought up the defender role as their purpose for being. Usually it was protecting white women from black men who they imagined were just waiting to rape "their women." The stories were long on emotional anger and short on specifics. It reminded me of the kinds of stories one would hear in a high school boys' locker room that were embellished to make them more interesting. But there was a kind of thrill to be at a Klan meeting where everyone really enjoyed being jacked up by stories that were based more on fear than fact.

The issue of "race-mixing" came up in every rally. One speaker up on stage likened it to letting a "mongrel bull" get loose with defenseless, "pure-bred cows." In small groups it was discussed as the most disgusting thing one could imagine. There was always a sexual connotation, and there was always a theme of defending of the "white race." The fear was the intentional weakening of the white race by "Jews" and "Niggers." It was described as an insidious plan that ordinary people wouldn't know about unless they came to a Klan meeting.

One night, after a rally, there were five young men in street clothes who sat outside with me on a park bench about 30 yards from the burning cross that cast a bright glow over the departing crowd. One of the younger men said he felt like the Civil Rights Movement was "threatening his way of life" and that he had to "fight back." Another said black people were getting financial help from "New York Jews." The five men displayed their own uncertainties, saying that they were really on their own with no "outside help." It seemed a great irony that these working-class men, who liked to talk about terrorizing black people, had cast themselves in the role of American patriots. The burning cross, just a short distance away, seemed to give them a sense of self-importance in being involved in a cause that was bigger than life.

In another group, one man asked if I would try to reach northerners to tell them about the dangers of the Civil Rights Movement. He said the Klan was just trying to "save America." He feared what he called, "the mongrelization of America," where the white race would cease to exist because of interracial sex. When this man spoke of "defending our women," everyone else nodded their heads. There was the continuous theme of "standing up for America." They saw themselves in a lonely struggle with no support coming from the rest of the country.

In each of these conversations I brought up the question of why Klan members felt so strongly about opposing integration. They had an eager response: first came the denial that they "hated" anyone even though I had not used the word. Next there was a condemnation of the media that they said focused on the few cases of violence that had occurred. But the main message always turned to being forced to go to school with "Niggers."

One thing I noticed was that the topics were always discussed in absolute terms with no gray areas. There were no doubts about the political scene. Washington, D.C., was the "hotbed" of enemies; the Congress, White House and the Supreme Court—all sympathetic to "Kikes, Niggers, and Papists." The Klan was the only group that they could depend on. As the evening progressed, they relished telling personal stories about how their "daddies" had raised them to defend the white race and stand up for America. Then they asked me the question, "Wouldn't you stand up for your family?" Of course, I had to nod and agree.

There was an ever-present sense of history in the discussions. The aftermath of "The War Between the States" was brought up as an example of how the rest of the country was insensitive to their needs as a people. Several times they spoke of how Christians in the South had been a friend to "Negroes," and how secure and orderly life had been for black people before the Civil Rights Movement. The message was that northerners were badly "misinformed" about history. Newspapers like the *New York Times* and *Washington Post* were the main culprits.

No one mentioned slavery, but it was lurking in every conversation as they discussed how it "used to be." Phrases like, "we all got along real well" were code for defending the Old South. I could sense that segregation had a psychological value to these unskilled white men who were near the bottom of the social structure. It must be satisfying for members of the Klan to have someone beneath them.

But at other times the conversations were a bit more threatening. The night I went to a local tavern was different from all the other evenings. That night, everyone had several beers as we sat at a table over in the corner near the shuffle board. I had one beer all night long. After two hours or so, the increasing number of beers seemed to make everyone a bit more confrontational. They spoke of "Niggers," and what they would do to get one alone on a dark street. In their excitement, they leaned forward and involuntarily spit in my face. At this point I stopped asking questions; they were interrupting each other in a continuous lecture about what the Klan would do to local black people they mentioned by name. The language got stronger and stronger. Taking notes was not appropriate. I just sat back and listened.

As the night wore on, individual members said they had to go home because tomorrow was a work day. Finally, there was just one man left with me at the table. The bartender said he wanted to close so we walked outside. At this point a small house cat walked up to us and rubbed against the other man's leg. While continuing to talk (he looked me straight in the eye), he reached down and picked up the cat and rung its neck, then dropped the dead cat on the sidewalk.

I was horrified, saying, "Why the hell did you do that?" His response, "It was only a cat." I asked again, and this time he seemed a bit put-off by my anger. Suddenly, I realized the ease with which he killed the cat, and I was struck by fear for my own safety. Never before have I seen such a cold, uncaring look in someone's eye. It almost seemed like a warning to me.

I raised my voice, saying, "That's it," as I walked away in disgust. The last thing I heard him say was, "But it was only a cat."

I drove to the next town looking for a motel. I didn't feel safe anymore in that community. That was my last Klan meeting. I still remember it like it was yesterday.

Despite their constant use of pro–American symbols, right-wing revolutionaries like the Klan have one large problem—difficulty in gaining a national following. While revolutionary reactionaries have attracted large groups in the past, mainstream America is turned off by internal violence. Average Americans are horrified by political massacres, bombings and assassinations. It is ironic that right-wing revolutionaries often believe violent acts will gain them recognition, but these kinds of acts almost always turn the public against them.

The Oklahoma City Federal Building bombing in 1995 was a case in point. The bombers, Timothy McVeigh and Terry Nichols, thought the bombing would activate others who wanted to attack the federal government. McVeigh said it was a "retaliatory strike" against federal agents who he called "fascist storm troopers." Actually, the bombing and inflammatory language brought about a sweeping rejection of anyone who would kill innocent men, women and children for a cause that had virtually no public support. McVeigh was executed for his role in the bombing and Nichols went to federal prison for life.

The aftermath of the bombing illustrated again that average people may sympathize with critics of the government, but they draw a sharp line when organized violence is employed. There are still pockets of right-wing militias that believe they are trying to "save America" through violent acts. The biggest problem for them is that so few people will follow them.

Questions for You

1. In your judgement, why is a sense of individualism so important for persons on the right? What evidence do you see that conservatives are focused on expanding the rights of individuals rather than the community? What is your reaction to this characteristic?

2. Read the 20 examples of policy objectives for the right and far right. Which one do you agree with the most? Why? Which one do you disagree with the most? Why?

3. Read through the 80+ individual statements in the "In Their Own Words" section. Do you generally agree with most of those statements? Which statement do you agree with most? Why? Which statement do you disagree with most? Why?

4. What does the letter-writer mean in the statement, "I made it on my own and I don't need to share it with anyone else?" Why does this statement bring out such sharp disagreement from liberals? Do you think private companies such as Amazon and Facebook should be subject to public regulation?

5. What elements of conservativism do you agree with the most? Which ideas from the right do you disagree with the most? What is your reaction to the so-called 1 percent group of conservatives?

6. What are the major factions within the conservative coalition? Why does the competing nature of groups within the body make it difficult for main-line conservatives to mount a national political campaign? How has Donald Trump affected conservatism?

7. In what way does the Mitt Romney example illustrate the problem for conservatives to win a national election? Do you have a recommendation on how wealthy candidates can avoid the rich guy image? How did Trump deal with his "rich guy image?"

8. Do you find it to be an interesting contradiction that right-wing revolutionaries usually come from lower-income groups and left-wing revolutionaries usually come from middle-class intellectuals? Why, in your judgment, is it not the reverse?

9. Google Mark Twain's quotation on patriotism. What is your reaction to the idea that patriotism can be "a refuge for scoundrels?" Do you think this is an accurate appraisal? Why or why not?

10. Read the typical goals of revolutionary reactionaries. Do you generally agree or disagree with these goals? Why or why not?

11. What is your response to *It Can't Happen Here* by Sinclair Lewis? Specifically, what do you think about the statement, "When fascism comes to America it will be wrapped in a flag and carrying a cross?" Do you take this prophesy seriously, or do you think it is an overly dramatic comment of little value?

12. In what way do the theories of right-wing revolutionaries stated earlier match the interview with members of the Ku Klux Klan? Why do you think that the segregation of the races was a "satisfying relationship" for white working-class men?

How Do You React to Right-Wing Values?

Select one statement from the "In Their Own Words" section and present a convincing argument as to why you believe that statement *is not true*. Provide examples to support your point of view.

Select one statement from the "In Their Own Words" section and present a convincing argument as to why you believe that statement *is true*. Provide examples to support your point of view.

Do you see an ideological connection between the middle-right and the revolutionary-right? On which points do they agree?

8

Ideas and People
Move to the Right

There is another phenomenon in operation on the spectrum that happens so quietly that few people take notice. Within their lifetime, many people move across the political spectrum from left to right. With little fanfare, the young idealist, who may have embraced radical ideas, begins to turn slowly toward liberal causes, and finally, in advanced years, emerges as a conservative or even a reactionary.

The old maxim often quoted by conservatives on age and politics says it well:

He who is eighteen and not a radical has no heart.
He who is forty and not a conservative has no head.

There are several reasons for this phenomenon. First, history shows us that many ideas move from the left to right in politics. What was once a radical notion may be enacted into law a few years later by liberals and conservatives, and finally, after several decades later, defended by reactionaries. A prime example of this occurred in the American Women's Movement.

Before 1900, only a small band of radical women were pressing for the right to vote. Many men and some women resisted the idea. It was predicted by some that it would never be accepted by good women who "knew their place." But, after winning the right to vote, the practice slowly became more respectable across the nation. Today virtually all men and women accept the idea of a woman's right to vote.

Over the years, people became more accustomed to women voting—time made it more acceptable. But another major reason why the right to vote for women is no longer controversial is that radical women continued seeking new goals such as the widespread distribution of birth control information, the legalization of abortion, equal pay, an end to sexual abuse, and finally the move to add an Equal Rights Amendment to the U.S. Constitution.

These new topics made the old issue of voting rights appear less threatening. Proponents of equal rights demand full equality in employment, property rights, and prohibition of all sexual discrimination practices. By comparison, the right to vote now seems to be pretty non-controversial.

It is apparent that there are a number of women's issues still to be developed, and if the past is a guide, we will continue to see the movement of ideas from the left to the right. As in the past, the threat of newer ideas today lends greater acceptance to the radical ideas of yesterday. This same phenomenon is common in other areas of politics. Many policies and practices in government today began as an idealistic goal of a small group on the left, such as:

- Social security for the elderly.
- Same-sex marriage.
- Paid maternity leave.
- Civil rights for blacks and other minorities.
- A progressive income tax.
- Unemployment insurance.
- Animal rights.
- Voting rights for people without property.
- Rights of lesbian, bisexual, gay, and transgender people (LBGT).
- Separation of church and state.
- Legalization of abortion.
- Universal health care.
- Teaching of evolution in schools.
- Rights to organize labor unions.

This does not mean that all new ideas began on the left, nor does it mean that every idea promoted by the left will eventually be accepted on the right. The Equal Rights Amendment was a case in point. It was first proposed in 1923 and was approved by both houses of Congress in 1972, but it failed to be ratified by the states by the 1979 deadline. Another effort was made in 1982 to extend the deadline, but no more states chose to ratify the proposed amendment.

In recent times there has been a variety of groups attempting constitutional amendments to accomplish some changes in the law. The following are just some of the more notable proposed amendments:

- Legalizing prayer in public schools.
- Term-limits for members of Congress and state legislatures.
- Restricting campaign contributions.
- Declaring that human life begins at conception.
- Legislative district boundaries to be drawn by nonpartisan commission.

- Decriminalizing the use of marijuana.
- Defining marriage as being between one man and one woman.
- Direct election of the president by popular vote.
- Requiring a balanced federal budget.
- Banning capital punishment.
- Prohibiting the early release of convicted criminals.

The above is but a partial list of some of the serious attempts to amend the constitution. As one notices immediately, not all of them have originated on the left. But the trend of most successful political change coming from the left is clearly visible. Many of the controversial issues of the past are now established either by law or custom.

Public Reactions

Despite the enactment of new laws and the acceptance of new social codes, it should be noted that this process of political change is a source of enormous conflict. The following is a transcript from a recent local radio call-in show:

> It's so different now. Younger people just don't have the same values. Women act just like men. Black people want the jobs we have had for years. There are gay rights rallies right here in town. On television they show things that just aren't good for some people to see. When I was young, they just didn't do things like that. I just don't know what's happening to this country!

If a person lives a full lifetime (seventy years or more), he or she is likely to become a bit grumpy about recent changes. Some of these changes are a direct challenge to personal habits and beliefs that may be a part of family or religious training. Because of the tempo of change, it is somewhat unusual for an older person not to be upset by recent developments. Every generation in history has expressed alarm in how younger people no longer seemed to believe in things that "made this country great." Going back to the past has always been a safe proposal for political leaders.

Frequently, there is a direct backlash against the trend of change. In recent times, strong movements have developed to:

- Outlaw affirmative action programs.
- Pass laws that make it more difficult for minorities to vote.
- Restore the death penalty for serious offenses.
- Close down environmental agencies.
- Repeal and replace Obamacare.
- Deport recent immigrants.
- Close down abortion clinics.

- Reinstate prayer in public school.
- Ban same-sex marriage.
- Sell off federal lands for development.
- Weaken collective bargaining rights.
- Abolish the sale of birth control devices.

On social, economic, and political issues, an individual cannot stand still for very long. If a person maintains the same position over a period of several years, they will likely move to the right because new issues continue to press in from the left. This is especially true for political leaders with careers that span several decades. It is not uncommon for yesterday's liberals to be challenged today from the far left on the grounds that they have stood still, and are therefore too conservative in their outlook. Throughout the world, issues and people march to the right.

Self-Interest

Another factor that explains the movement of ideas on the spectrum is that individuals and organizations change their political philosophy to fit their economic situation. Movement to the right often occurs when a person abandons a leftist position held during personal hard times and substitutes a right-wing approach after attaining wealth and status. Financial rewards have a way of reducing one's interest in political change or reform. The labor movement is a prime example. One of the characteristics of labor has been the tendency of workers and their leaders to set aside their struggling spirit once they attain affluence. Some unions have moved from the position of genuine revolutionary radicals of the 1890s to a new situation of favoring conservative economic programs. This has been especially true among the rank-and-file members trying to block minorities and women from entering the labor market.

A major portion of the labor movement was spawned by revolutionary radicals who battled the police out on the picket line, but today they are moving more toward the middle of the spectrum. This is especially true in Britain where the name *New Labour* is used, in part, to suggest this major political party has moved away from its old radical roots. Labor today in Western democracies has become establishment—its basic economic needs have been secured by law. What began as an idealistic revolt has turned into a defense of gains achieved through collective bargaining, union contracts, and large pension funds. Labor's fervor has been diluted by success.

Violence still occurs on the picket line, but it now has a more institutionalized flavor; current conflicts between labor and management are seldom over ideological differences. Most strikes are void of political struggle and passion. Workers have specific pocketbook demands that hinge on negotiations, not upheaval. There is little interest in using their organization as a vehicle of political protest. Indeed, many union members are more conservative than management on the issues of civil liberties, aid to the poor, and hiring of minorities. There is little of the social consciousness remaining that was so prevalent in the unions of the 1930s.

Betrayal of Principles

Crusading religious and social institutions also move to the right. Many religions were founded by humanistic persons who preached equality and social progress. Their first followers were mostly poor people without power. The original leaders identified with the cause of the downtrodden, but over the years, these churches gained converts among the wealthy and powerful. Then the process of reinterpretation of principles began. After they became owners of property and large buildings, many churches had something to *conserve*. In many areas of the world, churches are well-known defenders of large landowners and military generals at the expense of the poor and the weak. It is an irony that some churches are now close allies to the authoritarian regimes that regularly oppose movements to aid the poor and underprivileged.

There is nearly always a great contrast between the original values of older ideological groups and the actual practices of the present. As the system moves to the right, the original principles are still repeated but seldom taken seriously. In older political systems, proponents of reform often come from the ranks of youthful idealists who have studied the original teachings of aging institutions. One of the major sources of left-wing movements today comes from young radicals invoking the ideals of a past revolution. They note the justification for sweeping reform cited by the founders of the system, take it seriously, and try to apply it to the present.

This tendency for organizations and political systems to drift to the right has been noted for many years. Thomas Jefferson, author of the *American Declaration of Independence,* noted that the leaders of political movements had an almost natural inclination to betray their principles after taking power. For that reason, Jefferson concluded that a revolution was necessary about every twenty years just to keep the leaders accountable to the principles of the system.

Jefferson was correct in his assessment. In real life, revolutionary regimes unusually fail to follow through on important promises. They also act quickly to close the door on anyone who wants to overthrow the government. The world is full of right-wing military-type juntas that began years ago when revolutionaries smashed a similar government. There's always a rhythm to the process as the next revolution is brewing in the wings.

Change and contradiction seem to be the constants of human affairs, and the political spectrum is a useful instrument to chart their movement. Pressure from the new ideas pushes old principles to the right. What seemed impossible a decade ago is now accepted because the old idea has been around for a time, and because an even more threatening idea has been introduced on the far left. The process has been occurring for centuries, but few seem to recognize it operating in their own lifetime. The political spectrum is one way of visualizing how yesterday's radicals in religion, politics, and economics have become the heroes of today's reactionaries.

During most of recorded history, strong governments in most parts of the world were dominated by royalty, church leaders, large land owners, or wealthy aristocrats. These folks used the political system to protect their interests, and to hold back the vast majority of people who had little political power, and almost no access to governmental decision-making.

Large central governments in early history usually served the interest of the monarchy and the established church. Institutions dominated by the well-born were thought to be the only hope for civilization. The common person was considered unfit to participate in political decision-making. The class system in most parts of the world afforded political power, wealth, and prestige only to those at the top. Most opportunities of life were enjoyed by elites in the upper echelons of society. The central government gave the aristocratic class the cloak of authority to continue in this elevated position for centuries.

Early theorists on the left were born into a world in which a large central government was an instrument of the privileged few on the right. In response to this situation, the left voiced a belief that the role of government should be reduced because, in their experience, government had always been the oppressor of the lower classes, the poor, and those without property. Early political leaders of the left proposed that the general powers of government be reduced so that freedom would prevail. There was an overall expectation that individual freedom would increase as the powers of government were diminished. Freedom, it was argued on the left, could only exist in the absence of governmental restrictions.

During early history two basic positions prevailed in Western politics. Put simply:

- The left opposed strong central governments because they seldom had any political influence in the system, and it usually acted against their interests.
- The right supported strong central governments because they usually dominated the political system and the policies usually favored their interests.

Revolution of the Right or Left?

The great hope of the American Revolution was that conditions would improve when the powers of government were diffused and diminished. But the experiment failed. The Declaration of Independence of 1776 had broken English rule in the 13 colonies, but the act of gaining freedom from a strong governing power didn't assure tranquility or prosperity.

While the revolution was still in progress, the 13 states met and formulated the Articles of Confederation (1781–1787) as their new national government. The Articles, launched in 1781, were designed to maintain the sovereign powers of each of the independent states. In their eagerness to be free, the central government was not given the crucial powers to regulate commerce, to set the value of currency, and to collect taxes. While some individuals prospered at the state level, there was widespread chaos across the land. Money values fluctuated wildly between the 13 states, tariff barriers were set up that restricted commerce, and the national government (with no dependable source of revenue) went deeply into debt.

Independence under a weak national government was a mixed blessing for the typical American. There was a legendary account of a chicken farmer in New Jersey who had a thriving business before the revolution crossing the Hudson River to sell chickens and eggs in New York City. But the farmer went bankrupt because the New York legislature set up a tariff (tax on incoming goods) to protect their chicken farmers from competition. It wasn't long before trade dried up between states because individual states were afraid to open their borders to free trade. The new American republic was off to a rocky start.

The central government (under the Articles of Confederation) was unable to act to restore an orderly trade between citizens of different states, it could not stabilize currency values, and it had no means to avert a growing financial crisis at the national level. Each state jealously guarded their independence and refused to work together. There was political/economic turmoil across the 13 states as European governments anticipated the downfall of the entire union.

The value of currency became a political question in several states. In Rhode Island, for example, debtors controlled the state government; they wanted an inflated currency that made it easier to pay off their debts. There were stories that the currency printing presses could be heard operating during the night to print more money. Next door in Massachusetts, creditors were in control of state government; they wanted a currency of stable monetary values. There were actual cases of debtors chasing creditors trying to pay off debts with money worth only a fraction of the original loan. Passing more restrictive state laws didn't help the situation. Bands of armed, insurgent debtors started a rebellion to protect farmers from foreclosure. The general population was alarmed, especially those who feared political instability.

Bankers, landowners, and investors were very concerned about the inability of the central government to maintain order and assure an orderly economic climate. Groups of troubled leaders planned a meeting for the next year to consider reforms that were necessary to stabilize the entire government.

The Constitutional Convention that met in Philadelphia in 1787 was dominated by conservatives who were specifically interested in reintroducing stability into the governmental structure. Their major goal was to devise a political system that would restrain the human appetite for the excessive freedom that was causing disorder. They set about the task of designing a government that would check and balance the popular will.

The Constitutional Convention of 1787 was charged with the task of revising the Articles of Confederation to make them more workable. However, the delegates decided that an entirely new document was necessary. The one point that united them was the conviction that a stronger central government was their only chance to save the republic. Amending the Articles required unanimous agreement among the states. Noting that it was impossible to gain support from all the states, they decided to set the Articles of Confederation aside and began drafting a new constitution.

At the outset, the delegates knew they were acting illegally by drafting a new document. The Articles of Confederation were considered perpetual with no legal means of being abolished. But those who met behind closed doors were practical, well-educated men who recognized that their legal concerns should never override a political necessity. Many of them had a personal self-interest in building a new system, but they were also drawn together to save the country from an uncertain future. To this end, they went into a secret session that was to last throughout the entire summer of 1787. From personal diaries, we know that the summer was unusually hot, but the windows in the hall were kept closed so no one outside the building would know they were plotting to overthrow the prevailing government. It was a very well-organized, peaceful political coup d'état, pure and simple.

Through the new constitution, the founding fathers succeeded in diluting the principles of a decentralized democracy that had prevailed since the revolution. The new document was to be a mixture of novel constitutional devices which appealed to both the left and right. Checks and balances were set in place to avoid what many of them believed to be the excessive democracy that plagued the Articles of Confederation. In the best tradition of American politics, it was a bundle of compromises that suited the interests of the small and large states as well as those regions where slavery was still practiced.

The first and most pressing issue was the question of how powerful the central government would be. The concept of federalism was implemented as a compromise between those who wanted a stronger central government, and those who favored protecting the powers of states.

In a flurry of eloquent debates, the framers of the constitution launched a very effective drive for ratification of the new document. Radicals and liberals in the camp of Patrick Henry and Thomas Paine were slow to mount an opposition, and the Constitution was quickly approved by a series of state conventions. By the standards of the eighteenth century, it was a well-organized, blitzkrieg operation that was approved before the opposition could mount a real campaign against the new constitution. The whole process of writing the document to launching the government took just 13 months.

But the entire process from 1776 to 1787 featured a very important shift in leadership from the left to the right. The 56 persons who signed the Declaration of Independence were mostly radicals and liberals; the signers included Thomas Jefferson, John Hancock and Thomas Paine, all of whom were clearly left of center. They were outraged by the actions of the English King and Parliament. Eleven years later in 1787, there were 39 signers of the Constitution; this group included well-known conservatives like George Washington, Alexander Hamilton, and James Madison. They were motivated to bring more order into the system.

Only six individuals were signatories of both documents. When Thomas Jefferson heard of the meeting in Philadelphia, he was heard to say, "I smell a rat." Many of the liberals and radicals thought they were being sold out by conservatives who were willing to sell out freedom in exchange for order. In a real sense they were correct.

In terms of political philosophy, the entire process to establish a new government was instigated by radicals, propagated by liberals, rescued by conservatives, and opposed by reactionaries who fled to Canada to continue living under the Crown.

But in a real sense, the debate about the power of the central government has continued to this day. The disagreements between the left and right are still very apparent. But the really interesting point is that both sides have switched sides and they have each traded political slogans to cover up their real self-interests.

The Flip-Flop

Conservatives of today can hardly talk for more than five minutes without declaring that they favor a more "limited government." It's the opening statement in nearly every campaign as they extoll the virtues of a small government. Generally, the feeling on the right is that smaller governments (local, state, and federal) promote more freedom because they can't intrude so easily on the citizens. The implication is that liberals want a larger government. Folks on the left seldom admit there're going to increase the size of the government, but they usually do increase it.

The left and right have flip-flopped on this important topic, and they each did so to benefit their own self-interest. It turns out that both sides switched their enduring beliefs for selfish objectives, and neither side talks about the switch today.

If a book had been written on the American political spectrum in the year 1800, it would have quoted two famous American leaders of the day: Thomas Jefferson, the liberal, and Alexander Hamilton, the conservative. Each had built their political philosophies around what each thought would be the ideal society.

(Remember the three "Eternal Questions" from Chapter 3 as you read on.)

On the left, Jefferson favored farmers and folks who lived in small towns. He opposed a large federal government because he saw it favoring large land owners and emerging business interests. He feared the corrupting influence of a centralized political/economic system, and favored instead small autonomous wards to be set up across the nation so people could govern themselves without the intervention of wealthy banking interests and large industries. Jefferson idealized an Agrarian Society with frontiersmen, farmers, villagers, and small shopkeepers in the interior of the country, with a down-home wisdom about public affairs. One can almost imagine the paintings of Norman Rockwell with strong, sturdy, regular people working closely with their neighbors. He romanticized the worker with dirt under his fingernails. Jefferson had a life-long fear of far-off banking institutions that would maintain the hard value of currency and therefore make it more difficult for lower-income debtors to pay off their mortgages. He believed that federal authority should be confined strictly to those powers enumerated in the Constitution and that all other matters should be left to the states and to individuals.

On the right, Hamilton favored a stronger federal government that would govern from above. He had no faith in common people, and he actually feared the excesses of public participation. Hamilton trusted the natural aristocrat who lived in the big house on the hill. As the leading conservative of his day, he believed political and economic affairs should be guided by the strong hand of the wealthy and well-born that possessed a special insight to govern. Hamilton imagined smoke stacks dotting the future horizon as the nation produced a wide assortment of products. He hoped there would be an opportunity for the classes to profit together, but with a definite hierarchy set into place. In his lifetime, Hamilton sought a strong central government, led by national elites, that would promote sound currency values, and investment opportunities for bankers and business leaders, but he thought it would also provide employment for workers. Hamilton's Commercial Society would be stable and well-organized by community leaders who had a firm grip on political and economic power.

From the very beginning, American politics was like a religion in that the beliefs were established by leaders and filtered down to the members like a religious dogma. In the early years of American history, liberals at the local level extolled the virtues of a weaker federal government while they jealously guarded the powers of individual states. Conservatives, on the other hand, saw a strong centralized government as their friend, and they fully expected they would dominate national government policies in the future.

The ideas of Hamilton were fortified by the Supreme Court during the early years of the nineteenth century. Chief Justice John Marshall, a conservative, used his position on the Supreme Court from 1801 to 1835 to bolster national power by defending the federal government's right to:

- Build a strong judiciary with an independent voice within the central government.
- Establish the power of the national government to regulate interstate commerce.
- Assert the power of the federal regulations over state governments.

Before the Civil War began in 1861, most conservatives upheld the doctrine of a strong national government because it still benefited their interests to do so. Liberals also continued to advocate their political doctrine of a limited national government. But this was about to change as the United States went through a major transformation following the Civil War.

Several factors developed which were to change the way both the left and right saw the role of the national government. High-sounding ideals were used to cover up the real motives on both sides. But the flip-flop enabled both of them to change their views to fit three new realities of the time.

The first reality was that, after the Civil War, the nation went through an unprecedented economic boom: industry, railroads, and agriculture all developed at a greatly accelerated rate. The second half of the nineteenth century was a time of rapid growth, inventions, and industrialization. The westward movement continued as new towns sprung up across the nation. Thousands of new immigrants flooded into the country between 1865 and 1900. It was the time when the United States began to realize its full potential.

The second change was that the economic expansion brought forth huge personal fortunes into the hands of a few. The new captains of industry became so powerful that they wanted to expand and operate without the national government's interference. It was now in their self-interest to argue against a stronger national government because they feared greater regulation from that government. The practical solution for these new industrial leaders was to stop quoting Alexander Hamilton and to begin using the arguments of Thomas Jefferson to minimize the power of government and block further regulations from elected representatives.

And the third factor that brought change was that the economic boom also affected the left. Many of the farmers, workers, miners, small shopkeepers, and others found themselves at the mercy of large industries, railroads, banks, and various trusts and monopolies which were seeking enormous profits with little concern for the public interest. The old Jeffersonian belief of keeping the government weak was of no value to these workers and farmers. Slowly they began to realize that, with their increased numbers at the polls, the left could use the ballot box to take over the governments at all levels, and use new regulatory powers as an instrument to promote their own economic/political interests. They could see that a stronger national government was to become their greatest ally.

The flip-flop that began in the 1870s was complete in the 1930s as liberals instigated many new governmental regulations to benefit their voting bloc and conservatives argued more for limiting a government that was detrimental to their clientele. It was then, and still is, all a matter of self-interest.

Increased voter support and new government regulations were the two factors that reversed the position of both parties. Expanding the right to vote and bringing more voters to the polls favored the election of liberals who used the central government to aid those with the least political/economic power. Since then, conservatives have favored measures reducing the number of registered voters and making it more difficult to vote. They know that a smaller voting base would more likely favor business interests, cutting government regulations, slashing taxes on upper incomes, and repealing programs that aided lower-income groups. Conservatives of today are still trying to suppress the right to vote for individuals who want to regulate business.

Both the left and right changed their overall philosophy on a stronger central government to fit their new self-interest:

- Liberals came to favor the growth of a strong central government because it could be used to promote their own economic/social/political goals.
- Conservatives opposed the growth of a strong central government because they feared new policies that would minimize their economic power.

Before the flip-flop, both sides had a simple, honest message—promoting a situation that favored their economic segment of the population. After the switch in philosophy, the situation became more complicated. Liberals had an advantage because they could openly take a positive position of using the government to aid the working class. But conservatives had greater difficulty because they had the negative task of blocking the expansion of the government so they could avoid public accountability, but they could hardly say that out loud. Leaders on the right invented philosophical cover-ups by insisting that a weaker government at the state and federal level would promote more freedom for everyone. Next, they had to apply it to real cases and make the argument believable.

An example occurred in a court case involving the so-called freedom of contract doctrine. In *Lochner vs. New York* (1905), the U.S. Supreme Court struck down a New York law that attempted to reduce the hours of people working in bakeries by limiting workers to a 10-hour day and 60 hours in a week. The New York law was favored by labor who wanted a shorter workday in bakeries. A conservative majority on the Supreme Court, in a 5 to 4 decision, ignored the drudgery of working long hours in a hot bakery and declared that the state law violated the "freedom of workers" to work more hours in a day. This line of thinking (that supposedly favored the workers) ushered in a whole new era of permitting robber barons and business monopolies to dictate longer hours under the guise of giving workers "freedom" to work more for less money. Reducing the role of government to regulate was, of course, the real goal.

Conservatives of the 20th and 21st centuries have chosen to depart from their Hamiltonian strong government approach and take on a limited government position. They even paraphrased Jefferson with the motto, "The government that governs best, governs least." In recent years, leaders on the right have used the "limited government" doctrine as they advocated slashing government regulations and programs aimed at helping the poor and disadvantaged. But today the claim of limiting government (to promote freedom) is really a cover-up for economic and political goals that are less praiseworthy.

It can be argued that conservatives have little interest in the size of government—their real interest is to eliminate government regulations, cut social welfare programs and reduce taxes for upper income persons. But that wouldn't be good public relations to say that out loud. That kind of naked self-interest would be unacceptable, even to most conservatives. It has to be said in code as a promotion of "freedom" to cut the size of government.

Truthfulness has become a rare quality in our political discourse, and in recent times, some lie every day as falsehoods pile up high in the public square. Then there is the ethical question that applies to the public. "Why," some people ask, "should any of us tell the truth when leaders look us right in the eye while they tell lies? What is the future of democracy when liars can win elections with the continued support of voters who know that they lie?"

More or Less Freedom?

Conservatives of today have developed a strategy that gives them an advantage in nearly every area of politics. They advocate "freedom" as though they invented the word, and because of this position, they see themselves as the true ally of all the people. The right argues that freedom would be extended to everyone by reducing the size and reach of government. Who, they argue, would oppose increasing freedom for everyone?

Liberals find it difficult, if not impossible, to defend various regulations when they are presented in this context. Freedom is one of the most positive words in our language. The public never seems to tire of hearing about how they can enjoy more freedom if they cut the restrictive rules set down by government. It is argued very persuasively that no person, group, or enterprise should be targeted for unreasonable regulation—more freedom should prevail in all areas of life. It goes without saying that everyone should be free to improve private property without restrictions such as building codes or zoning laws. All employees should be free to contract themselves without regulations. The marketplace, they contend, is where real freedom prevails.

The more important point, of course, is which side is the real beneficiary of increasing this freedom of workers: labor or management?

One of the most attractive aspects of the freedom strategy is that it doesn't cost the taxpayer anything up front to repeal government regulations. Conservatives have a long list of laws they want to repeal because the laws restrict the freedom of choice. These may involve banking practices, consumer affairs, racial equality, ambient environmental standards, union rights, and safety codes. In each case it costs nothing to peel off the restrictions placed there by others. It is comparatively easy to use a common-sense approach by cutting all the red tape that seems to be everywhere in daily life. Many will find the following to be reasonable expansions of freedom. It is argued that:

- Hotel, pub, and restaurant owners should be free to refuse service to any customers on their private property.
- Stocks and bonds should be traded in a free market with no governmental restrictions or regulations.
- Banks and insurance companies should be free to speculate in the marketplace using funds from their customer's accounts.
- Local public school boards should be free to require religious prayers to be recited daily in the classroom.
- Individuals and organizations should be free to contribute as much as they please to legislative lobbying and political campaigns.
- Everyone should be free to buy any type of weapon and carry it in public places without a permit.

But how about other examples?

- Labor unions should be free to collect union dues from all workers in an industry without restrictions.
- Women should be free to have a safe abortion locally without any government restrictions or regulations.
- Persons in the LBGT community should be free to use the public restroom of their choice.
- Folks should be free to grow, distribute, and use marijuana in every locality in the nation.
- Undocumented children brought into the US illegally should be free to obtain citizenship without restrictions.
- Same-sex couples should be free to marry legally and adopt children in all states across the country.

All of the above issues (on both sides) have been the subject of public regulations. Emotions run high when any of these activities are discussed. These are the hot-button issues that divide people all over the country. And the most interesting point: *it's all about freedom.*

Conservatives focus on freedom for the individual as an end in itself. They tend to idealize a society where restrictions are kept at a minimum—where capable people can prosper on their own initiative. Government is viewed as an adversary that takes more than it gives. There is an effort to repeal the rules that hold people back from enjoying their rightful place of being free. There is an underlying belief that everyone is on their own and responsible for their own welfare—that government just restricts freedom and holds us back.

Liberals see it differently. They argue that uncontrolled freedom often promotes the interests of one group at the expense of another. The left emphasizes that government should first protect the freedoms of the most vulnerable—those with the least bargaining power in economic and political affairs. Liberals say they are trying to protect the freedom of the "little guys" who can't fend for themselves

These two views on freedom come into conflict when the left asserts that it is justifiable to restrict the freedom of some in order to increase the freedom of others. For example, it is argued that it was necessary to restrict the freedom of a white majority to practice segregation in order to liberate a black minority—or in commerce, when the freedom to engage in monopolistic practices is prohibited for the sake of the consumer. But the right insists that inequality and inequities are a normal part of life and that government has no right to try and create a "nanny state" that protects people who don't want (or need) to be protected. The left counters by saying that *freedom is not an absolute good,* that government has a right to restrict the actions of some individuals for the sake of the public welfare.

This issue has been debated endlessly by the left and right for hundreds of years. In recent times, it has become one of the most important question facing governments in all parts of the world. Bring up the subject of government controls and loss of freedom is guaranteed to be discussed. Freedom is more complicated than we think.

In reality, both the left and right believe in promoting and restricting freedom. But they each have a rather narrow version in their heads as to who should be free to do what.

- Liberals are eager to extend freedom to low-income minority groups, but are less interested in granting more freedom to large private business in economic affairs.
- Conservatives are supportive of expanding economic freedom that benefits private business, but less interested in extending freedom to low-income minority groups.

When discussing this topic, we often speak of freedom and liberty interchangeably, as though they were synonymous, but there is a very important distinction between these terms. Freedom is a more general term; it signifies an absence of restraint, whereas liberty is a guarantee of a particular freedom protected by an outside source. Early in our history, it was more common to speak of liberty when discussing opposing points of view. President Abraham Lincoln spoke of liberty while discussing the merits of slavery in 1864, during the American Civil War:

> With some the word liberty may mean for each man to do as he pleases with himself, and the product of his labor; while with another the same word may mean for some men to do as they please with other men, and the product of their labor.

Lincoln went on to say that the two views are incompatible:

> The shepherd drives the wolf from the sheep's throat for which the sheep thanks the shepherd as his liberator, while the wolf denounces him for the same act, as the destroyer of liberty, especially if the sheep was a black one.

Lincoln went on to say, "the wolf's dictionary has been repudiated."

Does government consistently play the role of liberator by protecting us from harm, injury, and exploitation? Some would say individuals should be free to make their own choices despite the personal risk. Many contend that too much protection diminishes personal freedom even if the protectors mean well through their laws and governmental restrictions. One can almost hear an overprotected child say, "Really mother, I'd rather take care of myself."

The debate goes on, because there is a built-in conflict between freedom and protection. You can't have it both ways. Reasonable people have disagreed about where to draw the line. But as the debate continues, the expansion of government continues as well, so the issue is still dividing the electorate.

Years ago, a person could dump raw sewage or garbage into a creek without much concern that anyone could stop them, even if there were people living downstream. In rural areas or even in large cities, there was a prevailing belief that individuals just had to adjust to life around them. If someone wanted to build a smelly or unsightly chicken coop next to your home, you had little choice but to accept the situation.

Throughout American history, most problems (great and small) were not considered to be governmental matters. *The roots of the American Revolution were anti-government.* There was a strong tradition of opposing government controls that ran through our history. Because of this strong custom of nonintervention, new regulations have always clashed with the tradition of everyone doing as they pleased. Then and now, there are many who resist the idea that government has the right to interfere in one's personal affairs.

With this as a backdrop, it's easy to see that there's always going to be a debate between the wolves and the sheep—between freedom and protection. It comes right down to the question of how much freedom needs to be given up in order to live in a crowded twenty-first century America. It's a moot question with no clear answer except to say that it will probably continue to be one of the most contentious issues of our times. The question of individual freedom versus the public welfare will never be completely settled.

Negative and Positive Freedom

Most people idealize freedom as a black or white concept, assuming that a person is either free or not free. The earliest concept of freedom was that it existed whenever there was an absence of external restraint. For example, conservatives argue that if the government does not require everyone to belong to a particular church, individuals are free to worship as they please. The assumption is that if a certain practice is not prohibited, individuals are free agents. But liberals note that the absence of restrictions didn't automatically bring real freedom—other factors have to be considered.

Perhaps the best example of this lack of real freedom came about when slavery was outlawed after the Civil War. The Thirteenth Amendment to the Constitution prohibited slavery in 1865, but everyone knew that black people were not really free. The social/racial community standards in the United States maintained a different form of bondage in which black people faced all forms of discrimination, including enforced segregation, and in extreme cases, death by lynching. This was a clear example of *negative freedom*. There were no legal constitutional obstacles, but real freedom was a cruel fiction. African-Americans were still not as free as white folks. It turned out that freedom was on a sliding scale.

Positive freedom, in the case of black people, began to expand when the government created certain conditions that preserved their freedom. Real freedom did not really exist until the government enforced civil rights for black folks in real-life situations.

Negative freedom has generally been seen by right-wing groups as an end itself. Conservatives believe taking out the legal obstacles is the key; once they are removed, everyone is on their own. Individuals should shape their own destiny and make it on their own without government help. Examples would include public response to the LBGT community or members of a minority religion. Conservatives assert that everyone can be as free as they wish; it is all up to the individual—government should not intervene to aid one person over another.

Positive freedom is often pursued by left-wing organizations because they recognize the power of social codes that create an unequal playing field. Liberals declare that real freedom is an individual right that should be protected and enforced. This position goes to the heart of liberating people at the bottom of society from social, political, or racial discrimination. Gaining greater freedom for the dispossessed is a much more difficult task. It often involves protest movements and governmental intervention. There are often groups who try to block government promotion of freedom. That's what the Civil Rights Movement was all about.

The gap between negative and positive freedom was ignored for many years in the United States. The Constitution appeared to defend basic freedom through the First Amendment to the Constitution, but in fact it did little to protect individuals from daily discrimination. The First Amendment was misleading in its language:

> Congress shall make no law respecting an establishment of religion, or prohibiting the free exercise thereof; or abridging the freedom of speech, or of the press; the right of the people peacefully assemble, and to petition the government for a redress of grievances.

From the beginning, the freedoms of press, speech, religion and assembly were not protected at the state or local level. Individuals were protected from Congress violating their rights, but the most of the abuses were occurring at the local and state level.

Let's imagine it's during the early 1920s, and several things occurred in your hometown. The local school board denied the right of racial minorities to receive a public education. The mayor shut down the local newspaper because the editor criticized his administration. And the chief of police decided to ban all public meetings because outside civil rights advocates were motivating local people to protest against the law.

All of these acts were a clear violation of basic constitutional rights and you would expect the First Amendment would have protected those rights against infringement, but you would have been wrong. Read the amendment again. It states clearly, "Congress shall make no law..." You were *not protected* at the level where you needed it the most.

Why did the founders in 1787 protect people against the federal government rather than the states or localities? There was a mistaken belief that the greatest danger to individual freedom would come from above. The federal government was distant from everyday life, and was thought to be a threat to personal liberties. There was a faith that local people could be trusted more to defend basic freedoms than those who lived in far-off places. Built into the American belief system was the myth that people you don't know well would try to restrict your freedom, but you could feel comfortable with folks down the street. And so it followed that the Constitution should defend against governmental restrictions from outside your locality rather than local political bodies. There was a persistent faith that local government was the most responsive to everyone, regardless of an individual's race, culture, religion, gender, or nationality. There was a built-in fear of a central government that would infringe liberties.

Those who wrote the Constitution in 1787 were believers in negative freedom; they had decades of adversarial experiences with a distant government headed by an English king and parliament. Their apprehension of a centralized authority was shaped by real examples of autocratic rule from a government above them that was far away. Their struggles with the Crown forces convinced them that central governments were to be feared while local governments were more likely to preserve individual freedoms. But it soon became evident that they were wrong.

Then and now, real life experiences teach us that highly homogeneous populations at the local level often repress minorities. When a community is made up mostly of people who think, look, and act the same, there is a higher likelihood that they will be unsympathetic to those who don't fit in. When nearly everyone has similar outlook, there is a tendency for the dominant group to want to defend their privileges—they often become headstrong and turn against those who are different. There is a long history in the U.S. (and around the world) of local majorities discriminating against those outside the fold.

Just ask new immigrants that came to America—black families that tried to move into all-white neighborhoods—foreign people who don't speak English—Muslims who set up a local Mosque—gay people who want a same-sex marriage, or people who just don't "fit in" to a small town. Otherwise good folks can become intolerant and mean-spirited when they they're in a large majority. Hostile discrimination is a common reaction. Homogeneous groups can flex their muscle and come down hard against people of another race, religion, nationality or sexual orientation.

But that situation feels very different within the majority. A homogenous group may offer acceptance and security to its own members because they believe, look, and behave like everyone else. Life in the neighborhood can be heaven on earth if a person fits in. If you are of the same race, religion or nationality, there is little fear of mistreatment or discrimination—there's no difficulty when everyone shares the same values.

It is important to note that the concept of negative freedom was observed throughout the United States for more than the first 130 years of our history after the Constitution was written, but it was a problem that many ignored. Minority religious, ethnic, racial, and nationality groups were not enjoying the same levels of protection as the majority. Freedom of speech, press and assembly was generally secure for the majority, but less so for a minority. Depending on where one lived, some Americans were second-class citizens and there was little they could do to improve their status.

Finally, the Supreme Court moved to defend the freedom of speech at the local level. In *Gitlow v. New York* (1925) the Court held that the guarantees of the First Amendment could be enforced at the state level through provisions in the Fourteenth Amendment. In a series of cases during the next 20 years, the Supreme Court declared that a citizen's due process would now include uniform enforcement of First Amendment rights at all levels of government. It dramatically changed the way we interrupted the First Amendment. But in reality, the problem of discrimination continues. Like other issues in politics, there may never be a real uniform application of freedom.

As a consequence of judicial actions, it has usually been the federal courts that have stepped in to rescue minorities from abusive majorities. Local and state courts have had little sympathy for unpopular groups that were out of step with the majority. Surprisingly, it was the government in Washington, D.C. that came to the aid of local dissidents who favored racial integration or defending the freedom of religion. It was the federal courts that often defended minorities who spoke out against measures passed by state and local governments. The question: why was there such a contrast on the practice of upholding democratic values? Were there different sets of values at various levels of government?

Experience has taught us that heterogeneous groups are less likely to restrict individual freedom. *That is to say groups made up of many dissimilar parts are more diverse and therefore less able to restrict individual freedom.* When the majority is made up of more dissimilar parts, there is a greater likelihood that decision-makers will be open to bargaining and compromise, and an overall more moderate point of view will prevail.

By definition, the national government reflects the views of people from all over the country: folks with competing lifestyles, different political/economic orientations, religions, races, and opposing values. It's not that individuals within these diverse groups are more tolerant or understanding (there are bigots at all three levels of government), but no one group at the federal level can dominate the entire structure even if it wanted to. It is the varied composition of the government that often causes the leaders in Washington, D.C. to be more tolerant and willing to defend different minorities across the nation. It turns out that *heterogeneity is the key to personal freedom.* Overall diversity promotes the expression of minority interest groups at all levels. Racial, economic and religious minorities can gain some relief from stubborn majorities that are more likely to rule at the neighborhood, city, or state level. Think about it for a moment—maybe diversity is a friend of freedom.

Despite this clear record of freedom being abused the most at the state and local level, there are still many who argue that governments at the local level are the most responsive to the individual. The whole idea of trusting your neighbors to defend your rights comes right out of Norman Rockwell paintings. It sounds so true that it almost sounds un–American to say it's not true. But just ask America's minorities—they will tell many disagreeable stories about the suppression of freedom at the local level.

Interest groups that support the states rights' doctrine have had a different goal in mind—they represent the folks who live in the big white house on the hill, not those who live on the other side of the tracks. It is surprising how many ordinary citizens still believe the political folklore that local elites defend the rights of local powerless people. But again, just ask area journalists or local minorities—they will tell you the truth.

The New Reactionaries

Not since the early days of the 1950s has there been this much political/social/cultural activity on the far right. The new reactionaries are flocking to right-wing causes all over the globe. There has been a net gain of far-right political representatives in most Western democracies, plus right-wing groups are becoming more popular in less developed countries in the Middle East, Africa, and Asia. But the crowning achievement for the right was the election of Donald Trump as President of the United States. When he won the 2016 election, he surprised seemingly everyone, including himself.

When surveying the attraction of right-wing groups and those around the world, it is apparent that there are some common reasons why ordinary people are drawn to extreme right-wing politics. Here are some of the reasons that people to want to set up defenses:

- Increased number of immigrants coming over the border into the country.

- Upsurge of persons of other races and cultures that do not integrate into the majority.
- Barrage of conspiracy theories and distrust of mainstream media.
- Fear of growing cases of terrorism committed by foreign agents.
- Upset toward feminism and new codes of behavior from new gender roles.
- Suspicion of growing wealth in hands of upper-income groups.
- Anxiety about new ideas publicized by science, technology, and higher education.
- Distress over declining religious values and public respect for God.
- Preparation to silence the press and other media outlets that criticize national values.
- Eagerness to reinstate respect for flag, national anthem, and other symbols of the country.

There was an old orthodoxy that voters were primarily interested their pocket books—that upper income people backed conservatives, while blue-collar workers regularly voted for liberals. The logic was that economic issues were the most important factor in determining political affiliation. There were exceptions to this general rule, but the major parties were usually aligned along a liberal/conservative division which reflected economic interests and social class.

But the old rule of thumb has changed. Economics is no longer the *only* factor. Many working-class people are now leaving their old liberal affiliation and looking to conservative candidates because of cultural concerns rather than economic issues. These folks are really the new reactionaries of America because they are driven by their negative reaction to recent social changes that are very upsetting to their lifestyles. They blame liberals for promoting a society that has become permissive and immoral in their eyes. Many feel personally offended by the immorality of present policies, and they are now fighting back.

Many of the new reactionaries are convinced that the government has abandoned them. There is real anger that industries were allowed to move jobs out of the country—that big banks repossessed homes—that illegal aliens are taking their jobs—and that big business was reaping record profits while working families were creeping closer toward poverty. This group is outraged by the influence of big money and corruption (as outlined in Chapter 1) and they are especially angry at those in Washington, D.C., who are in the pockets of special interests.

This new assemblage of voters is still looking for leaders that feel their pain and speak their language. The one characteristic that they're looking for is someone who will shake up the system—someone who will tell them that their anger is justified. Donald Trump drew the support of millions of voters who fit this description. They were angry and Trump gave them a voice by ridiculing the establishment in both political parties.

The new reactionaries are searching for a brand of political leaders that promises to roll back the disturbing changes on all fronts. The catch is that the new movement combines outlooks that don't normally fit together. This new movement is a unique combination of right-wing morality merged with left-wing populism, but it's being expressed on the right side of the spectrum, advocating a return of a bygone era they seek to reclaim. The new reactionary is an unnatural combination of moral and economic policies that don't often co-exist in the real world.

Right-wing television and radio personalities have made a major effort to convince these two groups that freedom from government regulation is the major strategy that will take them to the Promised Land. The claim is that big government is undermining and corrupting society, and so it follows that dramatically reducing the size of that government can bring about a repeal of all the upsetting practices in society. That logic doesn't ordinarily stand up in the real world, but there is general agreement within this group to attack government as an institution.

Strong anti-government sentiments are increasing with many folks who used to be the backbone of a well-ordered political system. They have given up their moderate positions and have become the new reactionaries on Main Street America who have utter contempt for the government. Public opinion polls illustrate that they no longer have a reverence for the rule of law. They speak of everything being "rigged," including elections, the courts, the IRS and the FBI. Surprisingly, they even turned a blind eye to Donald Trump when he seemingly violated laws and got cozy with the Russians. These folks are bombarded every day by new conspiracies that explain why they should feel more anger. They feel betrayed by the leaders they once supported.

Former liberal leaders would turn over in their graves if they could see what has become of their old Democratic coalition formed in the 1930s. Progressives of today are dismayed that a major part of their former voting bloc has deserted the partnership. The old liberal majority was built on the expectation that people would continue to vote in their economic self-interest, but now that belief does not always hold true. Current leaders on the left cannot seem to understand why this reaction to recent changes has prompted so many working-class voters to line up to support candidates that enact some of the following policies:

- Lowering tax rates for the highest income groups.
- Easing the environmental standards for oil and natural gas exploration.

- Abolishing regulatory laws on speculation of stocks and bonds.
- Repealing programs providing for universal health care.
- Reducing benefits for disabled and unemployed workers.
- Gutting consumer protection bureaus.
- Cutting unemployment benefits.
- Enacting laws that reduce the membership in labor unions.
- Decreasing funds for public education.
- Eliminating environmental protection agencies.
- Using voter suppression laws to disenfranchise minority voters.
- Permitting unrestricted political campaign contributions.

Liberals of today continue to oppose these issues in an attempt to rekindle their old coalition. They are trying to remind people of their economic self-interests, but to no avail. Leaders on the left are hoping that these angry voters will come back to the fold when they recognize that they have been duped by right-wing leaders into supporting policies that do not favor their self-interest. Progressive leaders do not seem to understand that self-interest economic issues have become secondary to many who are more interested in cultural issues. The new reactionaries have a very new and different self-interest. In many cases they have become zealots in voting against their own self-interest.

Crusaders among these new reactionaries have unquestionably accepted freedom as an absolute good in all areas of life, economic as well as cultural. And as a result, they have accepted a whole host of policies that may actually be a detriment to their own personal welfare.

It is well known that converts to a religion frequently develop a more intense faith than people born into that religion; a converted person often turns against their former beliefs with a vengeance. (See Chapter 9, Moderates, Activists and Extremists.) When these new reactionaries departed from political parties of the left, they turned against their former political alliance with an explosive vengeance seldom seen in politics. The political label "liberal" has now become a dirty word in their vocabulary.

The new reactionaries have also expanded the conservative label to include many topics that are highly controversial. They are eager to take on social and cultural issues that would have been identified only with a fringe element in the past. Issues involving fundamentalist religion, sexual orientation, capital punishment, and abortion are now a part of the new conservatism platform. These topics have become the lead issues in many political campaigns. They are presented with a religious fervor that is new to moderates on both sides of the fence.

While there is general opposition to government controls on the right, there has been a recent expansion of governmental controls to block same-sex marriage, abortions, and teaching sex education and evolution in schools. The intensity of beliefs on these and related issues is so strong that traditional conservative groups have had to accept new government controls just to satisfy their far-right-wing base.

Old-line Republicans are uncomfortable with the inclusion of cultural issues that would have been considered out of bounds in the past. But they have nowhere to go. The new reactionaries are flexing their muscle and have become the new political base of the GOP. They are forcing old-line Republicans to line up with them on issues that used to be considered to be personal and not proper subjects for a political platform.

When the new reactionaries began to move into the existing Republican party, they were welcomed at first because it allowed the old-line GOP to become competitive in many electoral districts that were out of reach in the past. But now the tail is wagging the dog. There are signs that the new reactionaries are driving conservative party politics far to the right side of the political spectrum. This position is a clear disadvantage when campaigning in blue states. The loud voices and anti-government theme sound too strident to traditional conservatives who have lost control of their own political party. Independent and moderate voters may also be turned away by the rhetoric. Donald Trump and his supporters are a prime example. The GOP will not recover soon from their presence.

These new reactionary voices are shrill and angry. They are confrontational and not willing to accept any compromises or half-measures that might address the present situation. As stated earlier, religious faith and cultural morality can't be compromised.

Many in this emerging group have moved so far away from the old pocket book politics that they do not seem to recognize any economic issues that might benefit them personally. An example of this is in a person I know who owns a small dog-grooming shop. My first clue about her political point of view was viewing the bumper stickers on her car parked out on the curb:

- "You Can't Fix Stupid, But You Can Vote Them Out."
- "I'll Keep My Guns, Freedom & Money—You Can Keep the Change."
- "You Are Not Entitled to What I Have Earned."

Her physical appearance doesn't seem to fit her bumper stickers. She was a small, frail woman who doesn't look well. It was almost as if she were driving someone else's car. She seemed exhausted when I saw her last so I asked how she felt. Her reply surprised me: "I've got an advanced case of stomach cancer." I asked about surgery or any other treatment. She said she was too young for Medicare and didn't have any health insurance. In discussing her illness, she concluded by saying she knew surgery would extend her life, but she didn't have any money. Voicing my concern, I said, "It's a good thing we now have a government health-insurance program; you can get the surgery you need." Her response set me back: "Oh no, I don't believe in a government health program, that's the poor stealing from the rich. No, no, I wouldn't do that."

This new reactionary woman has a leader she says changed her life. Alex Jones has a following of several million right-wing folks who tune in to hear his radio show. He is the leading right-wing conspiracy theorist in American politics. His main message is, "You should be afraid—there is a conspiracy of globalists out to destroy our country and impose a world government that will place you all in slavery. These are among his most prominent theories of what is going on today:

- The destruction of the World Trade Towers on 9/11 was an "inside job" by globalists who wanted to spread fear across the country. A major in the U.S. Air Force was outraged because he was forced to train the terrorists who flew the airliners into the World Trade Center. The whole operation was conducted by the federal government to terrorize the American people so they would be willing to tolerate more government controls.
- Leaders around the world (the globalists) are planning to exterminate 80 percent of the world's population so they can rule the world without opposition. All the American patriots who oppose the globalists will be labeled "hate criminals" and eliminated by the US government. The goal of the globalists is to establish "one world government."
- The Carlyle Group is the biggest defense contractor in the world. It is owned jointly by the Bush and bin Laden families. Every war around the world adds to the fortunes of these two families who use their wealth to restrict patriots and increase their international power to establish a world government. The purpose of these wars is to create fear and distract public opinion while the government increases its hold on the American people.
- Mass shootings in the US were all faked to promote the globalists plan to enslave the world. Each shooting increases the call for gun control, and finally for gun confiscation. The globalist goal is to increase the fears of Americans so they are willing to disarm our own citizens, who are the only hope to oppose world government.
- Barack Obama and Hillary Clinton are the co-founders of Al-Qaeda; they are working with the globalists in a plot to take over the world. Every terrorist strike creates more anxieties among Americans; the panic justifies the government actions to increase so-called "security measures" that are designed to weaken the will of Christian conservatives who are fighting to defend the country.
- Children in elementary schools are being asked to reveal what kinds

of weapons are owned by their parents so they can be confiscated when the takeover occurs. *They want to take our guns!* There is also an ongoing effort to use chemicals in the school lunch programs to lower IQ scores and turn children "gay" so the birth rate goes down.

Alex Jones is the founder of *Infowars,* a media outlet that proclaims that there is a war against patriotic Americans. He offers (what he says) is the only "truthful" view on what is happening today. Jones pretty much limits himself to spreading propaganda, but there's an allied group that's willing to stand up for right-wing views out on the street.

The 2017 alt-right rally in Charlottesville, Virginia was a case in point. Hundreds of pro–Nazis marched through the city chanting, "Jews will not replace us," and "Our blood, our soil." David Duke, national leader of the Ku Klux Klan, was there to remind President Trump that the Klan appreciated his support. The right-wing militants clashed with local residents in a riot where three people lost their lives (one on the ground and two in a police helicopter).

"We want a homeland," is the demand of Richard Spencer and Jared Taylor, leaders of a band of self-described warriors of the alt-right, or alternative-right. "We almost had a homeland," Taylor says, but it is being systematically watered down by the influx on people of different races, religions and cultures.

The alt-right appeal makes perfect sense to many across the country who are overwhelmed by what they see as a loss of their homeland and their cultural identity. New members of the movement want to "clean out" America. From their perspective, the alt-right is the last chance to purify the white race. This cause is the most important thing they have ever done. They expect to be thanked by future generations.

From the outside, the alt-right appears to be a group of racist and fascist wannabes who flirt with Nazis paraphernalia, iron crosses, and swastikas. They are most easily identified by their strong opposition to Hispanics, African-Americans, Jews, Muslims and any other group that they define as non-white. They are also opposed to multi-culturalism, feminism, egalitarianism, globalism, the United Nations, and the mainstream media. They are comfortable marching in torch-light parades with Ku Klux Klan members and neo–Nazis. Out on the street, they've been known to use heavy clubs, metal shields and swords.

Most of all they fear that white, Protestant Americans will become a minority in their "own land." They argue that other nationalities have their own country where they are a strong racial majority—"why can't this country just be reserved for us?" The focus is on blocking immigration, especially from Mexico and the Middle East. Alt-right leaders contend that some races and ethnic groups have lower IQ scores and they don't want them mixed into the American gene pool. They caution other white people to stand up for their race, warning that ethnic and cultural diversity has weakened the United States from the inside.

The new Alt-right reactionaries appear on college campuses all across the country to present their views. They are not afraid to say their piece even when unfriendly students are shouting, "Go home!" They preach with a loud-speaker system to infuriate their foes, but they also win converts to the cause. Their numbers seem to be growing as more people find themselves feeling overwhelmed by recent events. The movement is gaining strength.

Perhaps the greatest fear of the alt-right is the danger of world government where they would be a minority forever. They are fond of saying that survival of the culture and race is more important that any one of them individually. They are ferocious fighters because they sense their backs are up against the wall. The Alt-right sees themselves as the modern "Minute Men" fighting off the invaders to their land. Their conspiratorial thinking arouses fear about the future. They are constantly citing books and studies that prove that they are trying to save America.

But there is another group (from the opposite side of the political spectrum) ready to fight them on every point. As we shall see, there is a grain of truth in the statement, "opposites attract."

The New Radicals

There are conspiratorial thinkers on the left as well. There is a whole new batch of theories and proclamations formulated by a variety of American radicals. These charges are repeated often and believed by many on the far left. The believers are a diverse group, ranging from a retired woman who would never consider violence to younger men armed with placards willing to go out on the street and risk being arrested. The new radicals are a highly motivated, diverse group. What they see convinces them that this country is in a real crisis:

- The financial donor class has taken over the entire economic and political system. Right-wing billionaires can dictate policy-making at all levels of government. Opposing candidates have been bought off by corporate interests that dominate the entire process. The strategy is to cut taxes for the rich and eliminate all programs that benefit the underclass. It's transference of wealth to the upper one percent.
- The Supreme Court has cleared the way for the mega-wealthy to dominate the government at all levels. The whole Donald Trump experience is a gigantic diversion to allow the deconstruction of democratic

institutions and eliminate the norms that have guided the State in the past—they are building a Fascist America! Activists of the left and right are kept busy fighting each other on cultural, racial, and gender issues that don't really matter to the ruling class. When the crunch comes down, the debate will stop. Until then there is a pretense of democracy while the deep state gains complete powers.

- Elections and voting are a sham. Both political parties are under the control of the same elites who always win. Voting machines in key states have been rigged to tabulate victories that destabilize the system. Opponents are permitted to win a few races so we think we still have a choice, but elite majority control is never jeopardized. Massive amounts of campaign funds and clever social media stories can mislead voters into supporting right-wing candidates that do the bidding for the governing elites.

- There is a master plan to demoralize the electorate and make them believe the country is degenerating into chaos. Right-wing cable news outlets are designed to make people angry and afraid, thereby dividing the United States and making it easier to stamp out reformers with democratic values. The result has been to create a tribal atmosphere where viewers are attacking their fellow countrymen. The police are given free rein to combat activists and add to the feeling that the entire system is unravelling.

- Donald Trump is a master at distraction. He is a "useful idiot" used by those who want to spread chaos and destruction of democratic institutions. Trump is a sick man who doesn't realize that he is being used by those above him. Leaders of the deep state are teamed up with fascists around the world to end democracy as we know it.

- Vladimir Putin is using President Trump to create an economic oligarchy whereby inequality will drive unemployed working-class people into the arms of a fascist regime. Tax cuts for the rich and deregulation of the economy are key elements of the plan. Fascism will be voted in by a dumbed-downed electorate singing patriotic songs. "Make America Great Again" will be the popular slogan that unites a fascist nation.

American radicals pride themselves as going to the heart of the problems. They feel like they are the only ones that see the depth of the problem, that everyone else has been duped by right-wing propaganda.

Antifa (anti-fascist) is the name given to a loose association of radicals who band together to deny a platform to right-wing organizations by interrupting reactionary events. These radicals are outspoken opponents of capitalism, racism, and sexism. Many identify as being anarchists, communists, socialists, or simply street people who believe in attacking white supremacists and right-wing groups. They got their start focusing on income inequality during the Occupy Wall Street and 99 percent movements around the world.

The roots of anti-fascism go back to the 1930s opposition to Adolf Hitler in Germany and Francisco Franco in Spain, but the most recent example of Antifa was their coming-out party after the 2016 election of Donald Trump. Spontaneous demonstrations popped up across America with the chant, "not my president." There was no formal organization—it just happened. Many cities were disrupted by the multitude of people who opposed Donald Trump.

Right-wing media outlets have labeled Antifa a "domestic terrorist group." Television accounts focused on the strong-armed tactics used by Antifa that included breaking store windows, manning barricades, starting fires, and fighting with the police. Proclamations from Antifa were repeated by right-wing groups in a manner that made Antifa appear to be a left-wing revolutionary group trying to bring down the government.

Antifa denies the charge and claims it has only one purpose: opposing what it regards as a fascist threat. They claim their reason for being is to combat right-wing groups that are a threat to democratic institutions. Antifa members are quick to point out they are trying to "save" the country from a fascist takeover. Not all radicals believe that fascism is in the wings, but there is a growing feeling that we are living in times when democracy is in danger. Radicals are especially concerned about how the government has been taken over by an oligarchy of the very rich. The radical point of view is that large banks must be broken up and regulated so that the political donor class is stopped from using large sums of money to buy off decision-makers in the Congress, the White House, and the Supreme Court.

Young people especially support issues raised by Antifa, but the establishment has labelled these ideas as "socialist" or "too radical" for the times. Old-line liberals see the radicals as proposing too much, too soon. In 2016, the Democratic Party found itself scampering to stay ahead of the social-democrat Bernie Sanders and other left-wing leaders who wanted to go much further than the Democratic Party had gone in the past.

But while this was happening in the United States, a whole new brand of radicals had been organizing around the world. As stated earlier, those on the far left are much more international in their outlook. They have taken to the streets in cities around the globe to protest what they see as the major ills of societies. The new radicals are outraged by sets of issues that they say are getting worse by the day. They are especially concerned about the following issues:

- World-wide trend of uncontrolled financial speculation.
- Unemployed workers who see no hope of having a satisfying life.

- Multinational corporations that make huge profits they conceal from taxation.
- Governments bailing out banks and insurance companies while small businesses fail.
- Large sums of campaign contributions that dominate elections and favor special interests.
- Cheap goods from sweat shops that flood the country and drive out established business.
- Wars in developing nations aimed at extracting oil and other natural resources.
- Homeless refugees all over the world fleeing war and repressive regimes.
- Great gaps of income between the very wealthy and the poor.
- Ignoring the signs of climate change caused by using fossil fuels.
- Political systems that are deadlocked by uncompromising groups.
- Taxation rates that favor the wealthy who shield their income from taxation.
- Oil and natural gas exploration that endanger the environment.

These and other issues are interrelated in the eyes of the new radicals who have occupied many public squares around the world. Many have never been involved in politics before, but they have taken to the streets because they are feeling angry and excluded by a political/economic system that only listens to military dictatorships and the corporate class.

There is also a very different brand of new radicals that has only come on the stage outside of Western democracies. Arab Spring and other physical uprisings were led by intellectuals and others rebelling against strongman rule in their countries. Unlike the new radicals in democratic societies, these rebels were putting their lives on the line to drive out tyrannical governments that do not allow political competition to exist. They started out by wanting reform—now they are dedicated to toppling the old political system.

To the surprise of many, these new radicals in various parts of the world have brought down right-wing dictatorships that had stood for decades. The cry of the far left is to:

- Free political prisoners who have protested the regime.
- Arrest former leaders and place them on trial.
- Renounce Western democracies that support the old regimes.
- Root out and eliminate the secret police.
- Block the importation of military hardware for the regime.
- Promote free democratic elections.
- Preserve the freedom to criticize the government.
- Gain representation for ethnic minorities.

- Dismantle military-type regimes.
- Reduce the role of fundamentalist religion.
- End discrimination against women and ethnic minorities.
- Introduce democracy into all social and political institutions.

The protesters have been willing to risk their own lives by taking on the old order in hand-to-hand combat. The televised account of these revolutions illustrates that many of these new radicals are idealistic youth who reject all the old established values of the past. They are driven by a sense of equality and want to build democratic institutions in parts of the world where none has ever existed. They are able to turn out thousands of protestors armed only with placards against troops with tanks and modern weapons.

Modern technology has opened up political options that were never thought possible a few decades earlier. The Internet has combined with international television and radio to spread ideas into areas that have never before tasted the fruits of democracy. These rebels are texting and tweeting across international boundaries. They are watching and listening to each other over a distance of thousands of miles. They've never met, but they have learned much from each other. A few years ago, the concept of a global village seemed farfetched, but no more. There seems to be no way to deny the idea that street action and global networking can bring down well-entrenched regimes.

Some governments have tried to shut down the Internet in their region because it poses a real threat to maintaining control. But pictures and videos have a way of seeping through and challenging the old patterns of life. These long-standing regimes still resist the influx of change; some political and religious leaders have turned guns on their own people. It is not a pretty sight, but the word is getting out: the people can overturn a government that seemed to be totally in control of every facet of life. It is a sure bet that the future will be full of more of this type of confrontation politics.

In the past, most sweeping political change came about at a much slower rate. In most Western-styled countries, democratic institutions emerged over decades, sometimes centuries. Today, however, the pace has accelerated. There is little time to digest all the new thinking that has come about with the Internet. Many political/religious/social/economic institutions in the developing world seem unable to bend—the result is they break. How will Western democracies respond to a world that is coming apart?

Instability has spread behind these new movements around the world. It is far too early to predict the direction of the new societies created by these mass movements, but it is interesting to speculate:

- Will new strongmen come into power in these emerging states?
- How will the old social, religious order respond to these modern ideas?
- Will right-wing groups bring religious fundamentalism back to power?

- What will happen if the world goes through another major economic crisis?
- How will climate change affect the political turmoil?
- Will right-wing groups use the Internet to divide people and undermine democracies?
- Who will these new revolutionaries line up with in their foreign policies?

* * *

The new radical and the new reactionary are a potent and explosive combination. They are political opposites in their goals in a world that is becoming a smaller place. In its own way, each has stimulated humanity as never before.

Modern technologies, communications, and weapons have shifted power to the outer edges of the political spectrum. It's no longer possible for large governments to keep the lid on world affairs. People who existed in primitive tribes just a decade ago now have the means to take on a super-power and promote wars that seem to have no end. As we look down the road, it seems apparent that tiny cells of these new reactionaries and new radicals will have a disproportionately larger voice in the future.

Questions for You

1. Why do ideas and people move to the right? Cite an example of this process that is not noted in this chapter. Have you moved to the right in your own lifetime?

2. Why do you think the liberals of yesterday are challenged by a new group on the left? Explain the process of standing still on political issues. Why is it a problem for elected officials?

3. Why have labor unions, churches, and other groups moved to the right? Why do some individuals lose their crusading attitude? Has this happened to you? Why or why not?

4. What is your reaction to the allegation that "leaders of political movements have an almost natural inclination to betray their principles after taking power?" Have you seen this happen in the United States? Why or why not?

5. Why did the Articles of Confederation (1781–1787) fail? In what way did conservatives come to the rescue in 1787?

6. Why did the author argue that the Constitution, drafted in 1787, was a coup d'état? In what way was the document a combination of principles from both the left and right?

7. After the Civil War, why did the left and right flip-flop on the question of promoting a strong central government? What do you think conservatives would say to the charge of flip-flopping? What would be the probable liberal response?

8. What is your response to the statement, "American politics is like a religion in that beliefs are established by the leaders and then filter down to the members like a religious dogma?" Is this claim an accurate appraisal today? Why or why not?

9. In what way have voting rights become the key to the struggle between liberals and conservatives? Do you see any current examples of that issue today?

10. Google the Supreme Court case *Lochner v. New York* (1905). How did the Court use the concept of "freedom" to promote the interests of business? Do you see any examples of "freedom" being used today to undermine the American labor movement?

11. Why is it charged that conservatives of today have little real interest in the size of the government? Are there other motives involved? What arguments would conservatives use to respond to this charge?

12. Why is freedom a two-edged sword? How can the restriction of freedom for one group be an expansion of freedom for another group?

13. Explain the political significance of the fable of the sheep and the wolf. If you were running for public office as a conservative, would you use the story as part of your campaign? Why or why not?

14. What is the difference between negative and positive freedom? If you were a liberal running for public office, which brand of freedom would you stress in your campaign? Why?

15. Why do the new reactionaries sometimes support economic policies that run counter to their self-interest? Outline the unexpected economic goals pursued by this group. Why do they support these objectives?

16. Compare and contrast the conspiracy theories of the new reactionaries and the new radicals. After surveying these opposing points of view, why does the author feel that the future is unpredictable? What do you think?

Do You Know Someone Who Has Changed Their Political Views?

Have you or any of your friends or family gone through a period of changing political opinions about some major issue? What was the subject area? Is it possible to say it involved moving the person to the right or left? Did the change increase or decrease political their interest in the topic?

9

Moderates, Activists
and Extremists

When violent behavior is encountered in politics, it is labeled as either being extreme right or left. The implication is that a revolutionary is merely an overzealous example of a more moderate position. But that's not really true. In terms of behavior, revolutionaries of the left and right have more in common with each other than either has with those in more moderate positions on their respective sides. And it follows that moderates on both sides have more in common than either does with the extreme positions. These observations have been largely overlooked in politics because the spectrum has been viewed as a one-dimensional, straight-line continuum with an emphasis on two opposing sides, left and right.

The regular political spectrum approach overlooks several factors that are similar at the ends of the spectrum and also in the middle. In reality, the political spectrum can be studied from a different dimension when presented as three sets of comparable perspectives that combine both the left and the right. The following three categories provide a different insight into political behavior:

- Moderates: liberals and conservatives
- Activists: radicals and reactionaries
- Extremists: revolutionary radicals and revolutionary reactionaries.

In each classification there is a similarity in the intensity of conviction, along with a striking parallel in political strategies. The comparative political spectrum illustrates that the terms moderate, activist, and extremist address both the political content (right or left) and also the intensity of ideological conviction (moderate or extreme). As one travels outward on the spectrum, participants are more highly motivated and they are also more inflexible in their political beliefs.

In the center of the continuum, politics is all about compromising issues, and at each end it is often a matter of life and death. It turns out there is a symmetry in the spectrum that makes it easier to contrast the various degrees of ideological commitment on each side, and also to note the shades of comparable tactics on the right and left. It's all about gradations and how individuals behave in a particular role. The great majority of people are in the middle of the spectrum, but the highest stakes and the greatest passion are at the ends.

This figure illustrates that the intensity for moderates is relatively low; activists are driven more strongly by their ideological beliefs, while revolutionaries on both ends have the highest motivation and intensity. The political spectrum has different degrees of political temperatures—ranging from lower levels in the middle to white hot at both ends.

FIGURE 9-1, A COMPARATIVE POLITICAL SPECTRUM

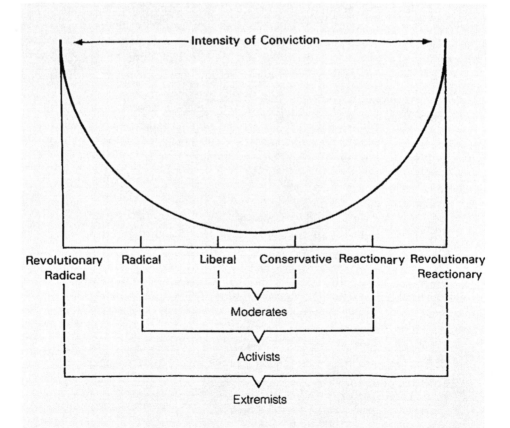

When viewing this specific spectrum, it is helpful to realize there is a definite correlation between the content of ideology and the passion of the believer. Those who are driven to remake the world may be willing to lay down their lives for such a sweeping change, while those in the middle may just want to change the tax laws.

Liberals and conservatives may be firm in their convictions, but they stop short in their willingness to risk their lives for an idea. By comparison, radicals and reactionaries are more intense in their convictions; they are willing to go out on the street to confront others, but they also avoid personal injury. Revolutionaries in both camps, however, are ready to devote their entire lives to their dream with little thought of their own welfare.

So much of political communication is emotion-based. Here is how the public typically responds to these three groups:

- Moderates: "He seems like such a nice man, I think I'll vote for him."
- Activists: "When they riot, they just destroy their own neighborhood."
- Revolutionaries: "That guy should be hunted down and locked up for life."

In American politics the general public is more comfortable with political tactics that are peaceful and non-threating. The problem for activists and revolutionaries is that those kinds of moderate-type tactics don't get much attention and are very slow in achieving results. Most people prefer a non-confrontational approach to politics. Middle-class America is conditioned to go through regular channels that include signing petitions and lobbying public officials. All of that is fine, except this process has no appeal for folks trying to bring about far-reaching change.

By definition, sweeping change involves sweeping tactics, especially if the proposed changes touch on racial, sexual or religious subjects. A quick review of the most contentious issues in the past 50 years illustrates that street confrontations were the method used by people who were trying to gain public attention on these continuous issues:

- Racial integration in public places.
- Bi-racial marriages.
- LBGT rights.
- Same-sex marriages.
- Immigration issues.
- Police treatment of minorities.
- Abortion.
- Capital punishment.
- Gun control.
- Prayer in school.

The above issues continue to draw in persons from many walks of life that range across the spectrum from left to right. But now we turn to those in the middle of the spectrum that are commonly referred to as "politicians."

Moderates: Liberals and Conservatives

Moderates are the conciliators of politics. They are the leaders we know by name; we see them on television—prime ministers, presidents, and members of legislative bodies. As a group, they can be characterized as those ready to make concessions to reach broadly-based agreements that include many interests. They consider themselves to be the natural leaders of democratic governments. Liberals and conservatives have a strong motivation to maintain public order; they both need a stable political system that accommodates many competing interests. Their long-range strategy is based upon voluntary cooperation of diverse groups within the system. They seek compromise and do not want to drive away prospective allies.

Of the three sets on the spectrum, moderates are the only ones who are constantly advising everyone to "play by the rules," and "work through the system." Liberals and conservatives are both able to win enough elections so each is convinced that success can be had if they are able to find a campaign formula that will return them to power. They are forever shifting people in and out of a coalition or party organization. Because of this ever-present promise of success, moderates almost never consider going outside the political system. In fact, the only time they did so in the United States was during the Civil War of the 1860s.

Moderates are often masters at turning down the temperature of politics. They present themselves as the only adults in the room as they try to minimize the impact of the more passionate members of society. Political party conventions, election campaigns and major legislative programs are all dominated by moderates. Familiar media outlets that feature moderate opinions at the national level are *The New York Times, The Washington Post, The Los Angeles Times, The Wall Street Journal,* CBS, NBC, ABC and CNN. Other media outlets and cable news shows are less inclined to voice a moderate point of view.

On a daily basis, moderates are dedicated to seeking solutions through the conventional channels of politics—drafting legislation, lobbying, constitutional amendments, and so on. They generally support the concept of majority rule because the majority almost always favors one of the choices provided by moderates. But they do show some alarm when activists move into their domain and try to seize control of a political party. The Donald Trump victory of 2016 was a case in point. Moderate leaders in the Republican

Party fought Trump's candidacy early in the campaign because it was outside the moderate mainstream. But when Trump became president, most Republican moderates accepted his unorthodox antics illustrating that moderates often have flexible principles when it comes to gaining and staying in power. Many GOP moderates had little respect for Trump, but it was widely assumed that they would use him to gain their political objectives. It should be noted that even establishment conservatives came on board with Trump only after he had won. At that point, some congressional members were even willing to defend him against the special council investigation of Russian meddling in the 2016 election led by Robert Mueller III. All of this demonstrates that moderates can sometimes be duped by an unconventional leader who can lead them into very dangerous waters.

Despite the Trump example, leaders in the center of the spectrum usually behave responsibly because they are in charge of the government. Every day they are involved in raising money for political campaigns by contacting lobbyists and special interest sources such as banks, labor unions, corporations and a growing number of billionaires who have come to dominate our politics. There's sort of a "good old boys club" mentality among them (regardless of gender) in that they share the same values and expectations of other officials. There are certain unspoken rules observed by moderates as they avoid calling each other derogatory names and questioning each other's motives. Clearly, they were bothered by the way Trump insulted his opponents, but they lacked the courage to do much about it.

But because of the increased polarization of American politics, there has been an upsurge of abrasive tactics used by liberals and conservatives. Twenty or thirty years ago, it would have been unthinkable for legislative members to separate into warring factions. Before the 1990s, it was common for leading liberals and conservatives to socialize with each other and show respect outside the legislative chambers. Today that rarely happens. Moderates on both sides have become more rigid and less willing to reach across the aisle.

Yet they feel the political system is in their hands. Their first order of business is to maintain public confidence and keep government and the economy operating. Indeed, maintaining order within society is the major function that liberals and conservatives share. They generally control the police, the courts, and the prisons. They can deal effectively with those who go outside the system and still maintain their moderate posture.

Liberals and conservatives realize that it is important that the law is obeyed because they fear any large-scale appearance that the system is playing favorites. More than anything, moderates fear a loss of public confidence and legitimacy. They don't ever want the people to consider using extra-legal means. They'll do nearly anything to avoid public unrest, but they will not hesitate to clamp down hard on any segment of society that preaches disobedience. Conservatives and liberals around the world are afraid of popular revolutions that spring from widespread public dissatisfaction. They want to keep the lid on society and keep people from going outside the regular channels of change.

Moderates of the left and right see themselves as the great bulwark of democratic institutions. Both are fond of recalling situations where they defended democracy (as they saw it) against the attacks of activists and extremists from both the left and the right. But sometimes moderates are rather timid when they meet up with unprincipled rogues.

There was a real test for regular conservatives and liberals during the so-called McCarthy Era of the 1950s when Senator Joe McCarthy (R) of Wisconsin began a series of investigations charging that there were Communists in the U.S. State Department, the U.S. Army and many other private and public institutions. The McCarthy hearings created a real hysteria charging that the U.S. had been infiltrated by disloyal people at the national, state, and local level.

Most moderates remained silent because they were afraid McCarthy would accuse them next of being communist sympathizers. Both Democrats and Republicans were privately relieved when McCarthy was challenged and discredited by the only woman in the U.S. Senate, Margaret Chase Smith (R) of Maine, who dared stand up to Senator Joe McCarthy. The witch hunts ended, but in this case, moderates seemed more concerned about saving themselves rather than standing up to Joe McCarthy.

An even more serious example of timidity among moderates occurred during the Trump years. The great majority of Donald Trump's congressional party remained conspicuously silent despite Trump's outrageous behavior. What follows is a partial list (at this writing) of some of the comments/actions taken by the President:

- Fired the director of FBI for failing to be personally loyal to him.
- Undermined international cooperation in worldwide climate change policies.
- Hired a paid agent of a foreign government to be his national security director.
- Advocated jailing his political opponents in the presidential election.
- Shared classified intelligence information with the Russians.
- Failed to condemn American Nazis, members of the alt-right, and Ku Klux Klan.
- Became a serial liar on a wide range of public and private issues.
- Bragged about the fact that he sexually abused women.
- Declared that the mainstream press was an "enemy of the people."

- Dismissed evidence that the Russians had interfered in American elections.
- Obstructed justice in matters relating to a special council investigation.

There were many more documented cases of shocking actions taken by Donald Trump that were far outside acceptable political and legal norms. Most Republicans declined to reject his activities because they apparently did not want to jeopardize their goals of repealing Obama Care, deregulating the economy, and cutting taxes for the highest income earners. In fact, a sizable number of his party tried to distract a special council investigation of Trump so they could protect the president and their own self interests. Not only did they fail to speak out—they actively engaged in cover-up operations that would shield the President from legal prosecution. This is the most serious case on record of moderates avoiding their constitutional responsibility while democratic principles were being violated. They did not stand up for the rule of law.

On a lesser level, moderates maintain the appearance of being homegrown public servants with local values. At public gatherings they display a down-home quality, feeling the need to shake people's hand, attend public picnics and support local business interests. If they step too far outside of that role, they take the risk of losing much of their support. Representing home-based prejudices and special interests is their full-time job. To win re-election, moderates usually tell voters and local special interests what they want to hear. Elected officials want to be seen as hometown people who support hometown values, but they squirm on national television news shows when they have to take a stand on controversial issues. They have made not answering a difficult question into an art form.

But it should be remembered that discriminatory laws against racial and religious minorities have been tolerated and enforced by moderates. There have been far too many cases where innocent people faced massive discrimination that was administered by popularly elected moderate leaders. Liberals and conservatives have been known to turn a blind eye to local groups like the Ku Klux Klan that terrorized defenseless minority groups. Moderates seldom stand up for unpopular causes; they seem more concerned with their own survival in electoral politics. They are often very popular at home, and it is not uncommon for them to be reelected by wide margins.

In their capacity as leaders, moderates are often guilty of masking their own self-interest in the political process. They claim to defend the public interest, yet they are fully aware of the many private interests—including their own. They are supposed to step aside when they have a conflict of interest, but they often keep it to themselves. Both liberals and conservatives propose certain government programs that benefit them personally, or favor easing a trade restriction that aids their particular interest. When moderates speak of free enterprise, they often have a specific enterprise in mind. It is not uncommon for them to profit personally from their public service.

Of the three sets on the political spectrum, moderates are the most likely to manipulate the political system for their own personal gain. Members of the U.S. Congress, for example, have used "insider" information to make personal investments. Neither activists nor revolutionaries seem very interested in their own economic welfare, but moderates have a great concern for their own financial interests and those of their supporters in their fields. It is of utmost importance for moderates to represent local powerful interests. And in return, they frequently accept gifts or trips to exotic places. It is illegal for elected officials to use campaign funds for their own expenses, but it happens often.

Public corruption is a real problem for federal, state, county, and city officials. Moderates of both political parties are often involved in scandals centered on influence peddling. Some minimum-security prisons have a long list of former legislators, lobbyists, and governors serving as inmates. Many moderates have had successful careers while turning a blind eye to corruption.

Despite their dominance within the political system, moderates usually see politics as only one of several important concerns in their lives; family and occupation are often their primary focus. On occasion, they may complain that political involvement is a burden that takes up too much of their time. But they usually continue to serve as community leaders, work on political campaigns, and sometimes seek public office.

The primary goal of moderates around the world is to manage conflict and promote incremental change. Their key strategy is to build consensus through compromise. Here are some of the major characteristics and goals shared by moderates of the left and right.

Moderates: Characteristics in Common

- Willing to cooperate and compromise through the political system.
- Raise huge sums of campaign funds from special interest groups.
- Support the democratic process at the federal, state, and local levels.
- Usually win most of the elections throughout the country.
- Have flexible principles when it comes to their own interests.
- Control law enforcement and the justice system.
- Dominate the two-party system at the federal, state, and local levels.
- Impose and support popular discriminatory rules against minorities.

- Avoid taking unpopular stand on critical issues.
- Often profit personally by using "insider" information to make personal investments.
- Assume joint responsibility for governmental leadership.
- Support incremental, evolutionary change.
- Defend the political system against activists and revolutionaries.
- Mask decisions involving their own self-interest.
- Involved in political scandals and corruption.
- Have the most to gain personally through the present political system.

Activists: Radicals and Reactionaries

These are the workhorses of politics. Persons in this category hold exceedingly strong opinions on specific issues. Individually they are constantly involved in all the most controversial topics and causes. Often they are focused on one or two issues they think are the most critical questions of our times. Politics is the avocation of radicals and reactionaries, and a deep passion is their motivating force. They seldom win elections, but in recent years there are an increasing number of people in Congress that have activist characteristics. Much of the gridlock in Washington, D.C. is caused by activists that are unwilling to compromise on cultural and social issues such as immigration and border security.

Opinion-makers for right-wing activists include Fox News and some religious broadcasters. MSNBC and the Nation magazine are recognized as an advocate for activists on the left. These media outlets often set the agenda goals for the entire country by uncovering scandals and noting issues that might be too one-sided for the moderate press. Activists often set off alarm bells for the nation. The media on the far right and left are not timid as they raise controversial issues that others may wish to ignore.

Most political change has been led by left-wing activists. Movements involving gender equality, civil rights, labor unions, voting rights, abortion, LGBT rights and a wide variety of social change started with radicals who went out on the street to advocate change. Activists on the left are usually the ones who fight for causes that are later accepted by moderates.

Activists on both sides are frustrated that the system is dominated by the opposition. They interpret nearly all political events as the result of conspiratorial actions taken by the "other side." Some of the conspiracies are unbelievable to moderates, but activists are driven by these controversial pronouncements. They are convinced that there are unseen hands controlling and deciding our fate behind closed doors as secret groups are undermining our future.

Right-wing activists, for example, are certain that the leaders of the nation's government, schools, businesses, churches, and media are all members of a radical conspiracy that is slowly taking over all of society. Reactionaries such as Senator Joe McCarthy of Wisconsin shared a belief that a communist conspiracy was soon to overtake control of the nation.

Left-wing activists today are certain that the Military Industrial Complex is sapping the nation's energies by diverting our resources to unwinnable wars that are motivated by big oil companies in bed with governments that discriminate against all reformers. These activists on the far left conclude that the poor are being used as fodder for the military machine that has destabilized whole regions of the world with a series of capitalist wars that benefit the one-percent financial community.

Both radicals and reactionaries warn there is little time remaining before the takeover is complete. From their perspective, it is an emergency of epic proportions. They are convinced that the opposition is gaining ground every day. Most activists trace the alleged conspiracies back to secret meetings and deals made by individuals in the opposing camp. A tremendous amount of energy is devoted to exposing this conspiracy. There is a prevailing belief on both sides that few important events can be explained by chance—they are part of a conspiratorial operation that is unfolding according to plan. There is a good deal of fear and paranoia expressed by activists on both sides.

Perhaps the best way to understand conspiratorial thinking is to relate an experience I had attending a public meeting where rock music was presented as being a part of a communist plot. It was a meeting at a local hotel on the subject of how a small group of Communists were using rock music to take over the United States. The presentation was given in a meeting room that had a floor to ceiling mirror covering the entire front wall of the room. I could sit in the front row listening to the speaker, but I could also look up in the mirror and see the faces of every other person in the room. You could have heard a pin drop as folks listened to every word.

The speaker said that all the music was composed with two hypnotic beats that had been programmed into the mind of every young person in the country that listened to rock and roll. He said these "beats" were included in every record produced and listened to by the public. But the shocking message was that every pop music radio station had a secret recording of a third beat that would be played only when the Communists gave the order. The third beat was designed to mesh with the first two beats in a way that all the listeners would become completely helpless zombies willing to accept orders like. "Go out and dynamite the local National Guard armory" or "do not obey your parents, teachers, or the local police."

I watched and listened to the presentation given to about 150 people who were hanging on to every word. The facial expressions reflected the fear in the room. No one had ever heard this message before, but there were no disagreements voiced. No one said, "Prove it!" The questions were all about how they could expose this situation? Would it help to call the radio station managers? Does the government know about this? Can we trust our own children?

Once people accept one conspiracy theory, it is very easy for them to accept the second and the third—conspiratorial thinking can become a way of life. In this case, nearly all the people in that room were over 50 years old, and the message of rock music being a communist plot meshed with their general annoyance of loud music that was so popular at the time. It seemed to make them feel better that the music they disliked was also a threat to the country.

Later that night I started thinking that the meeting itself was like the "third beat" that made people into political zombies who would believe anything. Meetings like this opened a scary door. Everyone in that room felt powerless and afraid. Several expressed anger that elected officials had not warned them before. And perhaps the scariest thing was: they could all vote.

There are also cases of left-wing activists believing in a political make-believe that is far outside the mainstream. The largest utopian commune in recent American history was established near the small town of Antelope, Oregon (population 46) in the mid–1980s. It was started by a devoted group of religious followers of an Indian mystic and spiritual leader, Bhagwan Shree Rajnessh. The group bought the 64,000-acre Big Muddy River Ranch, and in a few years, it was transformed into a city of 7,000 people with its own police and fire departments, several restaurants, a crematorium, hotels, a sewage treatment plant, a public transportation system, a 4,200-foot airstrip, and its own zip code, 92741. People from all over the world heard of the communal living arrangements and flocked to the growing commune.

I visited Rajneeshpruram in its heyday and found it was many things to many people. It was a paradise for most of the residents who all dressed in red and orange, working together building roads, growing food, practicing free love, and following the teachings of their leader, "the Bhagwan" (the blessed one). Nearly everyone I met had a smile on their face.

I talked to many people there, but I especially remember a woman from Switzerland who told me she had arranged to marry a U.S. citizen at the ranch so she could become a legal American resident. She met her spouse briefly for the arranged marriage to gain her resident status, and in return she made a generous contribution to the ranch. Another person I remember was a retired high school teacher from Los Angeles who signed over his entire retirement income to the ranch in return for a "lifetime membership" in the commune. Both people were completely happy with their decisions and were certain that they would be happy for the rest of their days.

There were many television sets at Rajneeshpruram, but there was only one channel. It played lectures from the Bhagwan, 24 hours a day. He was never out of site or out of mind. There were nightly meditation sessions in a canvas-covered building housing 4,000 people. The half-hour sessions featured complete silence which gave me a mind-altering experience—thousands of folks sat on the floor for 30 minutes without making a sound. There were no locks on any doors or the hundreds of bicycles that were parked everywhere. It appeared to be a paradise on earth where everyone could be trusted to love each other.

But there was another world that was just outside the perimeter of the compound that most people seemed to ignore. There were guard towers on the borders of the ranch manned by men with high-powered rifles. Police inside the commune were armed with automatic weapons. All of this was said to be for the protection of the residents, to keep out other nearby Oregonians who were not happy with the attempt to take over the government in the local county.

It turned out that the ideal life on the ranch was inside a bubble. There was trouble brewing on the horizon. Rajneesh leaders bussed in 2,000 homeless people and registered them to vote in an effort to install their own people as elected officials of the local county. Rajneesh leaders also came up with a scheme to decrease the vote of longtime residents on Election Day by lacing 10 salad bars in nearby towns with a salsa that contained salmonella.

The reaction was immediate to the poisoning episode. Within days, federal and state officials descended on Rajneeshpruram. The Oregon Attorney General charged that Rajneeshpuram was a religious community that violated the principle of separation of church and state. Enforcers of Oregon environmental laws charged that the Rajneeshees had converted rural lands to urban use without going through the correct procedures. Immigration and Naturalization officials charged that federal laws had been violated by so-called "marriages of convenience." Arrests and deportation orders followed quickly. It wasn't long before there was an auction on all the equipment left behind. All the "paraphernalia of paradise" was put up for sale. Soon after, there were lots of used red and orange clothes in local secondhand clothing stores.

Since Rajneeshpuram folded, there have been many political conspiracies that have disrupted American politics even more. In this Trump era of "alternate facts," and "make-believe thinking," distrust in the government follows almost naturally. One of the most damaging byproducts of conspiratorial thinking has been the decline of trust Americans have for their government. When lies and the fears are muddled together with racism and ignorance, democracy is in jeopardy.

* * *

Despite their different conspiratorial views of the world, radicals and reactionaries are very similar in their personal political habits. Both gain an incredible amount of personal satisfaction from discussing and advocating their political theories. They choose friends on the basis of their political beliefs. Individually they spend a great deal of time promoting causes they believe are absolutely essential to the community and the nation. Both are constantly involved in persuading people to join their cause. They are tireless political workers with very firm convictions.

Virtually every women's march, pro-life group, pro-choice meeting, Trump rally, right to bear arms meeting, gun-control gathering, and the immigration demonstration has a large number of activists involved from both sides. Every protest rally brings out activists to agree or disagree. They are the ones that are heard chanting or protesting at public gatherings.

In recent years, activists from both sides have spent an inordinate amount of time and energy picketing the U.S. Supreme Court. There are hundreds of people carrying placards in front of the building cheering or jeering major court decisions. It is easy to see that our politics have become tribal. In contrast, moderates across the nation may approve or disapprove of judicial verdicts, but they almost never demonstrate out on the street.

Majority rule is embraced in theory by the activists on both sides because they believe that the people will ultimately be attracted to their cause. But if majority opinion runs counter to their primary goal, activists are more than willing to override the majority. From this perspective, it is sometimes lonely for activists who perceive themselves to be saving the people from a great disaster because the majority seldom appreciates their involvement. The public is often disinterested or openly hostile to the controversial goals sought by activists.

Unlike moderates, who direct much of their attention to economic pocketbook issues, activists are more inclined to take on social or cultural issues where there are moral or international implications. The following topics invite activists from both the left and right:

- Abortion issues.
- Climate change.
- Woman' rights.
- Birth control.
- Police shootings.
- Capital punishment.
- Environmental protection regulations.
- Settling Middle East refugees.
- Gay and transgender rights.
- Mass shootings and gun control.

- Illegal immigration.
- Voter ID requirements.
- Race relations.
- Same-sex marriage.
- Minimum wage.
- Prayer in public schools.
- Union rights.

Moderates generally avoid these types of issues because it divides public opinion on an emotional level, but activists are drawn to these topics because of their strong personal convictions. Activists expect controversy and they are rarely disappointed.

The aftermath of the Trump election created more activists on both sides. Some said they were going to make America great again—others thought the followers of Trump were destroying American democracy. The antics of Trump raised the temperature in public meetings across the country. Wherever people gathered, there were contending activists taking sides: they had the loudest voices on TV talk shows, and they even invaded the coffee shops on Main Street America.

But these new activists were different than the groups of 30 years ago. The old brand of activists was only interested in changing public policy on issues like prayer in school, or civil rights—they didn't declare that their opponents were their enemies. After the election of Donald Trump everything changed. He wound up folks by intentionally dividing groups and inflaming the electorate. Conspiracy theories were everywhere. Some of the President's supporters became so single-minded that they were willing to undermine the principles of democracy. There were attacks on the rule of law. Telling the truth was no longer expected. Politics took on a destructive fervor that was remindful of the McCarthy era of the 1950s.

Activists: Characteristics in Common

- Favor sweeping change throughout society.
- Appeal to the frustrated element in politics.
- Eager to be involved in public confrontations.
- Spearhead the nation in promoting political change.
- Demonstrate an idealistic faith in their ideology.
- Choose friends for ideological reasons.
- Expect that a dramatic change will improve society.
- Fear that the opposing side is controlling the system.
- Believe in the conspiracy theories of history and politics.

- Lack of tolerance for people with competing ideas.
- Attempt to take over moderate political parties.
- Faith in common people to save society.

Extremists: Revolutionary Radicals and Revolutionary Reactionaries

Extremists are revolutionaries ready to engage in any tactic, including political violence. Individuals in this very small cell group see their involvement as a full-time, life-and-death struggle against the political system. They are completely certain that their view of the future is the most important goal in the world. Revolution is an all-encompassing task—they have few other personal interests.

During World War I and II, combat soldiers were trained to throw their bodies on the barbed wire so other troops could step on them and run on to engage the enemy. Revolutionaries of the left and right are similar in that they are willing to sacrifice themselves so the main body will go forward and triumph. But this kind of politics is always a long shot; it takes a special kind of person to risk their lives for a movement.

Winston Churchill said a fanatic is one who "can't change his mind and won't change the subject." In fact, fanatics come in all makes and ages—they may be religious, political, economic, sexual, or racial. There are some who are so committed to their ideological view of the world they are willing to kill; they plant bombs and carry guns while others have elaborate schemes for how they will use violence to overturn the government, or resolve some wrong.

In Northern Ireland there was a sign with the inscription, "Terrorists are not easy to spot. They look just like us." That's true of a lot of folks who pass for normal, but in politics they are wolves in sheep's clothing. They don't really believe in democracy because they would subvert it immediately to close down those who disagree with their views.

Tolerance is the one word that never passes from their lips—it is completely outside their experiences. From their point of view, tolerance is a sign of frailty. It is a weakness that comes from not recognizing how powerful certain enemies are in this society. I recall with some apprehension how much some people I have known (left and right) love to talk about their hate.

I knew a Cuban refugee in Washington, D.C., that was eager to kill anyone that aided Fidel Castro. He truly hated the entire Kennedy family for not fully supporting the Bay of Pigs invasion of Cuba in 1961. This man worked himself into an emotional lather talking about how he wanted to dedicate his life to killing all of the Kennedys, including their children. I'll never forget the look in his eyes as he spoke of how he wanted to torture every member of the family. He would relish any opportunity to cut their throats or pull the trigger. The look on his face, the words he chose to describe his feelings. His hatred had become his reason for living.

Extremists concentrate on their enemies, who they believe are responsible for all that is wrong with their world. Eric Hoffer, author of *The True Believer*, wrote that revolutionaries can exist without a belief in a god, but never without a belief in a devil. Their enemy is the greatest source of unification. Fighting their "devil" motivates them—it justifies violence. The devil symbol is often exaggerated as the sinister force behind all that is wrong with the world. Consider the following revolutionary groups and the focus on their devil:

TABLE 9–2, DEVIL SYMBOLS OF THE LEFT AND RIGHT

Left		Right	
Groups	**Devil Symbols**	**Groups**	**Devil Symbols**
Marxists Revolutionaries	Capitalists, imperialists, and landowners	Islamic State of Iraq and Syria (ISIS)	The United States and democracies of the world
Earth Liberation Front (ELF)	Logging Companies and groups that pollute the earth	Ku Klux Klan, Nazis of the United States	Blacks, Jews, Catholics, and foreigners

Revolutionaries not only direct their hatred against "the devil," they also exhibit a faith in their ideology that is not unlike a religion. They call for their followers to believe that the revolution will *save the people*. However, they see no value in debate because they have a *revealed truth*. Permitting the enemy to speak and voice an opinion is dangerous in their eyes. Extremist leaders profess the correct view to their followers and never tolerate dissent.

Political extremists of both the right and left have a commitment to the revolution that is full-time and unshakable. Personal friendships and family ties are broken if they interfere with the primary activities of the revolution. By necessity, personal contacts are only with people who can be trusted not to betray the cause. They don't have time for personal friends because they are constantly on the run, fleeing the law, and plotting their next clandestine action. They love to speak of the enemy as an overwhelming force. Often there is an exaggeration of all the enemy can do, giving them an even greater motivation to succeed despite the danger.

During the late 1960s, The Weather Underground was made up of a small cell of upper middle-class university students who broke off relations with their families and lived in abandoned buildings while they plotted a violent revolution against all American economic, social, and political institutions. Some of them robbed banks and others died a violent death when their homemade bombs detonated by accident. They even conducted their personal lives in a way that eliminated personal identities so they didn't think any more about their parents or siblings. It was reminiscent of the Mau Mau uprising in Kenya during the 1950s in which the members did unspeakable, personally shameful things together to wipe away any sense of individual identity. This practice is not unlike the initiation process that small, elite military units go through before they go into combat. It turns out that removing personal inhibitions are of great importance when launching a revolution.

The Symbionese Liberation Army (SLA) of the 1970s was similar in their behavior. They were self-described revolutionaries in the San Francisco bay area that kidnapped Patty Hearst of the Hearst newspaper family, and indoctrinated her to the point where she took on another name (Tania) and a whole new identity as a revolutionary. She took an active part in several robberies and other illegal SLA operations. The so-called "brainwashing" experience was disputed by her family, but it was clear that Patty Hearst changed her identity while in the group.

Revolutionaries not only take on a new personal identity, they also develop a highly regimented sense of purpose; extremists on the right and left exhibit a high degree of authoritarianism in their behavior. The ones I knew, who claimed to be allied with the Weather Underground, were completely single-minded. They had a highly disciplined command structure within their organization that reminded me of a military model where everyone knew their role. Among those I knew on the left in Berkeley, there was never a doubt about their identity, the movement itself or their revolutionary goals. I never heard one of them express any doubt or say, "I don't know." Right-wing revolutionaries I knew in southern Oregon had similar behavior patterns. They were also highly dogmatic and moralistic in tone. Both groups were out to remake society, and they exhibited a special fascination when describing the "terrible" reasons why that action was necessary, and why their violence would cleanse the world. Individuals within both groups had memorized the results of various conspiracies they had read about. There were well-worn books that they quoted several times. These writings were their group bible.

As stated earlier, conspiracies reign supreme among revolutionaries on both the right and left. One of surprising things I noticed was their willingness to believe and accept new conspiracies without checking them out. Often, I would bring up some idea I had heard from another similar group.

They would listen intently, saying they had never heard it before, but a few minutes later they would be using it as an example of why things were so bad. I found it interesting that they seemed to want to hear more "terrible things." They were actually eager to hear bad news with little or no thought as to whether it was true.

Revolutionary groups I encountered on the left in Israel, Northern Ireland and the United States were much more difficult to approach than those on the right. Groups on the left are almost always wanted by the law and therefore very reluctant to trust a new person. On the right, however, it is fairly common for the elected officials to "know" right-wing extremist personally and secretly approve of their actions. In Northern Ireland I knew right-wing paramilitary members who had close ties with the police. In some respect, the police and the paramilitaries in Belfast were working together.

One northern Irish Protestant loyalist I knew was given information by the police that enabled him to kill three Catholics. Five hours after the murder, the police arrested him and he spent fourteen years in prison. In Israel also, law enforcement officials were aware of right-wing extremists that targeted Palestinians. Across many parts of the United States, there have been communities where there was an "understanding" between the local sheriff and the Ku Klux Klan. In all these cases, the governmental authorities could claim to have "clean hands" because the actual violence was done by a civilian.

One characteristic I noted in nearly all the revolutionaries I knew on both sides in the United States, Israel, and Northern Ireland was that they seemed to have a broken self-image with very low self-esteem. There was a long list of personal problems that came up in casual conversations: sexual abuse, beatings as a child, anger toward their parents, being fired from a job, dropping out of school, and dishonorable discharges from military or police organizations. There was also a fascination with guns and violence. Often I got the feeling that a conversation was becoming dangerous as the anger level increased in the room. It was clear that these people were ready to blow emotionally, and I didn't want to be around when it happened. I knew they could turn on me in an instant. They sometimes joked about what they could do to me. I didn't think it was very funny because I knew it could happen.

One afternoon in Northern Ireland I took a ride with two Protestant paramilitaries who had just gotten out of prison. I knew one of them rather well, but I had never met his partner. The two of them acted suspiciously as they drove me to a remote area about 25 miles outside of Belfast up on a hilly, dirt road that overlooked the entire valley. When I asked where we were going, they replied, "Oh, you'll find out." Finally, we stopped and got out of the car and crawled over a fence. By then I was shaken and concerned for my safety. One of them turned to me and said, "When I was in prison, I used to think how beautiful this spot was. Today I wanted to show it to you." Then they both laughed at me and the three of us drove back to Belfast.

But there's a minimum of laughing among revolutionaries. Each of them has a rage to destroy a system which they believe has no right to exist. Behind that organized anger, there is an overwhelming conviction that someday their revolution will bring forth a new society which will benefit the great majority of the people. They are aware, however, that they may not live to see the day of victory—death may precede success.

Revolutionaries must be willing to risk their lives for a group they know only as "the people," despite the fact that large numbers of "the people" resist them, and are hostile to their principles. Whenever I brought up the unfavorable public reaction to their cause, they quickly changed the subject, saying the people would "come around" later when the TRUTH was known. Extremists of both the left and right believe the general public must be indoctrinated through a massive education after the revolution.

And then there is the matter of how far some were willing to go in confronting others with opposing beliefs. Moderates on the left and right may be content to press their points of view in legal language or lawsuits. Activists on both sides are eager to carry placards (and sometimes guns) as they engage in public protests. Devoted extremists boast that they are willing to give up their lives.

In recent years there have been more standoffs between self-styled militias and law enforcement officials. Frustrated people with weapons can gain public notice very quickly. There is always increased tension in the air when everyone is armed. Angry armed people are powerful figures on television. In these situations, it is difficult to tell the difference between an activist and an extremist—sometimes it is just a matter of waiting to see if they will back down or use their weapons. There is often a fuzzy line between an activist and a revolutionary.

But around the world there are many today who are eager to use violence. It is this small group who actually plan to kill opponents and/or innocent bystanders. People who strap bombs to themselves have become a fact of life in the 21st century. It is nearly impossible to stop those willing to die. Martyrdom is powerful.

Yet, the day-to-day problems of a revolutionary are awe-inspiring whether they are on the left or the right. Throughout the world, revolutionaries are wanted by the law as political criminals. Their chances of survival are slight, and the prospects of overturning the system may be even less promising. They are a rare breed in politics. Below are some of the major common characteristics of extremists.

Extremists: Characteristics in Common

- Belief that an evil force controls society.
- Have severed relationships with their non-members.
- Are willing to risk their lives and use violence.
- Have eliminated their own personal identity.
- Struggle against a largely exaggerated foe.
- See no value in debate because they know the truth.
- Are driven by a goal of spectacular change.
- Focus on a devil symbol as a source of common hatred.
- Have low levels of self-esteem.
- Rejection of democratic values that disagree with a revolutionary purpose.
- Willing to believe new conspiratorial ideas with no proof of validity.
- Have authoritarian personalities.
- Favor indoctrination over education.
- Attempt to close the political process to their enemy.
- Believe they have a license to kill on behalf of the revolution.

The mindset of an extremist is that of a "true believer." There is no room for compromise or adjustments to any new point of view. So what happens if there is some intra-organizational dispute involving revolutionary leadership disputes or major changes in strategy? If there is a split in a revolutionary organization, people on the losing side are usually purged, and in some cases executed. But those that survive (after being pushed out) often become so enraged that they turn against their former comrades and attempt to crush them by joining the group that was once the object of their hatred. Adolf Hitler recognized this factor among revolutionaries and he welcomed fallen-away Communists into the ranks of the Nazi Party. Hitler and others discovered that in politics—as in religion—there is no one more fervent than a convert from the other side.

While the ultimate goals of Marxism and Fascism are worlds apart, similarity of political strategies places the two close together in their appeal to the individual. Both provide an all-encompassing worldview of a violent struggle between good and evil. This level of commitment places each active revolutionary in a unique mental state. Once a person has taken steps into prolonged political violence, it is nearly impossible to retreat back around the circle to a more moderate position. Those who are uncontrollably furious with their former group are more likely to join the opposing side, and thereby become a "double revolutionary." This so-called horseshoe political spectrum below illustrates how a person can take the extraordinary step to jump across the ends of the spectrum and switch sides in a revolution.

FIGURE 9-3, THE DOUBLE REVOLUTIONARY

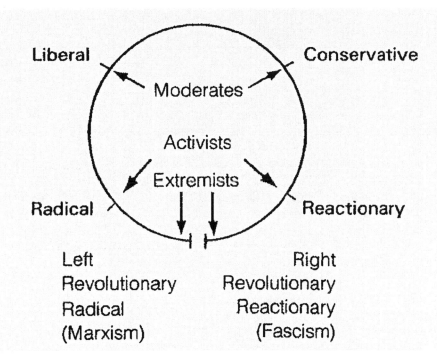

Because of the psychological conditioning that comes through violence, it is surprisingly easy to cross over the tips of the horseshoe. The tactics of violence seem to condition the individual to continue the revolution, even though the goals are reversed.

A similar dynamic applies to individuals who leave fundamentalist religious organizations. It is not uncommon for someone who leaves a church to turn against it later with a vengeance. I know a former member of a cult-like church who now hands out anti-church literature on the street corner. There is often a pendulum effect as individuals swing into another role of becoming an arch enemy of their earlier beliefs. The Internet is brimming with personal testimonies of those who say, "I know how bad they are, I used to be one of them."

The double revolutionary in politics and religion is usually more devoted to the second organization because there is a need for self-justification. He or she must prove that the defection was justified and correct. Often the past experiences supply the new convert with an opportunity to confess participation in the evil ways of the previous group, and to give an insider's view on how to fight that opposing force. The second organization often employs the transformed member to present documented evidence about the real intentions of the enemy. The technique is very effective and has a tremendous impact on the general public. After all, who would doubt information given by one who was a former member?

The Christian Anti-Communist Crusade was a popular group headed by the Reverend Doctor Fred Schwarz. The organization had a former Communist Party member as a regular speaker on their circuit. An element of drama was added when it was explained that the former party member went by an assumed name because he said all his relatives would become targets if his real name were used. His presentations were the highlight of meetings held across the country for more than 20 years. It was sort of a political "dog and pony show." For most people, it seemed to be the most persuasive part of the entire 4-day seminar. For some reason it was thrilling and exciting to actually see and hear the enemy. Conservative Christians lined up after his address to have their pictures taken with a person who they saw as the personification of evil. I often wondered about the security precautions when there were hundreds of pictures of the former Communists floating around the country.

I interviewed The Reverend Schwarz quite extensively about why he would place such importance on the views of a former Communist. Schwarz didn't really want to answer that question, but instead focused on how he never tired of hearing the former enemy confess to all the things they planned to do when the Communists took over the United States. In a real sense, Schwarz was building a devil symbol that his followers could all fear together. Somehow it was invigorating to hear how effective the devil was in misleading people around the world. Schwarz spoke passionately about how capable Communists are at enslaving people.

It is interesting to speculate why people would give so much credibility to a former member of the enemy camp. Why, for example, would the second group (Schwarz's audience) want to hear from a person who they once regarded as an agent of evil? Why, if the double revolutionary betrayed his or her comrades, would changing sides suddenly qualify him to be a trusted informer who gives an accurate appraisal?

Perhaps it is the condemnation that some people want to hear. Who cares that it is motivated by spite and personal hatred? Perhaps the double revolutionary is in such demand because he or she can tell people what they want to hear, confirming their worst fears.

In a real sense, revolutionary figures have a mystique in politics not unlike holy people or sports heroes. In Israel, Northern Ireland, and the United States, I found there was an overwhelming admiration for worthy opponents on the other side. On a very serious level, it was like a political/religious sporting game in which enemies were elevated to a star level and acknowledged in a way that revealed feelings of sincere respect. In politics, as well as sports, religion, and business, it is important to know what your adversary believes, what motivates them, and how to bring them down. It is this study of the arch-enemy that many really enjoy.

Strong anti-communists, like Schwarz, have a fascination with learning about the personal lives of historical and contemporary Marxists. For example, in our one-on-one conversations, Schwarz expressed a strong admiration for Vladimir Lenin. One day I asked Schwarz if he "respected" Lenin. He was taken aback by the word "respect" but finally did admit that Lenin was a "gifted revolutionary."

Extremists can't seem to get enough information about revolutionaries on the other side. There were some individual revolutionaries I knew that actually flirted with the idea of "switching." Paramilitaries on both sides follow the careers of soldiers on the other side that were living a similar life pattern. There is a certain level of admiration for their opponents.

I knew a police commander in Belfast who told me it was surprisingly easy to "turn" some fighters so they became informers. Interrogators learned to focus on how corrupt the first organization was in dogma. The focus was on how the leaders had betrayed the followers. "Then," the commander said, "It was just a matter of time before the fighter would become a spy for the police." It reminded me of my friend who rejected his religion and became an outspoken critic. I sometimes wondered if the act of fighting and belonging to a paramilitary group was more important for some than the cause itself. Why, otherwise do so many switch sides?

I remember an IRA man I knew in Belfast who kept saying that he felt like a "moth to a flame" in that there was something about risking his life that consumed him. He loved every minute of the danger and intrigue of fighting for the cause. There were a lot of people just like him in Jerusalem and across the United States. Many people get a personal high from political warfare. You can see their eyes light up when they talk about it.

There are always people looking for a new cause. Tomorrow's terrorist may well be today's young person looking for a political, social, religious, or ethnic identity. Regardless of the time or place in history, it's always been that way.

Questions for You

1. In your judgment, what is the value of the "comparative political spectrum?" Why is it so important that we consider the intensity of political convictions?

2. Why are moderates (liberals and conservatives) so committed to political order? What means do they have available to maintain an orderly political system?

3. How does the author explain the supportive behavior some congressional moderates have for Donald Trump? Why do you think some moderates have "flexible principles?" Do you agree or disagree?

4. Do you see any evidence that some members of Congress have activist characteristics? Why does activist behavior among members make it difficult to compromise in the legislative process?

5. What does the account of the communist plot with rock music and the Rajneesh commune tell you about activists' conspiracies? Why does the author think some people need to simplify politics? What do you think?

6. Why are conspiracy theories so common in American politics? Do you have any examples that you have noted in your personal life? What was your reaction to those theories?

7. Do you agree with the author that the election of Donald Trump promoted more activist behavior? Do you see any evidence that Trump has changed the temperament of the American people on a permanent basis? Did he change your views about politics?

8. Note some beliefs and practices among revolutionaries that are anti-democratic. Why, do you think, it is difficult for a revolutionary regime to evolve into a democratic society?

9. Why do revolutionaries need a belief in a devil? Why has the United States become a devil symbol in some parts of the world?

10. Why do revolutionaries sometimes find it necessary to eliminate their own personal identities? Why is conspiratorial thinking so prominent in revolutionary organizations?

11. What are the circumstances that produce a "double revolutionary?" Have you ever known a person that switched sides in politics? What were the person's reasons?

12. What is your reaction to the supposition that we often look for negative behavior in politics that we fear might be in ourselves? Do you suspect many of the scandals and stories of disloyalty are accepted by observers because it confirms their desire to hear "terrible things?" If this is true, what special problems does this create in a democracy?

Where Do You Fit on the Political Scale?

Would you classify yourself as a moderate, activist, extremist, or some other classification? Have you changed your behavior recently? Which groups in this chapter were close to your point of view?

10

Beyond Ideology

The politics of Donald Trump in 2016 were neither left nor right—he only cared about himself. His antics were based on expanding his personal standing by exploiting an underlying paranoia that already existed in the nation. He did not invent the situation that made him popular, but he did give it voice. Unlike anyone else, he knew how to tap into the anxiety and fear of folks who had lost faith in the future. He awakened the outrageous populist belief that political problem-solving was "simple," that government was "easy," and that he was a "winner" who could "Make America Great Again."

It wasn't apparent to other politicians at the time, but 2016 was a time when many people felt they had been deserted by the political establishment. Donald Trump was the only presidential candidate that tapped into their anger. He understood this state of mind and focused on it like a television preacher. Hearing him was like going to a tent show where old-time religion was mixed with off-color humor and outlandish proclamations. The country couldn't get enough of his self-centered political sermons. His profanities and simplistic solutions were greeted with cheers and laughter. While the nation looked on, he turned a crowd of thousands into an army of believers. They loved to hear him brag about himself and promise things that most knew were impossible. Trump's persuasive power was his style—his listeners didn't expect to hear a proper campaign speech, and he always fulfilled their expectations.

Voters who supported Trump had an utter contempt for the government in Washington, D.C., and for the mainstream media. They were sick of an establishment that didn't care about them. His pledge to "Make America Great Again" was a promise to make these people feel they were being heard; it also made them feel good to get revenge on those who had violated their culture. There were thinly veiled themes that were racist, homophobic, misogynist, nativist, and anti-internationalist. Again and again he targeted the media for disagreeing with his version of the truth. Press coverage that was critical of his exaggerations was labelled "fake news."

257

When people feel threatened and uncertain, they naturally turn to someone who is confident with a ready-made plan. Trump was absolutely certain about everything—he had no doubts and never backed down. He would build a wall on the southern border (and Mexico would pay for it), bring back lost jobs, and keep Muslims out of the country. Most listeners knew it wasn't possible, but they were delighted with his clarity. It came down to two vivid points: he gave them a simple version of what was wrong and who was to blame. His approach was blunt and easy to understand. Trump supporters were absolved of any blame for their own shortcomings—it was the fault of the establishment Democrats and Republicans, and it was going to be so simple to fix it.

In 2016, many thought the Trump phenomena was new, but it was not. We've had elections before that were based on blaming a target group. Depending on the era, it was international bankers, the railroads, labor unions, black people, Masons, Catholics, Jews, Communists, Mormons, big business, or some variety of foreigners.

Nearly every major ethnic, religious, racial, or nationality group has been the target at some time in the past. Today we may think that Americans are beyond targeting specific groups. In fact, there's always been that seed within us, it just took a crisis and a demagogue to give it life again. But 2016 was different in one respect. It was the time a leader threw a hand grenade into the American political system—and to make it more interesting—a sizable portion of the electorate sided with the guy who pulled the pin.

The 2016 election not only decided the winner of the presidency, it also affected many on an emotional level as well. An often-repeated comment was, "I've never seen so much bitterness and division." Trump supporters were surprised and happy to win, while Clinton voters were shocked and profoundly depressed. Hate crimes, racism, sexual abuse, bullying, and ugly graffiti popped up across the nation. I'll not forget one especially personal message scrawled on a wall outside someone's home after the election: "You don't count and neither does your vote."

Left and Right

Looking back to the election, we didn't realize how important the left and right were in our politics until both of them began to self-destruct before our eyes. Until 2016, we always had some form of predictable ideology operating on the presidential campaign stage. The choices weren't always textbook examples of the two philosophies, but they were fairly reliable clusters of opinion of what each political party stood for. There was always a good deal of overlapping in key areas; however, most politically active people had a working definition of the two brands.

The idea of what candidates stood for may have differed in particular sections of the country, but there was a clear expectation at all levels that neither party was going to make sweeping, unexpected changes that would cause turmoil. There was a certain level of civility in our campaigns also—none of the nominees ever said that the presidential nominee of the other party should be "locked up" or that the other candidate was "unfit" to be president.

Compared to 2016, American politics in the past may have been a bit boring, yet there was stability in knowing what to expect after the election. Everyone knew that change would be incremental, not sweeping. Usually it came down to degrees of difference along with the promise that neither party was going to lurch so far afield that the losing side would be fearful that the damage was irreparable. In the past I never heard anyone say honestly that they would be personally afraid if the other candidate won. I never witnessed a time after the election when folks held up signs saying, "He's not my President."

But 2016 was different. Voters on both sides were genuinely fearful of what might happen. It became a cliché to say that the United States was polarized at every level—from Washington, D.C., where the Congress was gridlocked, down to elementary schools where children were dividing into two camps at recess time.

Many of us looked back longingly at times when everyone seemed to get along with each other. In the 1950s, for example, some critics even thought that the parties were too close together in terms of their basic beliefs—that neither of them really offered a meaningful choice: it was Tweedledum verses Tweedledee. The often-repeated phrase came out of a nursery rhyme, *Alice in Wonderland*, which had two rather dull characters that were nearly carbon copies of each other. The implication was that both were shallow intellectually, with no original thought, and that neither of them had the courage to take decisive action—and because they were so similar—it really didn't matter which one won.

In 1968, Alabama governor George Wallace summed up Democrats and Republicans by saying, "there's not a dime's worth of difference between the two of them." In that era, members of the American Political Science Association, and other thoughtful critics, contended that the two parties should provide a "clearer choice" so voters had a better idea of how public policy might change after the election. The feeling in some circles was that they overlapped too much. That point of view isn't expressed anymore.

Predictability

The existence of two fairly coherent political parties performed several other functions for the public. Over several decades, voters developed a definite idea of what to expect from each party. The public anticipated that liberal Democrats would be sympathetic to the needs of blue-collar workers, and conservative Republicans would be more inclined to aid business interests. If either party had been in office for a few years, there was always the argument that "we need a change." There was an eagerness to give the other party a chance. Voters established a fairly well-defined account in their minds of what each had done in the past, and what they planned to do in the future. Again, it wasn't perfect, but it worked.

So why was the predictability factor so important? Perhaps the best way to explain this is to share a fictitious story I've told my students. I set up a situation in class by discussing a fictional candidate named Johnny Jones who was very flexible with the truth, and had no association with either party or any apparent ideological identity. In this simulated political campaign, Johnny Jones was exceptionally entertaining as he promised to do great things outside the boundaries of regular politics. He was brash and spectacular in the campaign, but he failed miserably after being elected. Jones had a strong, dominating voice, but had no understanding of how to govern. Johnny Jones brought chaos to the land. He lurched back and forth on a multitude of issues, but little got done. Some people even thought he was mentally unstable.

The voters, of course, were unhappy with his performance, but there was little they could do except to say, "We'll never vote for Johnny Jones again." But four years later, voters were attracted to a new candidate, Sally Smith, who also was very colorful. Her campaign was limited to a pledge to repeal all the damage left behind by Johnny Jones, but Sally had no clear agenda. Again, voters flocked to this new figure who promised great things. When she failed, voters felt even more frustrated because they'd been led down the road again by another fast-talking candidate with no track record. There was a sharp decline in public trust. Elections campaigns became political sideshows that were dominated by crude behavior and outlandish promises. Big money moved in to fill the void as the governmental system lost all public credibility. The whole idea of democracy was seen as a scam, as something that didn't work.

This is what happens when the public can't keep scorecards on election decisions. They don't have a realistic idea of what to expect, and they don't know what to do when public officials fail to deliver. It's only then that we see how important it is to have groups of ideological candidates who establish a philosophical batting average with the voters. Without a known track record, election campaigns are just another shiny PR exercise where it is easy to con the electorate into buying an idea that may sound attractive, but in fact may be undoable.

It turns out that predictability is a critical factor in a democratic system—without it, campaigns can degenerate into a 2016-style, free-for-all series of rallies with unpredictable results and chaos. Our democracy may be more fragile than we think.

Electing a traditional conservative or a crusading liberal isn't a guarantee for public satisfaction; however, regular political party members permit a clearer line of succession than candidates with no track record. Political brands are extremely important in our political system. Voters routinely associate candidates with the established record of political parties that is either left or right. The logic may be rough, yet we hear the following kind of comment: "I'm going to vote for them again because the last time they were in office they did so and so, and I guess I can expect more of the same."

Liberal Democrats and conservative Republicans have a public reputation based on a record built up over several decades—they are held responsible for their past performances. Most of the public remembers what each one of them did the last time they were in. If voters are unhappy with long-term performance, they can pledge never to vote again for that party. That's a much more responsible basis for voting than just saying, "I'll never vote for Johnny Jones or Sally Smith again."

The 2016 presidential election was noteworthy because the standard identities provided by the left and right were largely absent. Donald Trump (the Republican candidate) wasn't a conservative or a liberal; he wasn't even recognized as a real Republican. He was an off-color, opportunistic, TV celebrity, populist that seemed to make it up as he went along. He had never held public office and had no track record from the past. Voters didn't really know what he stood for because so many of his pronouncements appealed to public emotion rather than to realistic policies. There was widespread doubt that he would follow any particular ideological line if elected. His opponent, Hillary Clinton was a traditional Democrat, but she carried a lot of political baggage from 30 years in politics. There was a good deal of suspicion among Democrats that Hillary had drifted too close to Wall Street and big business. She defeated U.S. Senator Bernie Sanders in the Democratic primaries, but she was unable to win over many left-wing Democrats who stayed home on Election Day; some even voted for Trump. Hillary Clinton couldn't hold together the old Obama Democratic coalition of blacks, blue-collar voters and young people. She never really made a positive case to the voters; much of what she said was just anti–Trump. There was no sense of left-wing solidarity or vision for the future in her campaign.

Donald Trump may well be remembered as a Johnny Jones figure. His lack of an ideological identity made him exciting but unpredictable. In retrospect, his election illustrated what can happen in a democracy when voters feel they have nowhere else to go. It was a perfect storm: millions of voters were adrift and Trump spoke to issues that were lurking just below the surface—racism, immigration, and a sort of reckless white nationalism. As stated earlier, "he tore the scab off" of political and cultural issues that had been festering for years. The most often heard expectation was that he would shake up the establishment, but no one seemed to know what he would do when he entered the White House, including the new president himself.

Political Manners

2016 will also be remembered as the year parents didn't want their children to hear some of the comments made by presidential candidates. In the absence of competing ideological campaign issues, candidates sidestepped the issues and turned on each other in a personal manner. Candidate's spouses were attacked, comments were made about the probable size of a candidate's genitals, reporters with physical disabilities were mocked in public, and charges were made against various nationalities, ethnic, and religious groups. It was entertaining, but chaotic. No one had ever seen a campaign that was so dirty and personally destructive. But the media covered every charge and countercharge. Looking straight into the TV cameras and telling lies became the new normal. Truth was said to be "relative" and there was a new phrase, "alternative facts," that was a fancy term for lies.

Certainly, we can't attribute all the unorthodox behavior of 2016 to the absence of traditional party involvement; however, it is clear that it was like no other campaign in terms of the general conduct of the candidates. Fear and anger were used to wind up voters so they responded on an emotional level. Promises were made that most everyone knew could never be kept. The rest of the world looked on as the leading democracy in the world degenerated into a political free-for-all without the general rules of civil conduct.

Regular conservatives and liberals winced as they watched the campaign become a sort of political black hole—sucking in legitimate leaders and making them look ridiculous. After their national convention, the Republican Party seriously considered dumping their presidential nominee. In return, Donald Trump campaigned against his own Republican Speaker of the House, Paul Ryan. Many a traditional Republican wondered how the Party of Lincoln could become the laughingstock of the country. Clinton focused most of all on proving that Trump was unfit for office. But in her effort to demonize Trump, Hillary Clinton failed to advance her own policies as an alternative. The end result was that Trump dominated the airwaves, and sucked up all the attention. His free-wheeling style won out at the end because he spoke the language of the guy down at the end of the bar who had one too many. He promised to "shake up the system," and that was something voters thought they understood.

People who do not understand what motivated Trump voters do not understand what it was like to be angry and have neither party reach out with a helping hand—they do not understand how sweet revenge can be in a system that gives huge tax cuts to the rich while ignoring voters who are desperate for a job—they do not understand why folks who feel they are locked out of society can be eager to tear it down—they don't understand why many Trump voters are still proud they voted for him—and finally, they do not understand how much some people enjoyed giving the middle finger to leaders who always seemed beyond their reach.

It's always risky to attempt an analysis of a current event. How do we know for certain what caused all of this? In truth it is a combination of many things, some that are systemic and other factors that may just be a reflection of the personalities involved. But the trend is unmistakable. The old rules of decorum are no longer operating, party loyalty ties are being broken, and a new, narrower, form of partisanship is out of control. The country has degenerated into tribes that want to destroy each other. There aren't many regular liberals and conservatives who expect good manners to return soon, if ever.

Trump versus Anti-Trump

A strange (maybe temporary) realignment of our two parties has taken place. It is too soon to know if it will last, but the battle lines are being drawn in a way that we have never seen before. The incumbent president, Donald Trump, took over the Republican Party while the Democratic Party was being held together by an intense opposition to Trump. Old-line conservative Republicans were afraid to confront the president for fear that he would oppose them in their re-election campaigns. There was almost no evidence of the old liberal/conservative model that was so prevalent in the past. No one knows for sure where this will lead. Are we seeing the beginnings of a Johnny Jones/Sally Smith scenario? Will this become the new normal?

The most important side-story of 2016 was the question of what will happen to the Republican Party. The GOP won an election with someone at the top of the ticket that many Republicans found repulsive. In private, moderate leaders were nearly unanimous in their contempt for the bully who knocked down regular Republicans in the primaries and won the nomination without much opposition. Main Street Republicans across the country were visibly distraught as they wondered how the old guard could reclaim their party.

Early polling results in the summer of 2016 indicated that the Democratic candidate (Hillary Clinton) would win for certain, so the fallback position for Republican moderates was that they could pick up the pieces after the election. GOP moderates were planning to unite around the effort to stop

President Hillary Clinton, and perhaps impeach her before she could enact any major legislation.

But then the unexpected happened: Donald Trump won the election and the Republican Party had to face the unsettled prospect of dealing with a presidential leader they didn't even respect. But Trump's support among the Republican base of voters was strong so they couldn't reject him. How would GOP congressional leaders respond to the crude, unorthodox ways of Donald Trump who was not really a Republican? Would they acknowledge his leadership? Would they stand beside him and accept his outrageous policies of building a wall on the southern border? Would his goals become their goals? And then there was the evidence that the Russian government had gotten involved in American politics by releasing information that was harmful to Hillary Clinton—plus Russians tried to manipulate the vote in several states. Would congressional Republicans vigorously block an investigation of Russian involvement? Would Republicans become complicit in Trump's willingness to destroy public trust in the government just to save himself? In addition, Trump insisted that the press was the "enemy of the people." Would Republicans join in the chorus in undermining the media? All of this was going on as regular Republicans were trying to achieve their own goals (repeal Obamacare, government deregulation, and passing huge tax cuts) without being tarnished by the new president.

Privately, Republicans were aghast because there were no attractive alternatives; they had to face reality. Trump had taken over the Republican Party—he was going to call the shots. The nagging question wouldn't go away: would they throw in with a president who was taking the nation in a direction that was fraught with danger? Would gaining their goals be enough to justify the risks? Did they have any choice? How would moderate Republicans respond to the White House attempt to delegitimize the free press? What would be their reaction to the White House plan to "deconstruct the administrative state?" Would they turn a blind eye to a chief executive as he weakened long-standing collective security pacts with allies around the world?

Democrats were also at a crossroad. After the 2016 election, it was really tempting for Democrats to jump on the anti–Trump bandwagon. The marches and chanting crowds that showed up at town hall meetings were anti–Trump, not pro–Democratic Party. The new-found support for the Affordable Care Act (Obamacare) had come about, not because the Democratic Party had convinced people it was a good program, but because Trump and the Republican Party were threatening to repeal it.

There was a real danger that if the Democratic Party gained voter support in the future, it would be because Trump has overreached and acted unconstitutionally, not because the Democrats had offered any reasonable alternative. At the time of this writing, Trump is dominating both parties; he has taken over the Republican Party and is stealing the thunder of the Democrats who want to win on the basis of their own policies. Trump has come to dominate the process of government just as he did in the campaign. It is too early to know for certain, but it seems like we are beginning to live in the era of Johnny Jones and Sally Smith.

Perhaps the only way to regain our civility in public life is for Democrats and Republicans to join hands (as unlikely as that sounds) and illustrate that the two parties can reject the ideas of a bully and bring back the politics of the left and right. It's been said a couple of times before that our system is not perfect, but it works.

A Recipe for Disaster

Some would argue that winning has made America great, that our competitive spirit has been our greatest asset. But maybe it's not a sign of our strength. There may be a good chance that the focus on winning has caused some of us to sacrifice our collective soul for the price of victory over others. It may be good to remember that *every* American depends on maintaining a workable political system, and the first order of business should be to preserve it. This pronouncement sounds like something one might hear in a ninth-grade civics class, but the preservation of the democratic system is, in fact, more important than any particular issue.

It seems pretty clear that much of our dysfunction has come about because we haven't realized yet that our political system is quite fragile, and that if we continue to abuse it, the result may be systematic failure. Some folks have pushed the system to the brink without realizing it could go over the edge; they are willing to undermine the rule of law to gain narrow political objectives. In their eagerness to win, they are fouling our own nest. With an almost blind, foolhardy faith they keep saying our best days are in our future, but as time goes by, that forecast seems to be overly optimistic. Maybe we are close to real trouble, but it hasn't really hasn't sunk in yet. Perhaps we are ignoring some of the probable consequences down the road.

Just because it's legal, doesn't mean it's good for us. It may be time to weigh political practices and ask ourselves: are rather narrow one-sided goals important enough that we will risk bringing down the political system? We've never been this close to the edge since the Civil War. Can our constitutional system survive some of the recent stresses? Here are ten permissible facts and practices that have brought us to the point of a systematic crisis and a near complete loss of public confidence. These are some unsettling changes and possibilities that have come about in American politics:

- The Supreme Court can be staffed by politicians masquerading as judges.
- Unlimited sums of money can be donated to dominate political campaigns.
- Foreign governments can use covert tactics to influence U.S. elections.
- Legislative districts can be drawn to grossly underrepresent specific groups.
- Public officials can be elected without disclosing personal conflicts of interest.
- The president can use his office to promote his own financial interests.
- Refugees can be blocked from entering the country based on nationality/religion.
- The free press can be marginalized and branded as the "enemy of the people."
- Political officials can lie to the public without any fear of accountability.
- Voter suppression laws can be used to discriminate against specific groups.

Clever political operatives have manipulated the legal system so that critical political norms can be violated without raising legal red flags. The Supreme Court has become politically predictable as it dresses up partisan issues in a legal form so it can make political decisions that undermine the democratic process. It's all happening out in plain sight. It's very different than it was a few years ago. Changing the rules of the game has encouraged corruption throughout the political system.

It is now time for the left and right to recognize that they have a joint interest in saving the system that makes our form of government possible. If the ten practices noted above continue to compromise the process, our democracy may drift perilously close to an authoritarian model that permits a takeover without firing a shot. The vitality of liberals and conservatives offering alternatives will be replaced by authoritarian practices that we haven't yet experienced.

There's also an over-confidence in the American character that may be a fatal flaw. We see ourselves as being so capable that it is difficult to imagine our own built-in vulnerabilities. We see ourselves as winners that will always land on our feet. We can fend for ourselves and not be trapped in the slow demise of our constitutional liberties. There is something inside of us that makes us feel that we are everlasting. Other countries can slip into decline—but not us. Many of us think God has ordained the United States as his favorite and we'll always be on top.

Until now, we've been able to avoid the temptations of authoritarianism—of one-man rule that bullies the free press and shuts down legitimate opposition. Our democracy has always been messy and noisy. The word "politician" is almost a dirty word. We have distasteful pictures in our minds of Democrats and Republicans making deals behind closed doors. Collectively, we have become cynical and complacent. We seldom acknowledge that making deals is really what democracy is all about.

There have been times before when a leader has tried to short-circuit the political process. In these times of crisis there's been an enticement to trade freedom for order. Fortunately, we've always had the wisdom to avoid that temptation, but today it is even more serious. We may not be fully aware of the threat until it's too late.

The Dark Corners of America

There's a mistaken belief that Donald Trump is the sole reason for "Trumpism," that he alone is answerable for all the outrageous practices that are now synonymous with his name. Yet many of the anti-democratic practices that aided Trump were firmly rooted in the political system before he ran for office. There was a built-in readiness for Trump that few realized.

First of all, Donald Trump couldn't have singlehandedly created such anger against the establishment, nor could he have developed the willingness for so many to go along with the outrageous promise that he alone could "Make America Great Again." There were a multitude of reasons why voters were attracted to him, many of which we may never fully understand. But we can understand that the Trump phenomenon did provide a chance for voters to take revenge against a political system that they felt was unresponsive to them. His biggest applause came when he charged that everything was "rigged." In fact (Trump may have been correct) it was, and still is, rigged by big money, gerrymandered districts, and voter suppression laws. There was a lot of anger out there that had been overlooked by regular Democrats and Republicans.

To the surprise of nearly everyone, Donald Trump was able to harness a segment of the electorate that had not been united at the national level since the days of George Wallace in 1968. Trump, like Wallace, knew how to read a crowd and exploit all the resentments that had been building up on the fringes of society. His crude language and unbelievable pledges were a welcome relief compared to all the hollow rhetoric they had heard before. Trump was a showman that knew which throw-away lines would bring out the most raucous applause.

But the important point to remember is that there had to be a willingness to accept those sentiments before Trump could exploit them. The American character had a multitude of dark impulses just below the surface that were activated easily by an Elmer Gantry–like figure that knew how to play to fears and antipathies in a tent-show setting. The fictional character Gantry had a lot in common with Trump. They both found that, more than anything, unfulfilled people wanted to believe in something; whether it was true or false made little difference. They wanted to believe in a message that explained complex issues with no grey areas. Both of them embellished the truth on a regular basis, and they did it with certainty. That was the key.

There was a thirst in America for certainty. Everything in the world seemed to be changing. Folks wanted something to hang on to. Trump cleared up all the ambiguities with a series of absolute positions: "zero tolerance" on immigration, "American First" in foreign affairs, and the United States was to be the only nation in the world to deny the facts of climate change; it was to be the only nation to start a trade war with our allies, and everything that went wrong could be blamed on Barack Obama and Hillary Clinton. To top it off, Trump used his twitter account to mix in a little racism and condemnation of the press. The Donald Trump rallies undeniably drew their strength from all those dark corners of politics that existed long before election day. Some of Trump's critics have said that this was not the America they knew, but in fact it was, and still is, a real part of America that we don't like to acknowledge.

Elected conservatives and liberals were well aware of the angry, raw emotion scattered around the country. They knew there was a large group that wanted simple, short answers to very complex problems. They also realized that intolerance, bigotry, prejudice, white nationalism, and inclinations towards authoritarianism were brewing out there, but those who felt that way were regarded by the establishment as a fringe element that could never win control of the White House. Many in power viewed this group as the "unwashed masses" that always made a lot of noise but never controlled any major part of the national political system.

As 2016 approached, the Democratic and Republican leaders didn't seem to notice that the foundations of democracy were being undermined by anti-democratic practices that caused voters to see Donald Trump as a reasonable alternative. Most of us didn't notice what was growing like a fungus in the dark corners of America. The following statements reflect some of the values and practices that were lurking inside the body politic well before 2016:

- Tolerance for ethnic and racial discrimination and racism at all levels of society.
- Demonization of immigrants and refugees who entered the United States.

- Acceptance of organized white nationalist sentiment in many communities.
- Abdication of control over the president's ability to act without restraint.
- Support of anti-democratic dictators and political strongmen around the world.
- Rejection of scientific findings that challenged basic religious or social beliefs.
- Failure to acknowledge that the upper one percent was ripping off the rest of us.
- Legalization of uncontrolled campaign funds that cause political corruption.
- Allowing the development of intense partisanship that causes gridlock.
- Permitting states to use anti-democratic methods to suppress the vote.
- Designing representative districts to underrepresent targeted groups of voters.
- Favoring the emission of greenhouse gases despite the threat of climate change.
- Abolishing the Fairness Doctrine in 1987, giving rise to propaganda in the media.

All of the above factors were present before Donald Trump came on the stage, and they will not go away when he leaves office. It was just a matter of time before someone filled the vacuum left behind by overturning democratic values. This time it just happened to be a man named Trump, a well-known TV personality who could con the electorate. He did not cause the paralyzing gridlock—he just knew how to capitalize on all the defects in the system.

Americans have a lot of reforming to do that does not involve Donald Trump. Political moderates should not make the mistake of blaming President Donald Trump or his underlings—they should recognize that they themselves laid the foundation for this constitutional nightmare. Regular Democrats and Republicans had already turned their backs on the folks that went to the Trump rallies. The foundation of American politics had already been corrupted by racism, big money, growing inequality, voter suppression, propaganda in cable news, and a war on the free press. All of this was in place before Donald Trump ran for office. If we really want to clean out the dark corners of America, there is a need for each citizen to take responsibility for what has happened. Blaming someone else will not revitalize our political system.

When explaining the rise of McCarthyism in the 1950s, the celebrated CBS commentator Edward R. Morrow pointed to the faults within the political system that aided Senator Joe McCarthy in undermining the principles of democracy. Morrow quoted the Shakespearian play, *Julius Caesar*: "The fault, dear Brutus, is not in the stars, but in ourselves."

Questions for You

1. Do you agree with the statement, "The politics of Donald Trump were neither left nor right?" Why, then, did he win in a system that was dominated by liberals and conservatives at every level?

2. During the 1950s and 60s, there was significant cooperation between Democrats and Republicans throughout the political system. What were the apparent strengths and weaknesses of a Tweedledum verses Tweedledee political party system?

3. Why was predictability so important in American elections? What are the lessons from the Johnny Jones and Sally Smith story? In your judgment, has the United States learned the lesson?

4. What special problems do regular liberals and conservatives have when campaigning against an unorthodox populist? In your judgment, how should moderate candidates and the media respond to an opponent that sucks up all the attention in a campaign?

5. Describe the possible realignment that has taken place since 2016. How would you describe the reaction of moderate Republicans since 2016? How have moderate Democrats responded during that same period?

6. According to the author, how may the American obsession with winning contribute to our own demise? Do you see examples of leaders who will sacrifice nearly anything for a political victory?

7. What is your reaction to the "ten permissible practices" in American politics? Why, in your judgment, is there not a public outrage on the continuation of this situation?

8. Do you share the view that Americans have overconfidence in their ability to survive a crisis? Do you see any evidence that there may be a change in that public attitude?

9. Do you see any evidence that there is a Man on Horseback on the horizon? Is that threat a real possibility or just an empty charge? Do you think an anti-democratic, authoritarian government might develop in America? Why or why not?

10. What is your reaction to "The Dark Corners of America" segment and the charge from Trump critics that "this was not the America they knew?" Do you think there was a "readiness" for Donald Trump before he came on the scene? If that is so, why do you think the American people seem unwilling to reform some of the "dark corners?"

What Are Your Predictions for the Future?

Prepare a predictive essay describing how American politics has changed since 2016. Pay special attention to the vitality of regular liberals and conservatives, and whether the United States has maintained a government where there is a lively competition between two political parties. Conclude with an evaluation of whether there are still many anti-democratic practices in the American politics. And finally, answer the question: is the United States still a divided nation? Support your answer with convincing logic.

Bibliography

Abramowitz, Alan. *The Polarized Public: Why American Government Is So Dysfunctional.* New York: Pearson Publishing, 2012.

Adorno, Theodor W. *The Authoritarian Personality.* New York: Harper Row, 1950.

Albright, Madeleine. *Fascism: A Warning.* New York: Harper, 2018.

Alterman, Eric. *Why We're Liberals: A Handbook.* New York: Viking, 2009.

Arblaster, Anthony, *The Rise and Decline of Western Liberalism.* Oxford, UK: Basil Blackwell. 1984.

Belfrage, Sally. *Autonomy Summer.* Charlottesville: The University of Virginia Press, 1965.

Bell, David. *The Radical Right.* New York: Double Day, 1963.

Bobbio, Norberto. *Left and Right: The Significance of a Political Distinction.* Chicago: The University of Chicago Press, 1997.

Branch, Taylor. *Parting the Waters: the King Years, 1954–63.* New York: Simon & Schuster, 1988.

Buckley, William F., Jr., *Getting It Right.* Washington, D.C.: Regency, 2003.

Buckley, William F., Jr., *God and Man at Yale.* Washington, D.C.: Regency. 1951.

Buckley, William F., Jr., *Up from Liberalism.* New York: Stein and Day, 1958.

Carmichael, Stokely. *Black Power: The Politics of Liberation in America,* New York: Random House, 1967.

Deneen, Patrick. *Why Liberalism Failed.* New Haven: Yale University Press, 2018.

Dimock, Marshall. *Political Polarization in the American Public, 1994–2017.* Washington, D.C.: The Pew Research Center, 2017.

Dionne, E.J. Jr. *Why the Right Went Wrong.* New York: Simon & Schuster, 2016.

Farber, David. *The Rise and Fall of American Conservatism: A Short History.* Princeton, NJ: Princeton University Press, 2012.

Fiorina, Morris P. *Culture War? The Myth of a Polarized America.* New York: Longman, 2010.

Flake, Jeff. *Conscience of a Conservative: A Rejection of Destructive Politics and a Return to Principle.* New York: Random House, 2017.

Flavin, Patrick. *Income Inequality and Policy Representation in the American States.* Newbury Park, CA: Sage Publications, 2011.

Frank, Thomas. *Listen Liberal: What Ever Happened to the Party of the People.* New York: Henry Holt, 2016.

Frank, Thomas. *What's the Matter with Kansas: How Conservatives Won the Heart of America.* New York: Henry Holt, 2005.

Goldwater, Barry. *The Conscience of a Conservative.* New York: Hillman Books, 1960.

Gray, John. *Liberalism*. Minneapolis: University of Minnesota Press, 1995.

Guttman, Allan. *The Conservative Tradition in America*. Oxford UK: Oxford University Press, 1967.

Haidt, Jonathan. *The Righteous Mind: Why Good People Are Divided by Politics*. New York: Random House, 2013.

Hartz, Louis. *The Liberal Tradition in America*. Washington, PA: Harvest Books, 1991.

Hayek, Fredrich A. *The Road to Serfdom*. London: Routledge Press, 1944.

Hoffer, Erik. *True Believer: Thoughts on the Nature of Mass Movements*. New York: Harper Row, 1951

Howe, Irving, ed. *The Radical Papers*. New York: Anchor Books, 1966.

King, Martin Luther. *Why We Can't Wait*. New York: Harper Row, 1964.

Kirk, Russell. *The Conservative Mind*. Washington, D.C.: Regency Publishing Company, 2001.

Kirk, Russell. *Prospects for Conservatives*. Washington, D.C.: Regency Publishing Company, 1954.

Kornacki, Steve. *The Red and the Blue: The 1990s and the Birth of Political Tribalism*. New York: Ecco Press, 2018.

Kristol, Irving. *Neo-Conservatives: The Autobiography of an Idea*. New York: The Free Press, 1995.

Krugman, Paul. *The Conscience of a Liberal*. New York: W.W. Norton, 2009.

Lackoff, George. *Don't Think of an Elephant: Know Your Values and Frame the Debate*. White River Junction, VT: Chelsela Green Publishing, 2004.

Lackoff, George. *Moral Politics: How Liberals and Conservatives Think*. Chicago: University of Chicago Press, 2002.

Lackoff, George. *The Political Mind*. New York: Viking, 2008.

Laird, Melvin, ed. *The Conservative Papers*. New York: Anchor Books, 1964.

Lavitsky, Steven and Daniel Ziblatt. *How Democracies Die: What History Tells Us About the Best Way Ahead*. New York: Crown, 2018.

Levendusky, Matthew. *How Partisan Media Polarize America*. Chicago: University of Chicago Press, 2017.

Lewis, Sinclair. *It Can't Happen Here*. New York: Signet Classics, 1935.

Lilla, Mark. *The Once and Future Liberal*. New York: HarperCollins, 2017.

Lofgren, Mike. *The Party Is Over: How Republicans Went Crazy, Democrats Became Useless, and the Middle Class Got Shafted*. New York: Penguin Books, 2012.

Lowi, Theodore J. *The End of Liberalism: Ideology, Policy and the Crisis of Public Authority*. New York: W.W. Norton, 1969.

Luce, Edward. *The Retreat of Western Liberalism*. New York: Little, Brown. 2017.

Meacham, Jon. *The Soul of America: The Battle for Our Better Angels*. New York: Random House, 2018.

Meulemans, William. *Making Political Choices: An Introduction to Politics*. New York: Prentice-Hall, 1989.

Meyer, Frank. *What Is Conservatism?* Wilmington: Intercollegiate Studies and Institute, 2015.

Nash, George H. *The Conservative Intellectual Movement in America Since 1945*. Wilmington: Intercollegiate Studies and Institute. 1976.

Ornstein, Norman, and Thomas Mann. *It's Even Worse Than It Looks: How the American Constitutional System Collided with the New Politics of Extremism*. New York: Basic Books, 2012.

Reich, Robert. Reason: *Why Liberals Will Win the Battle for America*. New York: Knopf, Double Day, 2004.

Roosevelt, James, ed. *The Liberal Papers*. New York: Anchor Books, 1962.

Rossiter, Clinton. *Conservatism in America*. Cambridge: Harvard University Press, 1982.

Rotunda, Ronald D. *The Politics of Language: Liberalism as Word and Symbol.* Iowa City: University of Iowa Press, 1986.

Sigler, Jay A. *The Conservative Tradition in American Thought.* New York: Capricorn Books. 1969.

Vance, J.D. *Hillbilly Elegy: A Memoir of a Family and Culture in Crisis.* New York: Harper, 2016.

Volkomer, Walter E. *The Liberal Tradition in American Thought.* New York: Capricorn Books, 1969.

Wald Kenneth D. *Religion and Politics in the United States.* New York: St. Martin's Press, 1987.

Wellstone, Paul. *The Conscience of a Liberal: Reclaiming the Compassionate Agenda.* Minneapolis: University of Minnesota Press, 2001.

Young, Andrew. *The Easy Burden: The Civil Rights Movement and the Transformation of America.* New York: HarperCollins, 1996.

Zinn, Howard. *A People's History of the United States.* New York: HarperCollins, 1980.

Index

Abbot v. Perez (2018) 141
activist issues 245–46
Adams, Brock 180
Affordable Care Act 107, 140; *see also* Obamacare
African-Americans move North 133
Akin, Todd 181
Ali, Muhammad 158
Alinsky, Saul 164–66
Allen, George H. 180
Alt-right (anti-fascist) 225, 228
Amazon 183
American Exceptionalism 56
American Labor Movement 57
American Main Street Culture 112
American Medical Association 49
American Nazi Party 26
Antelope, Oregon 243
Anthony, Susan 154
anti-democratic practices 4, 268–69
Arab Spring 229
Aristotle 177
Armour, Richard 179
Articles of Confederation 205
Aryans 91

Baker v. Carr (1962) 138
Bannon, Steve 142, 182
Barnum, P.T. 104
Bay of Pigs Invasion 247
Beal, Howard 147
Bell, Alexander Graham 48
Bentham, Jeremy 153
Bezos, Jeff 183
Bhagwan Shree Rajneesh 243–44
Biden, Joe 158
Black Lives Matter 64
block busting 106
Bloomberg, Michael 158
Boehner, John 181
Bonnie and Clyde 57
bonus army 168
Bradley, Bill 157

Brandeis, Louis D. 21
bribery 3
Bridges, Harry 169
Brown, H. Rap 66, 157
Brown, Jerry 157
Brown, Sherrod 159
Brown v. Board of Education of Topeka (1954) 134, 137–38
Bryan, William Jennings 178
Buckley, William F., Jr. 178
Buffett, Warren 158
Bureau of Alcohol, Tobacco and Firearms (AFT) 65
Bureau of Land Management (BLM) 65
Burke, Edmund 27, 72, 177
Burwell v. Hobby Lobby Stores (2014) 141
Bush, George W. 17, 23, 180
Bush, Jeb 181–82
Bush v. Gore (2000) 140

Cagney, James 59
California State Assembly 96
California State Senate 96
California State University at Bakersfield 96
campaign spending 3, 21, 29
Carlyle Group 224
Carmichael, Stokely 157
Carnegie, Andrew 177
Carson, Ben 182
Carter, Jimmy 23, 157
Castro, Fidel 247–48; in Cuba 166
Catholics 91
Charlottesville, Virginia 225
Chavez, Cesar 96, 156
Chief Joseph 154
Chomsky, Noam 157
Christian Anti-Communist Crusade 254
Churchill, Winston 178, 247
Citizens United v. Federal Election Commission (2010) 140
Civil Rights Act of 1964 10, 25, 101, 138
Civil Rights Movement 17, 25, 57, 135–36
Clean Air Act of 1963 138

climate change 94, 111
Clinton, Bill 23, 97, 140, 148, 158
Clinton, Hillary 2, 109, 160
Cold War 134
Common Cause 32
Communication Workers of the America v. Beck (1988) 139–40
communist conspiracy 242
Communist Party 169–71
conservative, male role 4
conservative Republicans 98
conservative values 39
conservatives resist New Deal 130–31
conspiracy theories 144
Constitutional Convention of 1787 205–6
corruption 11–15
Coulter, Ann 181
crime and punishment 116
Cronkite, Walter 148
Cruz, Ted 182

Darrow, Clarence 154
Dawkins, Richard 156
Democratic Convention of 1948 and 1968 101
Democratic Party 21, 150, 163
Dennis, Eugene 169
Dennis, Peggy 169
Dennis v. United States (1950) 137
deprivations and expectations 127–29
desegregation of armed forces 137
de Tocqueville, Alexis 177
Detroit 106
District of Columbia v. Heller (2008) 140
Dodge City, Kansas 29
Donner Party of 1846 59
double revolutionary 252–53
Duke, David 225
dysfunctional family 6

Earth Liberation Front (ELF) 248
Eastman, George 48
Edison, Thomas 48
education 116
Einstein. Albert 155, 165, 178
Eisenhower, Dwight 25, 93–94, 105, 136, 155, 178
Elementary and Secondary Education Act of 1965 139
Employment Act of 1946 137
Engle v. Vatale (1962) 138
Environment Protection Act of 1970 139
Environmental Protection Agency (EPA) 40, 112
Epic Systems v. Lewis (2018) 141
Ettor, Joseph 154
expectations and deprivations 127–29
extremism 66

Facebook 184
Fair Deal 161
Fair Housing Act of 1965 139

fake news 148
Falwell, Jerry 179
Fascism 37
Federal Bureau of Investigation (FBI) 107
Feinstein, Dianne 157
Foote, Shelby 156
Ford, Henry 53
Fourteenth Amendment 218
Fox News 103, 109, 241
Frank, Ann 26
Frank, Barney 158
Franklin, Benjamin 177
freedom of contract doctrine 211
Friedman, Milton 180
Frontier Thesis 60
Fulbright, J. William 155–56
functions of ideology 90–93

Galbraith, John Kenneth 159
Gantry, Elmer 268
Garofalo, Janeane 159
George, Henry 154
Gerry, Elbridge 15
gerrymandering 4, 15, 21
GI Bill 132
Gill v. Whitford (2018) 141
Ginsburg, Ruth Bader 158
Gitlow v. New York (1925) 218
Giuliani, Rudy 182
globalists 224
Goldwater, Barry 66, 95, 179
Gompers, Samuel 154
Gore, Al 158
Gould, Jay 177
government regulation 184
Graham, Franklin 182
The Grapes of Wrath 59, 131
Great Depression of 1929 130–31
Great Society 101, 161
Greely, Horace 178
Grylls, Bear 159
gun control 54–55, 116

Hall, Gus 169
Hamilton, Alexander 177, 207
Hancock, John 207
Hannity, Sean 181
Harrington, Michael 155
hate crimes and racism 258
Hayden, Thomas 157
health care 2
Hearst, Patty 249
Heinlein, Robert 178
Hell's Angels 188
Heston, Charlton 191
heterogeneous groups 218
Hitler, Adolf 72, 228
Hobbes, Thomas 72
Hoffer, Eric 248
Hoggart, Simon 156
homogeneous groups 218

Hoover, Herbert 168
Hoover, J. Edgar 179
horseshoe political spectrum 253
hot-button issues 128–29
Housing and Urban Development Act of 1965 138
Huckabee, Mike 182
Huerta, Dolores 96
Hughes, Charles Evan 129
Humphrey, Hubert 100, 155
Husted v. Philip Randolph Institute (2018) 141

identity politics 108
ideology 90–93
ideology fits self interest 202–3
immigration 2, 133
income inequality 3
individualism 119
Infowars 224–25
Internal Revenue Service (IRS) 65
Internal Security Act of 1950 137
Irish Republican Army (IRA) 64, 67
Islamic State of Iraq and Syria (ISIS) 64, 248
It Can't Happen Here 190

Jackson, Andrew 154
Janus v. American Federation of State, County, and Municipal Employees (AFSCME) (2018) 141
Javits, Jacob 10
Jealous, Ben 160
Jefferson, Thomas 154, 177, 203–4, 207
Jewish Defense League (JDL) 64
Jews 91
Jim Crow Laws 24
John Birch Society 95
Johnson, Lyndon 10, 25, 66, 101
Jones, Alex 224
Julius Caesar 269–70

Kennedy, John F. 25, 95, 101, 155
Kennedy, Robert 101, 156
Kennedy, Ted 186
Kerry, John 158
Keyes, Alan 180
King, Coretta Scott 156
King, Martin Luther, Jr. 25, 101, 156
King, Steve 181
King v. Burwell (2015) 141
Koch, Charles 181
Kristol, Irving 181
Ku Klux Klan 24, 26–27, 58, 64, 66, 91, 136, 192–97

labor unions 95
LaPierre, Wayne 181
law and order 45
League of Women Voters 32
learning political values 93–98
left-wing principles 150
left-wing thought, ancient and modern 153–60

left-wing values 40–41, 150–72
LeMay, Curtis 179
Lenin's Russia 92
Lewis, C.S. 179
Lewis, John 156
Lewis, Sinclair 190
LGBT practices and rights 109, 111
liberal Democrats 98
liberal, female role 4
liberal values 39
Limbaugh, Rush 97, 181
Lincoln, Abraham 177, 214
Locke, John 72, 177
Lockner v. New York (1905) 211
Lodge, Henry Cabot 178
Los Angeles 106
Loving v. Virginia (1967) 139

MacArthur, Douglas 178
Madison, James 207
Make America Great Again 64, 227
Malcolm X 157
Mandela, Nelson 157
Manifest Destiny 56
Manning, Brennan 156
Mao's China 92, 166
Mark of the Beast 146
Marshall, John 177, 209
Marshall, Thurgood 155
Marx, Karl 72, 154
Marxian model 166
Marxism 37
McCarthy, Joseph 137, 238
McConnell, Mitch 23
McGovern, George 156
McVeigh, Tim 197
Mead, Margaret 155
Medicaid 43, 161
Medicare 43, 161
Mellon, Andrew 178
military industrial complex 242
militia members 54
Milk, Harvey 158
Miller, Zell 179
Moore, Michael 158
Morgenthau, Hans 58
Morrow, Edward R. 269–70
Moscone, George 96
MSNBC 241
Muir, John 155
Murdock, Evelyn 169
Murdock, Steve 169

Nader, Ralph 157
National Association for the Advancement of Colored People (NAACP) 25
National Federation of Independent Business v. Sebelius (2012) 140
National Rifle Association (NRA) 55
Nazis 64
negative freedom 215–16

neo–Nazis 26, 91
Network 147
Neuberger, Dick 13
New Deal 93, 111, 161
New Frontier 101, 161
New York Times 57, 103
Nichols, Terry 197
Nixon, Richard 17, 95, 101, 139, 179
nonpartisan redistricting commission 32
Norquist, Grover 144, 180
North Carolina Agricultural and Technical State University 31
Nugent, Ted 182

Obama, Barack 17, 23, 25, 97, 140, 159, 183
Obama, Michelle 159
Obamacare 17, 43; *see also* Affordable Care Act of 2010
Obergefell v. Hodges (2015) 141
Occupy Wall Street 63
O'Donnell, Lawrence 159
Office of Economic Opportunity Act 138
Oklahoma City Federal Building bombing 197
O'Neal, Tip 18
overlapping political bell curve 9

Paine, Thomas 207
Parkland, Florida, shootings 191
Patton, George 178
Paul, Ron 180
Peace Corps 101
Pelosi, Nancy 108
Pence, Mike 182
Penn, William 177
Pentagon Papers 57
Perry, Rick 181
Pittsburgh 106
Pol Pot's Cambodia 92
political corruption 266
political extremism 66
political labels 63–64
political socialization 93, 89–110
political spectrum 36
political thermometer 37
political threats 76–81
Politics Among Nations 58
Poor Peoples Conference 81–89
Pope Francis 159
positive freedom 216
Posse Comitatus 146
privatization 119–20
public funding of campaigns 15
Putin, Vladimir 227

racism and hate crimes 24–26, 258
radical revolutionary goals 167
Rambo 59
Rand, Ayn 179
Randolph, A. Philip 155
Reagan, Nancy 180

Reagan, Ronald 18, 96, 139, 179–80
reapportionment 132
recession of 2017 52–53
Redford, Robert 158
Regents of University of California v. Bakke (1977) 139
Reich, Robert 159
Republican Party 21, 173
Reuther, Walter 155
revolutionaries 37; of the left 166–67; on the right 188–90
revolutionary reactionary 64
Reynolds v. Sims (1964) 138
right to work laws 46–47
right-wing principles 173
right-wing thought, ancient and modern 176–82
right-wing values 40–41, 173–97
Rizzo, Frank 182
Robber Barons 57
Robertson, Pat 179
rock and roll conspiracy 242–43
Rockefeller, Nelson 10, 95
Rockwell, Norman, paintings 112
Rocky 59
Roe v. Wade (1973) 139
Romney, Mitt 180, 186–88
Roosevelt, Eleanor 80
Roosevelt, Franklin 93, 130–31, 155
Roosevelt, Theodore 178
Rosenberg, Ethel 137, 170
Rosenberg, Julius 137, 170
Rousseau, Jean-Jacques 72
Royko, Mike 181
Rumford Fair Housing Act 106
Russell, Bertrand 154
Russell, Richard 10
Russian influence in 2016 election 141
Rustin, Bayard 156
Ryan, Paul 181

Sanders, Bernie 4, 21, 41, 160, 228
Sanger, Margaret 154
Santorum, Rick 181
Seale, Bobby 159
secularism 133
Seeger, Pete 170–71
segregation 135–36
Shelby County, Alabama v. Holder (2013) 140
Shelby v. Holder (2013) 29–30
Smith, Adam 177
social conservatives 185
Social Security 43, 161
Social Security Act of 1965 138
Socialism 41–42
Solid South 10, 17
Spencer, Ricard 225
state rights' doctrine 219
Steinbeck, John 161–62, 131
Steinem, Gloria 159
Stevenson, Adlai 94, 155

Streisand, Barbra 159
strong central government 204
sundown law 95
Sununu, John 182
Supreme Court 3
Symbionese Liberation Army (SLA) 249

Taft, William Howard 178
Taft-Hartley Act of 1947 137
Taylor, Jared 225
television and violence 66–67
Thatcher, Margaret 180
Thoreau, David 154
Till, Emmett 26
Tindley, Charles Albert 154
The True Believer 248
Truman, Harry 25, 155
Trump, Donald 3, 17, 22, 25, 32, 38, 45, 64, 104, 141, 145, 147, 182, 185, 191, 221, 227, 238–39, 263–65
Turner, Fredrick Jackson 60
Twain, Mark 178, 189

undermining the electorate 15–17
University of Alabama 101
University of Wisconsin 101

Veterans Administration 108
Vidal, Gore 157
Vietnam War 17, 57, 101
violence and television 66–67

violence and welfare state 81
violence as a dividing line 73
voter ID laws 21
voter suppression 3, 16
voting reform 30–31
voting rights 29
Voting Rights Act of 1965 3, 16, 25, 101, 139

Walker, Alice 156
Wall Street 53, 140
Wallace, George 25, 136, 161, 259
War on Poverty 162
Warren, Elizabeth 159, 183
Washington, George 67, 177
Washington Post 57
Water Control Act of 1965 138
Wayne, John 59, 179
Weather Underground 146, 249
welfare state and violence 81
Wheeler, Burton 154
white supremacists 24–27
Whole Women's Health v. Hellersdedt (2016) 143
Wilson, Charlie 45
Wilson, Woodrow 25
Works Progress Administration (WPA) 93

Yates v. United States (1957) 138

Zinn, Howard 157–58
Zuckerberg, Mark 184